Negro Folk Music
U.S.A.

HAROLD COURLANDER

DOVER PUBLICATIONS, INC.
NEW YORK

HAROLD COURLANDER is a novelist, folklorist and specialist in the field of African and Afro-American cultures. He is the author of more than thirty-five books, including collections of folklore and tales from various regions of the world, studies of traditions and life in the Caribbean, and novels about Afro-American life, one of his best-known being *The African,* published in 1967. His most recent novels include *The Bordeaux Narrative,* set in Haiti, and *The Master of the Forge,* set in the Western Sudan. His study of the life and lore of the Haitian people, *The Drum and the Hoe,* is widely regarded as one of the definitive works on Haitian traditions. He is also the author of several books on the Hopi Indians of Arizona.

Among his published collections of African and Afro-American oral literature are *A Treasury of African Folklore* and *A Treasury of Afro-American Folklore.* Some of the traditional music that he recorded in such places as Haiti, Cuba, Ethiopia and the American South was released on records by the Ethnic Folkways Library (Folkways Records), now issued by the Smithsonian Institution in tape format.

Mr. Courlander is a Guggenheim Fellow, and his work on *Negro Folk Music, U.S.A.* was assisted by grants from the Wenner-Gren Foundation for Anthropological Research.

Copyright © 1963 by Columbia University Press.
Copyright © renewed 1991 by Harold Courlander.
All rights reserved under Pan American and International Copyright Conventions.

Published in Canada by General Publishing Company, Ltd., 30 Lesmill Road, Don Mills, Toronto, Ontario.

Published in the United Kingdom by Constable and Company, Ltd., 3 The Lanchesters, 162-164 Fulham Palace Road, London, W6 9ER.

This Dover edition, first published in 1992, is an unabridged, slightly corrected republication of the work originally published in 1963 by Columbia University Press, New York. The drawings throughout the book are by James and Ruth McCrea. This Dover edition is published by special arrangement with Columbia University Press, 562 West 113th St., New York, N.Y. 10025.

Manufactured in the United States of America
Dover Publications, Inc., 31 East 2nd Street, Mineola, N.Y. 11501

Library of Congress Cataloging-in-Publication Data

Courlander, Harold, 1908–
  Negro folk music, U.S.A. / Harold Courlander.
      p.   cm.
  Originally published: New York : Columbia University Press, 1963.
  "The music" (unacc.): p.
  Discography:
  Includes bibliographical references and index.
  ISBN 0-486-27350-4
  1. Afro-Americans—Music—History and criticism. 2. Folk music—United States—History and criticism. 3. Folk songs, English—United States—History and criticism. 4. Afro-Americans—Music—Discography. I. Title.
ML3556.C7 1992
781.62′96073—dc20   92-35475
                                                                      CIP
                                                                      MN

Preface

THE SUBJECT OF Negro folk music has been with us for a long while now, and, when I began to put this book together, I entertained the thought that perhaps there was really nothing new to say about it. There had been, and continues to be, a tremendous effort in the direction of collecting Negro folk songs and analyzing them, in relating them to their environment, and in searching for prototypes and comparable oral materials in non-Negro cultures. Musicologists and, more recently, ethnomusicologists have probed relentlessly into the musical structure of Negro songs. Collectors in the past few years, if they were seeking undiscovered songs, have had to be content, in the main, with finding variants of already-known themes. Even the seemingly spontaneous, improvised tunes often contained familiar elements of words or melody, or both. What, then, was left to be said about Negro folk music in the United States? Merely that it was one of the prime sources of jazz?

In looking at Negro folk music as a whole, however, rather than just at spirituals, work songs, cries, or pentatonic scales, it seemed to me that quite a bit remained to be said about the subject to put it in a larger framework. For there is more to it than haunting melodies, humor, and plaintive themes. Among many other things, there is a cultural continuity, often only dimly perceived, and a relationship with other existing traditions. Running through American Negro folk music and lore there is unmistakable evidence of a large and significant oral literature. If we look at any single spiritual as just a "song" or an "example" we are missing the larger picture altogether, for it is in fact only a single point of contact with a rich and integrated religious view of life. And that view is not naïve or quaint unless all other religious views are naïve or quaint. It may safely be said, I think, that Negro folk music today is the largest body of genuine folk music still alive in the United States, and this alone justifies an effort to see it in the round.

I want to acknowledge here the assistance of the Wenner-Gren Foundation for Anthropological Research, which made grants available for the collection and transcription of Negro folk songs, a number of which appear in this book; and of the John Simon Guggenheim Foundation which supported a project to study the relationship between American Negro musical tradition and the traditions of the West Indies. Among the many individuals who helped me greatly in my collecting work in the South were Ruby Pickens Tartt of Livingston, Alabama; the late Thomas M. Campbell, who was field agent for the U.S. Department of Agriculture at Tuskegee Institute; S. W. Boynton, who was county agent for the Department at Selma, Alabama; C. J. Hurston, who was principal of Dallas County Training School at Beloit, Alabama; Rev. E. D. Tuckey and Mrs. Rebecca Anderson of Shiloh P. B. Church at Bogue Chitto, Alabama; and my wife, Emma Courlander, who assisted me on my 1950 recording expedition.

I also want to thank the various singers who provided me with many of the songs appearing throughout this book, especially Rich Amerson, Earthy Anne Coleman, Dock Reed, Vera Hall Ward, and Annie Grace Horn Dodson—all of whom gave very generously of their time. To Folkways Records and Moses Asch, I express appreciation for making their recorded materials available to me for use in this project. And to Alan Lomax and Harry Oster, thanks for their permission to notate several examples from their collections.

Most of the music transcriptions appearing here were prepared by John Benson Brooks and Mieczyslaw Kolinski from my own tape recordings, and other examples have been taken from selected pressings and Library of Congress recordings. Transcriptions by Dr. Kolinski are signed M. K., and those by Mr. Brooks are signed J. B. B.

May, 1963   HAROLD COURLANDER

Contents

The Music

Negro Folk Music, U.S.A.

I. The Setting

IT IS A LITTLE LATE in the day to apologize for reference to African traditions in discussing Negro folk music in the United States. Whether a large number of Negro spirituals developed out of white spirituals or not is of minor importance when one considers American Negro folk music in its entirety. The field is vast, and it is difficult to explore it or understand it properly without recognizing the African heritage. This is not to say that United States Negro music is African, but that many characteristics of African musical styles persist to this day. Some of those characteristics are melodic or rhythmic concepts. Some are to be found in the relationships between voices, and between voices and instruments. Others are in the instruments themselves, and in the use of those instruments. Still others are found in concepts of vocal and instrumental sound, in accidental conflicts with traditional Western scales, in motor actions associated with singing and dancing, and in attitudes toward music and music making.

That Negro folk music in the United States is preeminently "American" is all too evident. It could have come into being only in the United States, where elements of specific cultures were brought together under conditions that were not exactly duplicated anywhere else. European and African elements mingled to produce one result in the Spanish islands of the Caribbean, another in the English islands, a third in the French islands. The result was still different in Brazil and Venezuela. In all of those places, the process of cross-fertilization of musical styles continues, but elements of European and West African tradition survive, sometimes in pure form. In the days when analysis of Negro music in the United States depended on comparison with notated European and West African tunes, it was perhaps easy to accept the notion that European traits—primarily English, Irish, and Scottish—had almost obliterated the last vestige of African musical tradition. We are aware now that the evidence for a considered conclusion was inadequate. Among other things, African samplings were relatively sparse, and our conventional system of notation was not adjustable enough to properly set down various characteristics of African music. And finally, it is doubtful that the American Negro examples then analyzed represented a true cross section of the repertoire, spirituals being the choice exhibits.

Since the days of earliest interest in this subject, our knowledge of both the American and the African scenes has increased tremendously. We now have a vast reservoir of recorded folk or traditional music from Africa, the Caribbean, and Negro communities of the American mainland. Much work has been done in the field by ethnomusicologists, and anthropological observations have added a new frame of reference. We know that there is a wide range of styles in West African music, with differences within specific cultures as well as between regions. Some traits of Negro music in the United States that were once believed to be exclusively European have been found to exist also in Africa. Furthermore, certain heretofore unnoticed traits of United States Negro music have come to be recognized, and can now be related to specific African ways of doing things.

When it is appreciated that other elements of West African life and thinking have survived in the United States until recent times—and, indeed, even to the present moment—the surprise at finding a modest number of African musical traits is less, and it is easier to understand why American Negro folk music is different from American white folk music. Some of the resistance shown toward the fact of African survival has had a social rather than an intellectual character. There have been members of the Negro community who felt that the existence of African survivals was a disparagement of their group, that mention of such matters only served to belittle the cultural accomplishments of the Negro American. Conversely, there were whites who held tenaciously to the view that when the African came to the New World he was without significant values and traditions, and that everything the Negro knew was gleaned from the white society around him. But various elements of African-derived custom, including attitudes and values, which are visible today in the United States, even in subtle or disguised forms, contradict both of these positions.

The Negro slaves of the New World came from many regions of West and West-Central Africa, and were recruited from some cultures whose accomplishments have only recently come to be fully appreciated. The Yoruba, the Fon people of Dahomey, the Ashanti, and various other tribes of West Africa had highly developed religious systems, complex systems of law and equity, pride of history and tradition, a high order of arts and crafts, music and dance, a vast oral literature ranging from proverbs to epics, moral and ethical codes in large part comparable to those of Asia and Europe, and complex systems of social organization. It is only in recent years that the true significance of West African achievements has come to be fully appreciated. African sculptural art emerged only in this century into the full light of day as a powerful tradition; it deeply affected Western painters and sculptors, and art collectors and dealers have set a high price on their African wood carvings, ivory carvings, and brass castings. More recently, the true nature of African musical accomplishment is being comprehended as a far cry from "monotonous chanting" and tom-tom playing described by early visitors to the Dark Continent.

It is difficult to imagine that huge numbers of African exiles, gathered together in a new setting, would forget everything they knew and become a vacuum into which the attributes of another culture could be poured at will. In the ordinary course of adjustment, the African and his descendants absorbed and learned from the dominant culture in which they found themselves. Those attributes of the master culture which were essential to their survival, or which were congenial to their past learning, were taken over most quickly, while they clung to those aspects of African life for which they found no satisfactory substitutes. The tenacity man has shown for clinging to old values is a constant source of wonder. Witness the presence of the Christmas tree, inherited, we are to understand, from pre-Christian rites, standing as a symbol in the midst of rituals dramatizing the birth of Christ. When we recall that African slaves were imported into the United States legally until early in the nineteenth century, and as contraband virtually until the Civil War, we realize that African motifs have been injected into this setting within the lifetime of some persons still living.

The nature of some of these motifs has been made clear by anthropological studies of the past two or three decades. Additional validity has been given to such studies by work done in other Negro communities in the Americas, providing a new base for comparison. Acculturation in the islands of the West Indies, in Brazil, Venezuela, and Surinam, for example, had one common element—African cultural inheritance. Certain muted, disguised, or filtered African survivals in the United States become more apparent when they are discovered to exist also in Jamaica, Haiti, or Trinidad in less disguised form. Our enlightenment on this score becomes more swift as we recognize the clues given so amply in these neighboring Negro communities.

In his book, *The Myth of the Negro Past*,[1] Melville Herskovits some years ago provided us with some valuable insights into New World African survivals. Some of those survivals are isolated phenomena; others are aspects of clustered phenomena which are held together by a central concept, for example, religious belief. Many are so commonplace as to go virtually unnoticed. The carrying of bundles on the head, the manner in which a young child is sometimes held so that it straddles the mother's hip, the woman's head wrapped in a kerchief or headcloth—all characteristic of the old South, and frequently seen today—are African patterns.[2] Hairdressing styles for girls—the plaiting into small designs and the binding or wrapping of tiny pigtails—so common until recently in the South, are characteristic of Africa and the West Indies. In Haiti, with its essentially African background, these hair designs are called "gardens." In the Georgia Sea Islands, rice was, and still is, winnowed in baskets or trays in the African manner, and at various places in the southern states, grain is pulverized in hand-hewn wooden mortars of the African type.[3] The way in which the mortar is used in the Sea Islands, with two or three women working together with long pestles, is clearly an African concept, as is demonstrated in photographic documentation in a book by Lydia Parrish, *Slave Songs of the Georgia Sea Islands*.[4]

A complex code of what we might be inclined to dispose of as "polite behavior" is noted by Herskovits [5] as having special significance in relation to African tradition. The conventionalized respect for elders, the aversion to "sassing" an old person, the turning of the head to demonstrate respect, the covering of the mouth when laughing, all are explained as manifestations of African attitudes. So are the interjections of "Ah-hah," "Do, Jesus," and other similar exclamations by a congregation in the course of a sermon, and of "Aint it so," "It's the truth," and "Yeah, man" by someone listening to a secular statement or narration. These exclamations are a reinforcement of, or applause for, the words of the speaker and are comparable to similar usage elsewhere in the Negro communities of the New World as well as in Africa.

The importance of fraternal orders, burial societies, and secret societies has been cited by Herskovits and others as having special meaning to Negro communities in the United States. With the breakdown of more ancient forms of social organization in the American setting, these organizations have been able to play a special role in assuring proper burial of deceased persons—a paramount consideration in West African life.[6]

Recent studies of the Gullah dialect of the Georgia Sea Islands have suggested that a significant part of the vocabulary has an African origin, rather than being, as stated by some earlier observers, a mispronouncing or corruption of English, or merely the survival of an early English dialect.

One spokesman for the earlier view, Guy B. Johnson, wrote that "the charm of the folk stories of the Sea Island people is inseparably bound up with the staccato tones of their speech and the quaintness of their idiom. . . . The first impression of the newcomer upon hearing the oldtimers talk is apt to be that he is listening to a foreign language. There are older Negroes in the Sea Islands who speak in such a way that a stranger would have to stay around them several weeks before he could understand them and converse with them to his satisfaction. . . . But this strange dialect turns out to be little more than the peasant English of two centuries ago, modified to meet the needs of the slaves. . . . From this pleasant speech and from the 'baby talk' used by the masters in addressing them, the Negroes developed that dialect, sometimes known as Gullah, which remains the characteristic feature of the culture of the Negroes of coastal South Carolina and Georgia." [7]

However, a study of the Gullah dialect by Lorenzo Turner found in the vocabulary of this region approximately four thousand words which appeared to be of West African derivation, in addition to many survivals in syntax, inflections, and intonations.[8] In Georgia, he recorded some songs with African word texts and others with mixed African and English words. He found that many African phrases had been rendered in English, while there were "whole African phrases . . . without change either of meaning or pronunciation." For comparison with his own findings, Turner referred to some earlier evaluations which dismissed African vocabulary survivals as negligible. He found that a considerable number of words that had been written down as though they were English or bizarre corruptions of English appeared to be Vai, Mende, and Wolof.

Not only workaday words but also many personal names have been demonstrated to have West African origin. Such names as Coffee (Ashanti: Kofi), Bilah, and Kwako (all heard at one time or another by this observer), and a number of others of West African provenience may be encountered almost anywhere between the East Coast and the Mississippi. In addition, many personal names in English, such as Tuesday, Thursday, Foreday, and Earthy, carry on a West African practice of calling children after special days or phenomena associated with circumstances of birth or other traditional considerations. Turner found that all twelve months of the year and all seven days of the week are used as names, in addition to Wind, Hail, Storm, Freeze, Morning, Cotton, Peanut, Hardtime, Easter, and Harvest.[9]

African vocabulary and grammar patterns have survived elsewhere in the Americas, as indicated in various studies of New World pidgin English (in Surinam) and Creole (the West Indies). Even tonal aspects of African speech may prove to have left their mark on Negro speech in the New World. The traditional "musical" quality of the Negro dialect, so-called, may well be related to African use of tone for semantic purposes.[10]

American Negro folk tales, which make up a large part of the oral literature, include animal stories, human tales, tales of magic, moralizing stories, and some tales that verge on the heroic or epic. A great portion of them stem from European oral tradition, some are from the Bible, and many derive from daily life in slavery and postslavery days; but in the view of this writer and a number of other investigators, an overwhelming number of the stories have prototypes in West and Central Africa. The African affinity is seen most readily in the animal tales first popularized in the white segment of the population by Joel Chandler Harris in his Uncle Remus series, but it is also apparent in stories of other kinds. Some tales have been found in which a king or another notable person replaces West African sky deities or culture heroes. Anansi, the Ashanti trickster hero (originally a spider), as well as his son Intikuma, is called by name in a large cycle of tales told in the United States and other New World Negro settings.[11]

Religious life, also, is marked by retention of persistent concepts and attitudes that were originally developed in the West African cultures. Among the more conspicuous retentions are the Negroes' regard for baptismal or water rites, their view of the ecstatic seizure as an orthodox expression of faith, and the unusual importance of music and—except where it has gone out of style through the desire to conform to white practices—rhythm. All of these elements are essentially a part of West African religious ritual, and are found to have persisted strongly in either pure or disguised form in a large part of Negro America, notably Haiti, Jamaica, Trinidad, the Guianas, Carriacou, Cuba, Venezuela, and Brazil. The ecstatic seizure—getting of the "spirit"— fundamental in African religious experience, is a commonplace characteristic of religious worship, "pagan" or Christian, throughout Negro areas of the Western Hemisphere. Water rites, sometimes called "baptising," pervade almost every aspect of Haitian religious practice. The significance of this aspect of worship has been set forth in a number of anthropological studies.[12]

If one goes back just beyond the turn of the century, he finds that Negroes in the Louisiana area were familiar with the names of a number of West African deities, such as Limba, Agoussou, Dani (Dan), Liba (Legba or Limba), and others, all of whom had become syncretized (as in Haiti, Jamaica, and Trinidad) with Christian saints.[13] Numerous rites concerned with burials, wakes, and other occasions for memorializing the dead have been shown to retain certain characteristics of African practice which are generally not present in Euro-American tradition. Not more than fifty or sixty years ago drumming and African-style dancing in church, at wakes, and at funerals were known at least in the Georgia Sea Islands, and probably elsewhere on the mainland. Remnants of the religious dance are found today in the shout, in which shuffling and handclapping are an echo of the common scenes of a few generations ago.

Having recognized the presence of specific African traits in Negro life in the New World generally, and in the United States in particular, we are in a somewhat better position to examine and evaluate non-European, seemingly African characteristics of American Negro folk music. That there was African influence is not to be doubted, and if the music reflects that influence it is difficult to reject the evidence out of hand.

To state the proposition another way, if we were to find in the body of our folk music a trait that was found elsewhere only, say, in Tibetan singing, we could not lightly attribute it to Tibetan origin in the face of what we know about our history. There was no Tibetan immigration to this country. Few, if any, of our immigrants had any contacts with Tibetans. Look as we might, it would be extremely difficult to find even a slim bridge between Tibetan culture and our own. Our newly discovered "Tibetan" musical trait, therefore, would in common sense have to be attributed to another source or to independent invention. But inasmuch as Africans came to the New World in great numbers, had a deep-rooted tradition of music and dancing, both secular and religious, and preserved many details of their home cultures, it would be something of a miracle if no vestige of their musical tradition remained.

The European elements that have gone into the making of Negro folk music in the United States are many. English, Scottish, and Irish folk tunes, sea chanteys, hymns, and white spirituals have made a deep impact. In Louisiana, various types of French influences were felt. French folksongs, folk dance music, and salon dance music must have been ubiquitous, first among the white population and then among the Negro freedmen and slaves. By the time of the Civil War, they were the common property of all. Cajun (Acadian) folk music, originally from rural France, arrived in Louisiana with the Acadian refugees from Nova Scotia in the eighteenth century. Though the Cajun style of singing is quite distinctive, and though it remains essentially the property of the Cajun community in or near the Louisiana bayous, Negro neighbors of these people have been much influenced by it.[14] Additional French influences came from the Caribbean area, along with a hybridized African style. There was a continual coming and going of French planters and their families between Louisiana and the French West Indies, and slaves were transferred from the islands to the mainland as required. The result was a Creole culture with a more or less unified character embracing Louisiana and the French Caribbean. The slaves of the West Indian and Louisiana plantations spoke a common language (Creole), shared common traditions of music and dance, and had a common folklore. Some songs are still sung in Louisiana that would be more readily understood and appreciated in Haiti and Martinique than in France or Alabama. Musicological studies are yet to be made to show the extent of Spanish influence on the folk music of the Louisiana region.

Although Africans or slaves of African ancestry had numerous contacts with Indians in various parts of the country (there were a number of Indian slave owners), there is no substantial evidence that Indian musical elements were absorbed by the developing mainstream of Negro folk music. Curiously enough, a study by an outstanding ethnomusicologist, George Herzog, indicated that at least one group of Cherokee Indians took over elements of African musical style from the Negro slaves.[15]

Even when the basic historical influences have been accounted for, however, the story is not complete. Various regional musical phenomena such as the so-called hillbilly style of the southeastern mountains, the western and cowboy styles, and the ever-changing "new style" music of the cities infiltrated, or at least affected, Negro folk music. Evidence of these tributary cultural streams is to be found in the repertoire of many a Negro singer. With the advent, first, of the phonograph and, second, of the radio in the twentieth century, an almost imponderable number of influences came to bear on all American folk music—Negro and white alike.

Records and radio introduced into the development of Negro musical tradition a new element which might be termed "feedback." A traditional type of folksong was picked up by a recording artist and sung in a new way. If the record became popular, a new generation of singers began to utilize some of the personalized contributions of the recording artist. In time, the new version, or elements of it, became, once more, folk music. When we become aware that the folk music of our day is drawing heavily upon records and radio, and that records and radio are in turn using folk music as a basic source, it is possible to comprehend in a dim way the permutations and combinations of the changes at work in the "feedback" process. One result of this activity is that we may hear cowboy tunes that are reminiscent of Negro blues; blues that sound like songs of the Golden West; hillbilly tunes and instrumental combinations that gallop through mountainized versions of John Henry or John the Revellator with jugs, jew's-harps and washtubs; jazz-like treatments of old religious songs; Calypsoish skiffle bands in New Orleans and Mobile; and gospel songs with a suggestion of "Moon Over Indiana" in them. This sort of thing is, of course, not essentially new. Musical acculturation between deep sea sailors and Negro stevedores, between Negro churches and white churches, and between Negro and white railroad workers has been going on for a long time. But the pace and acceleration of cross-fertilization in recent years probably never have been equalled.

In any discussion of Negro folk music the question of inborn musical talents is sure to come up. It has been a cliché, not altogether dispelled, that the Negro's sense of music is instinctive, or at least biologically inherited from his African ancestors. The nearest thing to an instinctive sense of music is the natural capacity that all men share, in greater or lesser individual degree, to make and to respond to music. An individual may inherit a capacity of this kind biologically, but there is no available evidence that any large ethnic group possesses a native talent for music greater than that of any other group. There is no racial or national monopoly on the art of music making. That there is a Negro inheritance is undeniable, but the inheritance is not biological but cultural. Negroes who have grown to maturity out of reach of Negro cultural influences may have no more sense of counterpoint and blue tonality, and no more ability to give a field cry, than the average Hudson Bay Eskimo. A Negro trained in France from early youth to choir-style church singing will give no hint that his forebears had any other tradition. Some Negroes in Louisiana sing in pure French or Cajun style. Negroes who are born and raised in a social setting which places no value on, or rejects, traditional Negro musical values may demonstrate only the most commonplace musical aptitudes. And clichés to the contrary, some Negroes are totally unable to keep time, dance, or sing anything but a sour note. In all of these respects they do not differ from people of any national or racial origin. It is not genes or blood, but social tradition—in short, culture—which is the carrier. In a setting where everyone sings, where music is found in some aspect in almost every important religious and secular situation, and in which group participation is a deeply rooted custom, the individual absorbs and becomes to some extent capable in the musical idiom of his culture. A non-Negro raised in a Negro community could be expected to have at least average awareness and feeling for Negro music.

Some years ago I was present at an Afro-Cuban secret society meeting a short distance from Havana. The activities of the society were remarkably African. African-style dances and rituals were accompanied by African-style drumming and singing. The membership was predominantly Negro, but participating were a number of white Cubans who had been admitted to the organization. Their dance postures and movements were in no way distinguishable from those of the Negroes, nor was their singing. Their voices had even acquired the peculiar timbre which is identified with the Negro voice. Living in close proximity to Negro esthetic values, these white Cubans found no difficulty in accepting such values and making them their own.[16]

All Negroes do not shuffle, boogie, sing spirituals and blues, and move with the beat. But where Negro cultural values have survived as a result of social factors, Negro musical traditions remain strong and dynamic.

II. Negro Folk Music in the United States

THE TERM "Negro folk music" is no less imprecise than "white folk music," and, for reasons that are readily apparent, the once favored term "Afro-American music" can be both inadequate and misleading. Yet, there remains the necessity of having an expression by which to refer to the musical and the musico-literary traditions of the Negro community in the United States. The term "Afro-American" in relation to Negro custom—musical or otherwise—seems to imply that African tradition is tremendously important and that Negro music-making in the United States has an essentially African core. Few scholars entertain this point of view, even though the true significance of the African contribution has become more and more clear. "Negro folk music," on the other hand, suggests, perhaps unwittingly, that race has something to do with tradition, a concept that is untenable in the light of modern knowledge. Influences that played a part in the development of music in Negro communities (in Africa as well as in America), as we have noted, were not racial. Thus, different settings, different local histories, and different social juxtapositions in the United States produced different kinds of "Negro" music.

The interplay of African and French traditions in Louisiana resulted in a music different from what African and British traditions produced in eastern Georgia. The former situation related the music of Louisiana Negroes more closely to the culture of the French West Indies than to that of the United States in general. In speaking of the music of Negro communities in the United States, we are dealing with variable elements. English tradition may be noteworthy in one place, French in another, and in some localities circumstances have contrived to perpetuate recognizable African characteristics. For all of these combinations and variations, we must have a convenient label. Where the expression "Negro music" or "Negro folk music" is used in this discussion, it is intended to refer not to a phenomenon of race, but to a complex musical development which took place, and which is taking place, within the Negro communities of the United States.

Negro folk music in the United States has both general and special characteristics which distinguish it from the folk music of pure European or Anglo-American origin. This is true, first of all, of the music *per se*—what it sounds like in tones, intervals, rhythms, harmonies, and so on. It is also true of the manner in which these effects are achieved, in the exploitation of instruments (including the human voice), and—on occasion—in the concept of sound as an aspect of motion. Negro music, furthermore, varies from other American folk music in the uses to which it is put, and the events and circumstances to which it is related. And it is significantly different in the literary sense—the specialized qualities of its imagery and the nature of the ideas with which the images deal.

We must not forget that this body of music is the result of an irrational blending process. Certain melodic lines may be indisputably European. Certain rhythmic patterns may be almost identical to rhythms found in the West Indies or West Africa. Certain images may coincide precisely with those found in songs of English or Irish derivation, and certain themes may correspond with similar themes known in the non-Negro mountain communities, or recall songs typical of the western ranch country. But, with all the permutations and combinations, there remains the reality that, taken as a whole, the Negro folk music idiom is an integral and somewhat separate phenomenon and has a character completely its own. This will be modified in time, and it is being modified now, to the extent that Negro music accepts more and more elements from other idioms, and to the extent that Negro music is drawn upon by jazz, popular music composers, and contemporary classical composers.

It is not likely that any over-all definition of the nature of Negro folk music could be stated, but it is possible to examine some of the elements and aspects of that music and to see how and where it may be distinguished from the mainstream.

A great deal of American Negro music has been found to use the pentatonic scale, which in its commonest form is made up of the tones corresponding to the black keys on the piano. Many Negro songs utilize other so-called "gapped" systems, such as the ordinary major scale lacking its fourth or its seventh—in other words, the pentatonic plus an additional note, either the major fourth or the major seventh. Other scales are the major with a flatted seventh, the minor with a raised sixth, the minor without the sixth, and the minor with a raised seventh; these four, according to some analysts, have been characterized as probable survivals of scales brought from Africa.[1]

A considerable part of the early day controversy over African influences in United States Negro music had to do with use of the pentatonic scale. Henry Krehbiel analyzed 527 Negro songs and found 21 percent of them to be in the pentatonic scale,[2] while other studies, with different samplings, showed a figure as high as 35 percent. To many scholars, this pointed toward a strong African influence. To others, it suggested just the opposite conclusion. Guy B. Johnson, for example, noted that examination of white folk songs of the southeast mountain area of South Carolina showed that the pentatonic scale was used in 21 to 28 percent of the tunes. "From this comparison," he said, "it is obvious that the spirituals have no monopoly on the pentatonic mode. Indeed, there is ground for suspicion that the similar proportions of pentatonic tunes in spirituals and in white folk songs are not entirely accidental, for it would be rather strange if a body of folk song with an English heritage should by mere chance have so near the same proportion of pentatonic tunes. The same holds for other traits—the absence of the seventh tone, the absence of the fourth tone, flat seventh tone, etc.—for these occur as frequently in the English-American folk songs as in the spirituals." [3] In further support of the conclusion that Negro spirituals are based on European melodic principles, which is shared by a number of students of American folk music, numerous examples are cited of the incorporation of whole tunes and bits of lyrics into spirituals from English or Anglo-American songs.

It seems apparent at this stage that when the African versus European controversy was launched, few of us had a full understanding of the African musical culture. It is only within recent times that we have had access to a large body of recordings of African music, but that short acquaintance has made it evident that African music has more in common with Western folk music than was heretofore recognized. It was once fashionable to speak of African musical attributes as being quite exotic. Africans were believed to use scales of their own devising and to be fairly ignorant of harmony. However, comparison of African melodic conceptions which has been made possible because of our present wealth of African recordings indicates that there are many parallels to be found in European and Euro-American folk music. It is further evident that African use of harmony is far more frequent than heretofore acknowledged. In some African areas, four-part harmonization is a fairly standard performance.[4] As seen by Richard Allen Waterman: "Almost nothing in European folk music . . . is incompatible with African musical style, and much of the European material fits readily into the generalized African mold. Thus, in the United States as in other New World areas controlled by English-speaking Europeans, folk tunes and hymns stemming from the British Isles were often seized upon by African slaves and their descendants and, after suitable remodeling, adapted as American Negro tunes." [5]

In evaluating the belief held by some specialists that United States Negro songs are almost entirely indebted to English melodic influence, it must be taken into account that many of the studies on which the conclusion is based dealt primarily or exclusively with the so-called "spirituals." If our conclusions are to be valid for Negro singing in general, where are our references to blues, field calls and cries, field songs, cotton picking songs, lumbering songs, rowing songs, railroad songs, preaching-singing styles, prayer singing, aberrational church singing styles such as those found in the sanctified cults, ring shouts, game songs, longshoremen's songs, juking joint songs, prison camp songs, secular songs of ridicule and recrimination, songs accompanied by percussion devices or banjo, and numerous others that quickly come to mind? One thing that seems obvious is that the whole church syndrome—brought directly to the Negroes by the whites—would be likely to include a larger percentage of European elements than would be the case in a situation where an entire, preformulated institution were not involved. Whatever the validity of conclusions regarding the English source for spirituals, they do not seem to apply to the field of Negro folk music as a whole.

Furthermore, closer familiarity with Negro folk music as it is heard in its natural setting, and with the problem of notating it without merely approximating it or distorting it altogether, unavoidably suggests that the notations from which much Negro music has been analyzed may be inadequate and include false implications. As an example, we might question how many times the partly flatted third and seventh notes have been transcribed as naturals or as simple flats.

Another observation concerns the assumption that the essence of Negro music—or any other music—has been adequately explored when melodic or scale characteristics have been probed. Melody is only a single facet of the problem. A growing interest in jazz origins has created a heightened concern in recent times with rhythmic aspects. Whether jazz enthusiasts are correct in assuming that rhythmic motifs in jazz are mainly African is beside the point. The point is that early studies dismissed rhythmic elements, and many others, as a style of presentation, not recognizing that a style of presentation is in itself an integral part of a musical concept. Also to be considered are harmony and polyphony, canonical elements, various relationships between singers, the use of the voice and the accepted standard of what constitutes good voice, the relationship between music and motor activity, the manner of projecting the music, tone requirements as they relate to instruments, the form of accompaniment, the content of the songs, the use to which music is put (which affects its character), and traditional attitudes toward singing in general.

Information gathered in recent years by anthropologists in West Africa and the West Indies, as well as in the United States, and the emergence of a body of specialists in ethnomusicology, have increased immeasurably our understanding of what we are hearing in a Negro folk song, as well alerting us to the possible significance of seemingly random, makeshift, improvisatory, or "accidental" characteristics.

One of the commonly cited characteristics of the Negro blues song is "blue tonality," the partially flatted third and seventh notes (E-flat and B-flat in the key of C). This commonplace of the blues in actuality is found in many different kinds of Negro folk music—work songs, religious songs, and others. In describing the style of a well-known gospel singer, the jazz specialist Marshall Stearns says: "Two areas in the octave—the third and the seventh in the scale . . . —are attacked with an endless variety of swoops, glides, slurs, smears, and glisses." [6] This difficult-to-define treatment of the thirds and sevenths is what produces the blue tones. The blue notes can be shown in various ways. If we use the symbol ↓ to indicate a tone somewhat lower than shown, but short of a full flat, the blues intervals can be depicted as in Example 1.

EXAMPLE 1

Thus we see that the third and seventh tones appear both as naturals and partial flats.

In the blues song shown in Example 2, we can observe the changing intonation of the third above the main note C. It appears as a natural, a flat, and a ↓ (a tone lower than natural but short of a full flat).

EXAMPLE 2

Again, in Example 3, we see the tone play centering on the seventh above middle C. There is a B flat, a B flat ↑ (a tone above B flat but short of B natural), and a B natural.

According to Stearns, the fifth tone is increasingly being used in modern jazz as a blue note.[7]

The cultural source for the partially flatted thirds and sevenths has not been established. According to the musicologist Mieczyslaw Kolinski, they are not a common occurrance in West African singing,[8] though some observers have noted their presence in African areas other than the ones in which Kolinski has done most of his work. Stearns quotes A. H. Jones, the British musicologist, as saying he never heard an African sing an exact third or seventh as it is known in our scale.[9] Some specialists hold that true blue tonality is not to be found in the European tradition.

EXAMPLE 3

Let me go home,_____ whis - key,
let me walk out____ that door._____
Let me go home,_____ whis - key,
let me walk out____ that door._____
Well___ I'm feel - in' so fine_____ but I
just____ can't__ take it no more._____

Kolinski, on the other hand, has observed the presence of blue notes in English folk songs.[10]

Is it safe, in the absence of hard evidence to the contrary, to regard this characteristic of Negro music as a New World development? Some people think so. But it is probably not safe to regard the blue tones as aspects of a rigid scale concept. Accurate transcription of Negro songs as they are sung in their own environment, rather than in detached settings, shows that some other notes of the scale, including the fifth tone mentioned by Stearns, on occasion are partly raised or lowered. As an infrequent thing, this might suggest simply a careless attitude toward established intervals. But as a fairly common occurrence it raises questions. One may ask whether certain "true" tones according to our scale are not regarded by at least some traditional singers as centers of gravity around which there is a microtonic play. One informant, a country-style blues singer in Alabama, explained that he "played with the notes" in the same manner that he "played with the beats." If understood correctly, this statement could suggest the existence of tone play comparable to syncopated time play. Kolinski disagrees with this possibility and holds that many of the partially raised or lowered notes are, so to speak, accidentals.[11] There undoubtedly are some grounds for this view. However, one notes that there are a variety of tones in African, Afro-Haitian, and Afro-Cuban usage which do not conform to notes in our tempered scale. In evaluating the partially lowered or partially raised tones heard in United States Negro singing— thirds, sevenths, and others—one must consider whether they are truly accidentals or whether they are the result of certain freedoms allotted to the singer within the tradition. Many of the singers "guilty" of these accidentals have a fine sense of music and are clearly capable of distinguishing one tone from another. And the Negro community at large is at least as aware in a musical sense as the white community. From the point of view of this observer, the occurrence of so many partially sharped and flatted tones in Negro singing cannot be explained away as the result of imprecision or accident. It might be well to consider whether they are not, for the most part, "incidentals" rather than "accidentals," and whether the blue "scale" is not something else than it has appeared to be.

One general impression that comes from listening to spirituals, worksongs, and other traditional forms of Negro music is that there is an absence of harmony. Group singing tends to be in unison, sometimes in octaves. But certain notes or groups of notes may be sung in simultaneous seconds, thirds, fourths or fifths. This is particularly true in church singing and gang singing. Responsive voices in one worksong,[a] for example, sang as in Example 4.

EXAMPLE 4

[a] See The Music, 26.

A two-voice gospel song [b] contained the figures in Example 5.

EXAMPLE 5

Some improvisatory and semi-improvisatory singing produces un-mistakable polyphony-like effects, as in the fragment of a prayer song given in Example 6. The top staff represents the voice of the "helper," and the bottom staff that of the leader.[12]

EXAMPLE 6

J. B. B.

While voice interplay of this type is most easily heard in the church setting, it is not unknown in secular singing situations, and it is possible to wonder whether jazz instrumentation does

[b] See The Music, 20.

not owe something to it. In any event, this kind of harmonization is solidly within the Negro tradition. The type of premeditated harmonizations used by various Negro quartets, glee clubs, and other vocal groups are latter-day developments shared with the non-Negro community.

In most traditional singing there is no apparent striving for the "smooth" and "sweet" qualities that are so highly regarded in Western tradition. Some outstanding blues, gospel, and jazz singers have voices that can be described as foggy, hoarse, rough, or sandy. Not only is this kind of voice not derogated, it often seems to be valued. Sermons preached in this type of voice appear to create a special emotional tension. Examination of African singing tradition indicates that there, too, "sweetness" of voice is not a primary objective, and that other considerations are regarded as more relevant to good singing.

When I was collecting musical materials in Haiti some years ago, some of my friends brought a woman who was described as one of the best singers in the region. As a singing leader, she proved to have a remarkable repertoire and a dynamic, compelling style which gave her complete command over the other singers and the drums. Her voice, however, was conspicuously raspy, a fact that went unnoticed by the Haitians present. Another singer with what seemed to me to be a marvellously clear, bell-like voice was quickly disposed of by them. They declared that she knew songs but did not know how to sing. It is obvious that similar considerations exist in Negro singing in the United States and that they are linked to old traditions. Apparently valued in Negro folk music is the "throaty" quality that has "body" to it.

Nevertheless, even body is no substitute for experience—that is to say, understanding of how a song should be sung. In the course of recording gang songs in Negro prisons in southern United States, Alan Lomax asked his informants what was required in a good singing leader. One man, reflecting the general view, declared:

"It wouldn't just exactly make any difference about the dependability of his voice, or nothing like that. . . . But it would take a man with the most experience, to my understanding, to make the best leader. You see, if you'd bring a brand new man here, if he could have a voice, why he could sing just like Peter could preach, and he didn't know what to sing about, well, he wouldn't do no good, see? Well, here's a fellow, maybe he aint got no voice for singing, but . . . he been on the job so long till he knows exactly how it should go; and if he can just mostly talk it, why, you understand how to work with him. . . . It don't make any difference about his voice. . . . The time, that's all it is. . . . You can just whistle . . . and if you know the time and can stay in there with the axes you can cut just as good as if you was singing. But you have to be experienced." [13]

Although singing for a team of woodcutters or track liners may have special requirements, the attitude that "it don't make any difference" about the quality of the voice itself applies equally to preaching, praying, blues singing, and street singing. The cultivated or smooth voice has no advantage over the hoarse, rough, or foggy voice owned by an understanding singer who knows what to do with it. It is clear that something of this folk value has carried over into jazz. In commenting upon the human voice in jazz blues, Leonard Feather states:

"[Louis] Armstrong symbolized what were then, and to some degree still remain, the essential qualities that constituted the Jazz singer. The parched, gutteral tone had something akin to the sounds that musicians then identified as jazz timbres. . . . Perhaps not by coincidence, many of those who followed Armstrong were also trumpet players whom nature had provided with gutteral voices that seemed to speak and sing the language of jazz. . . ." Ethel Waters is described by Feather as "adding a synthetic 'hot' touch through the use of occasional growling tones." [14]

There are various singing conventions in Negro tradition which, although not unknown elsewhere, are generally not found in other American folk music. One of them is the tendency to break into falsetto tones, sometimes for a note or two, on occasion for whole phrases or entire songs. This is not, as sometimes has been stated, the result of inability on the part of the singer to reach tones higher than his natural register. In Negro tradition the falsetto has an esthetic value placed upon it. African singers often use falsetto as an informal style for singing solo and in small groups, and men singing at work in the fields or forests may sing to themselves in this register. In Haiti, Jamaica, and other West Indian islands, where falsetto singing is commonplace, it is regarded as "delicate," "refined," or "private" singing. In Haiti when two men sing together at work—as, for example, when pounding grain in a mortar [15]—one of them may use his falsetto voice while the other sings in natural register. In Haiti, Guadaloupe, and Carriacou, Negro male singers may begin a traditional dance song in falsetto and drop to natural voice when the drums begin to play. The widespread use of the falsetto throughout Negro America most assuredly relates it to West African practice.

Although cowboy songs are occasionally heard, in part, in falsetto register, the device appears, in this case, to have been taken over from Mexican singers and Mexican yodelling cries. In any event, the cowboy song with falsetto effects stems from a different tradition than the Negro falsetto, and the two do not seem to be related. One popular American performer of English and Anglo-American ballads sings a large part of his repertoire in false voice, but his style is purely individual and aberrant.[16]

Other Negro singing elements that are noteworthy are humming and "moaning and groaning." They are found in religious songs, worksongs, old-style blues, and field cries. "Moaning" does not imply grief or anguish; on the contrary, it is a blissful or ecstatic rendition of a song, characterized by full and free exploitation of melodic variation and improvisation, sometimes with an open threat, sometimes with closed lips to create a humming effect. On occasion moaning is done in falsetto, or utilizes falsetto breaks. Elements of this kind are sometimes observed in preaching and in church prayers, where they may result in rudimentary polyphony. The ecstatic significance of moaning is reflected in a religious song which goes, in part:

When you feel like moanin',
It aint nothin' but love.
When you feel like groanin',
It aint nothin' but love.[c]

It is worth noting, in passing, that the term groaning is used among Jamaican and other British West Indian cults to describe

[c] See The Music, 11.

ecstatic religious activity of a somewhat different kind, related directly to supplication.[17]

Another characteristic that has been observed in a large body of Negro songs, particularly in religious singing but also elsewhere, is the alteration or softening of various ultimate consonants to produce a desired aural effect. Thus r's and l's may be converted into musical n's or m's, the resulting tone resembling humming. Father is sometimes sung as fathum, mother as mothum, angel as angun, hammer as hammun, steel as steem, somewhere as somewhen, there as then, and ark as arm. Such softenings are clearly musical devices and are not heard in conversational speech, which has its own formula for modifying terminal sounds.

One of the readily recognized characteristics of Negro group singing is the leader and chorus responsive pattern. Wherever group singing takes place, whether in work gangs, in the home, or in church (except where innovations have been taken over), there is a natural tendency for two-part singing, the first part being that of the leader and the second that of the group. In a typical call and response form, the leader makes a statement of one or more phrases, with the chorus coming in at some point to add to the statement. In some instances the leader sings the entire song, with the chorus joining in toward the end of a line or phrase. In others, the response may consist of a repetition of the line sung by the leader. In addition, there are numerous combinations of these patterns.

A frequently observed practice is for the leader's part and the responsive part to overlap. Thus, the leader may start a new phrase before the chorus has quite ended, or the chorus may come in before the leader has quite finished, with the result shown in Example 7.

EXAMPLE 7

Let   me   ride   oh   let   me   ride,   oh
                                              oh

Many songs of the responsive type completely change character when sung in solo. A soloist trying to sing a song normally sung by a group usually tries to compensate in some way for the absence of a second part or choral response. Sometimes he finds it useful to eliminate the response altogether. The result is a rendition which, at best, only approximates the original and which is devoid of its intricacies, subtleties, and embellishments. Some singers will not attempt to sing such songs unless at least one "helper" is provided.

In secular group singing, the relationship of leader and response is often developed by the singers according to their feelings. Once the pattern has been set, it is followed throughout. Responsive parts in religious songs are rarely improvised, however; there is a more conservative attitude about religious singing, and there is generally a recognized "correct" response. In the church setting there is a familiarity with the song repertoire and recognition of proper responses as set by custom.

The notion of response is deep rooted in Negro culture, and great, if implicit and unstated, value is placed upon it. It is apparent in numerous situations, some of them nonmusical in character, ranging from story telling and preaching to simple conversations. A man telling a story or yarn, particularly if his rendition is effective, will often stimulate conversational responses such as "Oh, Lord," "Yeah," "Aint it so," and "It's true" at appropriate places. The interplay of narration and exclamation sometimes sets up a rhythmic, near-musical pattern. In church preaching, the whole effect is greatly pronounced. Almost any sermon will produce this response pattern. But if the preacher delivers his sermon in a rhythmic, compelling, musical fashion, as is common, the interplay of statement and response becomes something akin to singing. The element of response in all of these situations is paralleled in Haiti, Jamaica, and other West Indian islands, and in West Africa. It seems apparent that it is part of a long-standing concept of the relationship between a speaker, narrator, or singer and the group, and stems out of a sense of community participation and the value of polite behavior.

Another commonly observed element in traditional Negro music is the part played by patting and handclapping. Clapping is a normal way of providing percussive effects and maintaining a rhythmic pulse for singing. Thigh-slapping or patting was a com-

monplace accompaniment to old-time social dances such as the
Juba and to certain kinds of singing. Patting and clapping are
integral to most old style church singing and are used in most
children's ring game and playparty songs. Clapping beats may or
may not coincide with melodic accents. Often the clapping sounds
fall squarely between the stressed voice tones and constitute a
regular offbeat. In some church singing and ring games, one part
of the group claps on the melodic accent and the other in mid-
measure, producing an entirely different effect than if the entire
group were to clap double time. In addition there are variations
on these schemes, some of them resulting in syncopated or rag-
time rhythms.

Handclapping as accompaniment to singing is found in many
cultures, but although occasionally used, it is not a standard fix-
ture in non-Negro settings in the United States. On the other
hand, it is normally present in children's songs, playparty songs,
and certain types of religious songs in the Negro West Indies, and
it is apparent that this musical device is of African derivation.

In worksongs, tools such as axes, hammers, and tampers provide percussion effects of a different though related kind. The
tempo of work with heavy tools is necessarily slower than handclapping. But the work beat can relate to the melodic accent in
various ways, as seen in the following fragments of timber-cutting
songs (Examples 8 and 9).

EXAMPLE 8

In describing the relationship of work accents to the voice parts
in songs of this type that he heard in southern United States, the
singer Peter Seeger stated:

"If all the strokes came in unison, they would occur normally
on the third beat of each four-beat measure. If two groups al-

EXAMPLE 9

ternated strokes, the sound would come on the first beat as well." [18]

Rhythmic characteristics of Negro music in general have been well explored in recent times because of the considerable interest in blues, jazz, and its precursor, rag. It is a commonplace that Negro church music and secular music not only "swing" but also have much more sophisticated elements of offbeats, retarded beats, and anticipated beats than does Euro-American folk music in general. The import of African tradition to the rhythmic element in American Negro music is more or less taken for granted. As remote as U. S. Negro rhythm is from the African today, it is certainly closer to it in rhythmic concepts than to either English or French folk tradition.

In an analysis of African musical style, Waterman found that whereas the accents in European melodies tend to fall on either thesis or arsis of the rhythmic foot, the main accents of African melodies regularly fall between the down- and up-beats. "The effect thus produced is that of a temporal displacement of various notes of the melodic phrase, in relation to the percussion phrase, to the extent of half a beat. Since the percussion phrase is dominant, however, this technique can best be understood as an artful flirting with the possibility of establishing, by means of the melody, another, competing and disorienting, beat at the same tempo as that established by the percussion." [19]

This musical notion is detected in various genres of Negro folk song in the United States, less clearly discernible, perhaps, and less predictable, where some form of percussion effects is present, as in gang worksongs. Group singing to accompany axes, hammers, or tie tampers frequently produces the "artful flirting" described by Waterman.

One other element in Negro folk music can claim our attention, even though it may not be possible to derive from it a significant conclusion—the clearly expressed interest in buzzing and rattling sounds which extends from country tradition into jazz instrumentation. The buzzing effects of the popular kazoo and the spluttering sounds that are often made with the harmonica and brass instruments cannot help but recall the value placed on such sounds in West African usage. Throughout a large part of West and Central Africa, buzzing and other vibrating effects are considered musically desirable. Membranes attached to balafons, and tiny metal jingles attached to the keys of the sansa, are devised to produce these effects. If we consider the uncertain, "impure" tones of African horns and trumpets—made of wood, ivory, and animal horns—we may find a possible explanation of the Negro musician's effort in the United States to modify brass tones by the use of a wide variety of "muting" gadgets, from hats to bathroom plungers, and to create flutter tones. The extent to which traditional concepts of sound survive in a new setting is an intriguing question which deserves further research and study.

When a broad view of instrumentation in Negro folk music and jazz is taken, there is at least an impression that a traditional, distinct approach exists. It is almost as though every instrumental device is intended to produce a percussive effect. This subject is a kind of no-man's-land in the absence of better definitions of what we mean by the term percussive. Alan Merriam has put forward the view that in African music there is a strong percussive tendency, not only in use of the voice but of stringed instruments as well. He notes that "the musical bow, one of the softest of musical instruments in terms of dynamic level, is struck with a stick or plucked with the fingers, producing a sharp, though soft, sound," and that "trumpets of many kinds are played for percussive effect, though the notes themselves are melodic." [20] In American Negro instrumentation one finds this same element in the playing of the washtub bass and the double bass fiddle of the jazz band, in the traditional "attack" on the harmonica, in the use of the banjo, and, indeed, to some extent, in the use of brass instruments of the jazz ensemble. It is as though the instrument is not emitting a tone on command but is being compelled or coerced. The nature of this elusive phenomenon is perhaps not adequately understood, but it is difficult not to be aware of it.

While many of the relationships between jazz and Negro folk tradition are self evident, what are we to make of the often heard assertion that jazz is a folk music of the mid-twentieth century? Is jazz truly a folk form of modern times? If not, where does folk music leave off and where does jazz begin? To properly answer such questions, one must in some way attempt to define the outer limits of the jazz genre and to recognize what is contained within those outer limits. Unfortunately, a number of specialists in the jazz field have been unwilling to go much further than to state, in effect, that if the music is jazzy, it is jazz. The paucity of serious studies and objective analyses of the jazz style has resulted in a long series of repeated clichés about its nature and its derivations, and a tendency to describe it in terms of itself, or by reference to what certain performers are known to do while playing or singing. Indeed, if some jazz commentators were deprived of the use of names of performers and performing groups, they would have great difficulty in talking about jazz at all. Some jazz specialists lay great stress on psychological factors—that is, the state of mind of the performers and a somewhat mystical power of "communication." Another alleged characteristic of jazz—supposedly one of its marks of distinction—is "improvisation."

Marshall Stearns tentatively defines jazz as "a semi-improvisational American music distinguished by an immediacy of communication, an expressiveness characteristic of the free use of the human voice, and a complex flowing rhythm; it is the result of a three hundred years blending in the United States of the European and West African musical traditions; and its predominant components are European harmony, Euro-African melody, and African rhythm." [21]

The jazz critic Nat Hentoff says of jazz: "Its essentials are a pulsating (but not necessarily regular) rhythm; a feeling of improvisation (it is possible to write jazz so idiomatically that written notes sound improvised); vocalized instrumental technique and, conversely, instrumentalized phrasing in jazz singing; timbres and polyrhythmic usages that are rooted in the Afro-American folk music of three centuries." [22]

From the composer's viewpoint, John Benson Brooks regards jazz, seemingly, as a general remolding process: "Any and all music (including the sounds of environment) is taken to be (1) recleffed in inflection, (2) regrouped in sonority, (3) recontoured in movement (this is mostly in the written models), (4) voice outlines are then recadenced, (5) tonalities respecified, and (6) compositional usefulness re-modalized, mostly by development of improvisation or written-down improvisation upon the previous conception." [23]

Jazz specialist Charles Edward Smith, like many others, believes that jazz cannot be easily defined, but he lists a number of qualities that he regards as characteristic. Three important qualities, he feels, are (1) the relationship of jazz to Afro-American oral traditions, (2) instrumental usage influenced by the latter, and (3) thematic material representing further assimilation and alternation of a complex of African-European-American musical materials. And he says, further: "Improvisation in present day jazz is often treated as separate from the musical performance as such. However, in folk music related to it, in much early jazz, and even in some contemporary jazz, improvisation is warp and woof of the musical fabric." [24]

On many points, these definitions, and those of other experts, tend to agree, though there are areas of difference. There are those who hold that improvisation is one of the cornerstones of jazz, for example, while others—as we have seen—prefer more cautious terms such as "semi-improvisational" and "feeling of improvisation." And we may note that at least two of our definitions include the possibility of "written" improvisations.

In the definitions or descriptions of jazz that have been cited, there is no intimation that jazz is a folk form. No one can argue convincingly that the two genres are of the same kind because some of the recognizable characteristics of jazz are present in folk music forms. The folk forms existed independently of, and prior to, the development of what we know as jazz. It is clear that jazz developed out of folk music, primarily Negro, but in some basic ways it has become completely dissociated from folk music. Not that it does not go back to its sources for refreshment and stimulation. But those forays into folk music by jazz are no more significant than forays into Afro-Cuban music, religious music, or show music. In fact, the persistent search for new motifs, themes, sounds, and rhythms; the constant seeking for innovation; and the emphasis on personalities and performers' styles certainly indicate that jazz is much more of a "pop" or "art" medium than a folk medium. As we know it at this stage, jazz is pulling in two directions at once—toward "tradition" (which has widespread appeal and a capacity for communication) and toward "freedom," "variation," "improvisation," and "change." The pull toward change and innovation, superimposed upon an ever more distant "tradition," places jazz in the same category as other modern popular or art forms. Although much of jazz is not strictly "literate" (that is, written, in contradistinction to folk music), there is considerable arranging, manipulation, rehearsing, rendition in the style of this or that performer, and stress on devices (instrumental and in musical style). Despite the theoretical freedom of improvisation, the performers nevertheless have a non-folk, non-unwritten approach to their music.

Furthermore, jazz lacks the social meanings and functions of true folk music, and the lack cannot be compensated for merely by constant delving into original folk sources for material. Though jazz in its usual form may be *related* to the chain gang song, the preached Negro sermon, the Negro spiritual, the early blues, the old fraternal bands of New Orleans, the Negro field cry, and African tribal rhythms, and though it has perpetuated some characteristics of these musical forms, it is distinct and separate. Folk music is a community tradition; it has immediate meaning in its own environment, is more often than not functionally integrated into community life, and is conservative and slow to change. Such changes and variations as occur come about through mis-hearing, mis-remembering, misunderstanding, and the blending and confusion of different things, plus adaptation of old materials to new settings or situations. Naturally there are new creations, because folk music is a living phenomenon; new songs come into being, and influences from outside are absorbed. But there is little value placed on "newness" or "variation" as such; there is no feeling of compulsion to have something very different this year from last year; and unnecessary alteration of a traditional way, custom, or form is frowned upon.

Thus, in becoming afficionados of folk music, many young people seeking an *avant garde* outlook are in fact choosing a more traditional and conservative concept than is to be found in the "pop" or popular art music of their generation, and the fastidious manner in which they sing folk songs, exactly as they heard them sung, even to the personal idiosyncrasies of the singer whom they accept as their standard of excellence, is notable. Jazz "tradition" at best is only a few years old, so short a time that one may use the term only by imparting special meaning to it, and there has been so much change and development, consciously motivated, that it has little in common with the social aspect of folk music.

There is, of course, a border zone between jazz and Negro folk music where the two are difficult to disentangle. If blues are taken as an example, we see that the urban and field blues in their original settings were true folk music. They were an integrated element of the scene in which they developed; the messages or comments that they conveyed were intimately related to the life around them, much like the Negro prison work songs; they were interpretative, reflective, and critical of matters common to their community. It is not likely that the first blues were sung by professionals, though this in itself would not have disqualified them as folk music. The emergence of the blues as an art form rather than a folk form did not take place as a chronological evolution but as a functional evolution. Blues sung under traditional conditions and with traditional motivations, with the social or personal comment a communicative rather than an entertainment function, are folk blues. In this friendly environment they have the force, meaning, and substance of the African social comment song out of which they originally were derived. However, at the point where the blues serve solely as an entertainment medium, contrived, tailored, and performed for mass audiences, where emphasis is placed on production and uniqueness, where they are integrated into jazz singing, and described in terms of styles and professional performers, they cease to be folk music and become an art form with clearly discernible folk origins. "Art" blues and folk blues exist side by side, sometimes distinguishable from each other, sometimes not.

III. Anthems and Spirituals as Oral Literature

NEGRO RELIGIOUS SONGS include a wide range of styles, idioms, and substance. There are staid, square-measured songs that strongly reflect white hymns of an earlier day; rocking and reeling songs that truly shake the rafters; two part prayer songs of polyphonous character; spirited tunes that are nothing less than marches; shouts that call for percussive effects by clapping and foot stamping; songs in which popular musical instruments such as tambourines, guitars, drums, and harmonicas provide instrumental dynamics; songs that are sung quietly and songs that put people on their feet; ecstatic moans and groans; religious songs of street singers that are almost indistinguishable from blues; strident gospel songs calling on sinners to reform; and songs which transpose scenes from the Bible into moving, immediate, colloquial, and, often, magnificently dramatic terms. So broad, indeed, is the realm of Negro religious music that the customary title "spiritual" is patently inadequate to describe it. In fact, this word is not used by some people who sing these songs, the term "anthem" being preferred. Although the range and variety to be found are considerable, most of them are within the limits of what we recognize as Negro religious and literary idiom. Musical elements were commented upon previously, and at this point Negro religious songs will be explored as oral literature.

Listening to Negro religious songs as they are sung in a great many churches, particularly in the South, one cannot fail to be impressed with an element that is best described as conservatism. In any community, there may be a large repertoire of religious songs upon which to draw. Selections are made according to circumstances—that is, songs appropriate to an occasion are sung. Despite an effect of spontaneity, innovation is not a daily phenomenon. Except in churches which favor the modern gospel-type song, old songs are called upon, and they are used in established ways, though there may be variations within the outer limits set by custom. A given piece may be sung "regular meter" or "long meter"; it may be done by a small choir in somewhat stilted fashion, perhaps with piano accompaniment, or it may be sung in free fashion by the entire congregation.

A good singing leader or a preacher can endow a song with a special, dynamic character. Songs may gradually move from one community to another, and a single church may have within its repertoire a number of variants of an old theme. But there is to be found nothing like the freedom of improvisation and invention that is characteristic of secular music. One perceives the richness of the oral literature only partially in the repertoire of a single community; its full implications lie in the composite picture. Some songs are heard in Mississippi and Texas that are not sung in Georgia and South Carolina, and many songs which are widely known throughout the country are sung differently in different places.

Many of the newer elements in Negro religious music come from individual street singers, gospel groups, and large urban churches. The religious street singers are fewer today than they once were. But it is inconceivable that countless performers such as Blind Willie Johnson did not affect more traditional styles of singing in churches. The gospel songs—composed or arranged airs—are among the most recent elements. They are self-consciously literary and formal, and many of them are designed primarily for performance by an individual singer or a choir. The urban churches have gone further in blending tradition with new styles than have the rural churches. Some urban services, in fact, are super-productions which employ professional gospel-type singers, instrumental ensembles, and even full-blown brass bands. This latter development is not altogether synthetic or illogical. A half century and more ago brass bands played at least a semi-religious role in Negro life. In some regions of the South, particularly, bands of fraternal lodges participated conspicuously in funerals, beginning at the church and ending at the graveyard, and in other similar activities. The style of instrumental music in some contemporary churches where it is heard has been affected by both secular tradition and jazz. In some small rural churches, the presence of instrumental musical support is of long standing, and the use of such devices as guitars, drums, harmonicas, and tambourines is regarded as traditional.

As for the main body of religious songs, we find in it a large number of themes projecting the Christian concepts of faith, love, and humility, with considerable emphasis on salvation. Another large segment pinpoints events and stories recorded in the Old and New Testaments; if these songs are arranged in a somewhat chronological order, they are equivalent to an oral version of the Bible. Each song presents in a capsulized or dramatic form a significant Biblical moment. It has been possible for lay preachers of an earlier day to go from church to church armed only with a knowledge of these songs and their meanings and give sermons that have met the best existing standards.

Why did Negro oral religious literature take the particular form that it did, and why did it eventually diverge so much from the white tradition, in view of the fact that Negro Christian converts were presented with ready-made songs (white spirituals and hymns), an established way of singing them, and a pre-selected set of images and symbols? The answer must lie in an assumption that the materials thus made available were regarded as inadequate, in some respects, in relation to Negro tradition. For psychological and cultural reasons, the earliest Negro congregations found it necessary to remold these materials.

We can only speculate on the religious attitudes of the first few generations of Africans in the New World. But we have learned enough in recent times about African cultures to know that the slaves brought to the Christian service religious traditions of their own, as well as established methods of treating musical and invocational ideas. They had clear-cut concepts of the role of music in life. Music permeated virtually every important phase of living in Africa, from birth to death. Singing related to religious activity had a specific character and specific requirements. Most West and Central Africans had their own concepts of a supreme (though not necessarily exclusive) deity. In many instances, this deity tended to be somewhat remote, and their dealings—supplicative, invocational, and placative—were with lesser supernatural beings, including members of holy pantheons. These demigods were full of personality, their actions were as predictable or as unpredictable as those of humans, and many of them had epic histories. In religious rites, epic and dramatic actions of the demigods, as well as their special powers and attributes, were recalled and extolled. Those who served such deities sang songs of praise which alluded to their various powers, behavior, and noteworthy deeds. Much of the oral religious literature of the African layman consisted less of "prayers" (as we think of them) than of dramatic statements, in the form of songs, relating to the deities.

Confronted with new religious patterns, the New World African found in the Bible prolific materials adaptable to the traditional dramatic statement and, occasionally, to the epic treatment. He felt impelled to translate and recast Biblical events into a dramatic form that satisfied his sense of what was fitting. The stories of the Bible thus transmuted became vivid images or, sometimes, poetry.

To enhance the drama, other subject matter was drawn from whatever portion of the Biblical literature, or whatever aspect of contemporary life, seemed suitable and useful. Thus there are interpolations from the New Testament into the Old, and from the Old into the New. Job, Jesus, Judas, and Joshua may be found in the same song, along with the twentieth century train that carries the sanctified. In some instances songs emerged in a form akin to the epic. Few Negro songs project mystical or abstract philosophical concepts. They tend to concentrate on particular events, episodes, stories, and revelations.

Any notion that Negro oral religious literature is primitive or naïve—an impression conveyed by numerous literary treatments —certainly does not survive careful reading or hearing. The song "All God's Children Got Wings," far from being quaint or childlike, is an expression of faith couched in symbols that were apparent to most pre-literate slaves and, later, liberated Negroes. While some people must have taken the inherent promises of this song literally, for most Negroes the wings, harps, and shoes must have conveyed simply the idea of relief from a hard and unrewarding life, either in this world or another. If Negro religious imagery is truly "naïve," then the burden of responsibility must be borne by the Bible, out of which the imagery is primarily extracted.

Negro religious literature, like the secular, is marked by an economy of statement, rich and fresh scenes, and the capacity to evoke recognition and response. The entire story of Jonah is presented in a song of fourteen lines, every one of which is visual and dramatic.[a] Many of the songs do not describe events so much as allude to them. Some telescope a variety of allusions into a few tight phrases.

There are certain standard images which are called upon again and again. The allusion to Elijah's chariot, for example, occurs frequently. The chariot represents not only Elijah's transportation to heaven, but the heavenly ascent of all who are saved. The image occurs, among other places, in "Job, Job"[b] and in "Rock Chariot, I told You to Rock,"[c] where the allusion to Elijah's chariot is clearly tied to each individual's fate:

Rock, chariot, in the middle of the air.
Judgement going to find me.
I wonder what chariot comin' after me.
Judgement going to find me.

The theme appears again in the song "Tip Around My Bed Right Easy":

[a] See The Music, 1. [b] See The Music, 2. [c] See The Music, 3.

Jes' low down the chariot right easy,
  Right easy, right easy,
Jes' low down the chariot right easy,
  Right easy, right easy,
And bring God's servant home.

Another widespread image is that of the train, which represents more modern transportation to the same ultimate destination for those who have found salvation. Among many songs, it appears in "King David":

Just as soon as you cease
  Good Lord,
Children, from your sins,
  Good Lord,
This-a train will start
  Good Lord,
To take you in. . . .[d]

The train motif has in it a certain excitement, an excitement that many people, regardless of background, have felt on seeing modern diesel or old fashioned steam locomotives at close range. The impression that the snorting, smoking engines of an earlier day must have left on Negro song makers is evident in the frequent resort to this image, and in the excitement which it has the power to evoke. A ring shout cited elsewhere in this book [e] actually takes on the driving character of a moving train, and it ties the train image to that of the chariot, for which it is only a modern substitute:

Who's that ridin' the chariot?
Well well well.
One mornin'
Before the evening
Sun was going down
Behind them western hills.
Old Number Twelve
Comin' down the track.
See that black smoke.
See that old engineer. . . .

In another song, the train has a slightly threatening character, with less glory and exaltation and more hint of judgement at the bar:

[d] See The Music, 9.   [e] See Chapter X, p. 197.

Oh, the little black train is a-comin',
I know it's goin' to slack;
You can tell it by its rumblin',
It's all draped in black.

The train we are singin' about,
It has no whistle or bell,
And if you find your station
You are in heaven or hell.

There's a little black train and an engine,
And one small baggage car;
You won't have to have much baggage
To come to the judgement bar.

The chorus of the song, interspersed between stanzas, goes:

There's a little black train a-comin',
Get all your business right;
There's a little black train a-comin',
And it may be here tonight.[1]

A song taken by Lydia Parrish in the Georgia Sea Islands refers
to a wild horse in a somewhat similar context:

Loose horse in the valley.
    Aye.
Who goin' to ride 'im?
    Aye.
Nothin' but the righteous.
    Aye, Lord.
Time's drawin' nigh.[2]

In recent days, some errant gospel songs have gone so far as to
supplant the train with an airplane.

There are a good many other standard images of this type, including the wheel of Ezekiel and the gospel shoes.

Considerable attention has been paid in recent times to the possibility that a large number of spirituals were not what they
seemed on the surface, but in actuality were songs full of hidden
meanings, hints, messages, and signals for slaves looking toward
escape. The spiritual "Steal Away to Jesus," for example, frequently has been pointed out as a double-meaning song—osten-
sibly religious in intent, but in reality an invitation to the slaves
to steal away to freedom:

Steal away, steal away to Jesus,
Steal away, steal away home.
I aint got long to stay here.
My Lord calls me, he calls me by thunder,
The trumpet sounds within my soul.
I aint got long to stay here.

Similarly, the spiritual "Go Down Moses" has been regarded as a significant double-meaning song:

When Israel was in Egypt's Land,
 Let my people go.
Oppressed so hard they could not stand,
 Let my people go.
Go down, Moses, way down in Egypt's Land,
Tell old Pharaoh, let my people go.

And a later stanza:

No more shall they in bondage toil,
 Let my people go.
Let them come out with Egypt's spoil,
 Let my people go.
Etc.

Reminiscences of former slaves and the accretion of legend and hearsay have pinpointed Harriet Tubman, the Negro antislavery worker and unofficial "conductor" of the Underground Railroad, as the Moses of the song.[3]

It is readily evident that songs of this kind could be interpreted in more than one way by the slaves. The situation of the Israelites in Egypt as described in the Old Testament was one with which people in bondage could easily identify themselves. It is a safe assumption that all Negro religious songs were understood by the slaves in the light of their own immediate condition of servitude. In singing of the Israelites' flight to freedom, or the promises inherent in the visions of St. John, or the prophecies of the prophets, or heavenly salvation, it certainly must have crossed their minds that there was a remarkable parallel to be seen. Songs about Moses and Joshua must have had a much more personal and immediate meaning to the Afro-American than to his white master. Indeed, one must consider the possibility that the appeal of Christianity to the New World African and his slave descendants lay to a significant extent in these obvious Biblical parallels.

ANTHEMS AND SPIRITUALS   43

Nevertheless, if songs of the type of "Steal Away to Jesus" and "Go Down Moses" are to be considered conscious disguises for political, temporal meanings, a large part of the religious repertoire must be placed in the same category. Every reference to crossing the Jordan could be interpreted to mean escape to the North; every battle of the Israelites might be read to mean the battle for Negro freedom; every reference to Elijah's chariot or the gospel train could be seen as allusion to the Underground Railroad; and every trumpet blast interpreted as Emancipation Day. But such a notion would be difficult to accept. Negro religious activity and belief are not based on the principle of secular or situational parallels. Negro religious music must be considered to be, in the main, precisely what it purports to be.

It may well have been, as legend has it, that to some slaves Harriet Tubman was Moses. Yet in the semi-isolation in which many slaves found themselves, Harriet Tubman probably was not a household word, and "Go Down Moses" must have been sung by some slaves in the belief that Moses meant simply Moses. A large number of spirituals and anthems were so worded that they could have a disguised meaning; but it is not safe to assume (or even take the word of persons who were born in slavery) that they were created as anything else but religious songs.[4]

As suggested previously, it would be possible to put a large body of Negro religious songs together in a certain sequence to produce an oral counterpart of the Bible; if printed, they would make a volume fully as thick as the Bible itself. To see how this generalization works out in practice, it may be worthwhile to take a look at various examples.

In Genesis, we read: "And the eyes of both of them were opened, and they knew that they were naked: and they sewed fig leaves together and made themselves aprons. . . . And Adam and his wife hid themselves from the presence of the Lord God, amongst the trees of the garden. And the Lord God called unto Adam, and said unto him, Where are thou?" This story, on which so much of Christian theology turns, is told in song this way:

Oh, Eve, where is Adam?
Oh, Eve, Adam in the garden,
    Pinnin' leaves.

Adam in the garden,
  Pinnin' leaves.
Lord called Adam,
  Pinnin' leaves.
Adam wouldn't answer,
  Pinnin' leaves.
Adam shamed,
  Pinnin' leaves.
Adam?
  Pinnin' leaves.
Adam!
  Pinnin' leaves.
Where't thou?
  Pinnin' leaves.
Adam naked,
  Pinnin' leaves.
Aint you shamed?
  Pinnin' leaves.
Lord I'm shamed,
  Pinnin' leaves.[5]

Following closely on the heels of the Adam and Eve story in Genesis is the epic of the flood, told in broad and general terms, without the wealth of imagery, detail, and poetry found in later portions of the Bible. But such details as there are in the original have provided inspiration for many Negro songs about Noah and the Ark, with dramatic images created by the song makers themselves. Although the Bible states that Noah was instructed to make his craft out of gopher wood, this song, found in Alabama, declares it was made in fact out of hickory bark:

Noah, Noah, who built this ark?
Noah, Noah, who built this ark?
Now who built this ark?

Noah, Noah, built this ark,
Built this ark out of hickory bark.
Oh Lord, who built this ark?
Noah, Noah, who built this ark?
Who built this ark?

Noah, Noah, built this ark,
Built this ark without hammer or nails,
Oh Lord, who built this ark?
Noah, Noah, who built this ark?
Who built this ark?

Called old Noah foolish man,
Building this ark on this dry land,
Oh Lord, who built this ark?
Noah, Noah, who built this ark?
Now who built this ark?
Noah, No'.[f]

In the Georgia Sea Islands, a quite different rendition known
as "Noah [pronounced Norah] Hoist the Window" was taken
down by Lydia Parrish.[6] Although the structure of the song is different, and the total effect is that of independent composition, the
presence of identical lines suggest that the two versions had a
common origin. The chorus and one stanza of the Sea Islands
"Noah" are given here:

Oh Noah, hoist the window,
Oh Noah, hoist the window,
Oh Noah, hoist the window,
Hoist the window, let the dove come in.

And the foolish man come ridin' by,
Oh hoist the window, let the dove come in.
Well he point his hand and he scorn at Noah,
Oh hoist the window, let the dove come in.
And he call old Noah the foolish man,
Oh hoist the window, let the dove come in.
You buildin' your ark on the hard dry land,
Oh hoist the window, let the dove come in.

We have already taken note of a song dealing with the role of
Moses. Next comes Joshua, whose warlike accomplishments are
the subject of comment in many religious songs. Probably the
best known is "Joshua Fit the Battle of Jericho," but it is not
often that the words of that song are read in tranquility; too often
the poetry is lost in the triumphant sweep and surge of the music.
One version of "Joshua" is sung this way:

Chorus (after each stanza)
Joshua fit the battle of Jericho,
Jericho, Jericho!
Joshua fit the battle of Jericho,
And the walls came tumblin' down!
That mornin',
Joshua fit the battle of Jericho,

[f] See The Music, 15.

Jericho, Jericho,
Joshua fit the battle of Jericho,
And the walls came tumblin' down!

Good mornin' brother pilgrim,
Pray tell me where you bound,
Oh tell me where you travellin' to
On this enchanted ground.

My name it is Poor Pilgrim,
To Canaan I am bound,
Travellin' through this wilderness
On-a this enchanted ground.

You may talk about the King of Gideon,
You may talk about the man of Saul,
There's none like good old Joshua
At the battle of Jericho!

Up to the walls of Jericho
He marched with spear in hand.
Go blow them ram horns Joshua cried,
'Cause the battle is in my hand!

Then the lamb-ram-sheep horns began to blow,
The trumpets began to sound,
Joshua commanded the children to shout
And the walls came tumblin' down!

David is the protagonist of numerous songs, and around the
scene of David playing his harp in the following piece there are
woven various Biblical references and modern preachments; the
final effect is a panorama with a great vista. There is an impression about this song that it was once smaller and more limited in
scope, and that over the years it accumulated a number of themes
which came from the preacher's pulpit.

King David was
     Good Lord
That shepherd boy.
     Good Lord
Didn't he kill Goliath
     Good Lord
And he shout for joy.
     Good Lord
Well the tallest tree
     Good Lord

In Paradise
   Good Lord
Them Christians call it
   Good Lord
Their tree of life.
   Good Lord

   Chorus (after each stanza)
   Little David play on your harp,
      Hallelu, hallelu,
   Little David play on your harp,
      Hallelu.
   Didn't you promise to play on your harp,
      Hallelu, hallelu,
   Didn't you promise to play on your harp,
      Hallelu.

Just watch the sun
   Good Lord
How steady she run.
   Good Lord
Don't mind, she catch you
   Good Lord
With your works undone.
   Good Lord

You got a true way to find
   Good Lord
Mister Hypocrite out.
   Good Lord
At the first thing gwine
   Good Lord
To church and shout.
   Good Lord
You goin' to meet Mister Hypocrite
   Good Lord
Comin' along the street
   Good Lord
First thing he show you
   Good Lord
His tongue in his teeth.
   Good Lord

Just as soon as you cease
   Good Lord
Children, from your sins,
   Good Lord

This-a train will start,
    Good Lord
It'll take you in.
    Good Lord
Way down yonder
    Good Lord
By Jordan Stream
    Good Lord
You can hear God's children
    Good Lord
Tryin' to be redeemed.
    Good Lord
Aint Jordan wide,
    Good Lord
Old Jordan wide.
    Good Lord
Well none don't cross
    Good Lord
But the sanctified.
    Good Lord

Sister Mary goin' to heaven
    Good Lord
On the springs of the sun.
    Good Lord
When Mary got to heaven
    Good Lord
Well her work was done.
    Good Lord
Just talk about me
    Good Lord
As much as you please,
    Good Lord
But the more you talks
    Good Lord
I'm goin' to bend my knees.
    Good Lord

Ever since my soul
    Good Lord
Children, been set free
    Good Lord
Satan act and lie
    Good Lord
At the root of the tree.
    Good Lord

Aint Satan just like
Good Lord
A snake in the grass,
Good Lord
He's always walkin'
Good Lord
In a Christian's path.
Good Lord
Old Satan got on
Good Lord
Them iron shoes.
Good Lord
It's you better mind
Good Lord
Don't he step 'em on you.
Good Lord [g]

The dramatic, epic-like saga of Samson, the half-tamed human lion, the "natural man" among Biblical heroes, has been recorded in a number of Negro religious songs, but the best known is one called "If I Had My Way." Over a period of time, many stanzas have appeared which were probably not a part of the "original" rendition. One version is sung like this:

Chorus (between stanzas, with variations)
He said, and if I had'n way, (×3)
I'd tear the buildin' down!
He cried O Lord,
O Lord,
O Lord Lordy Lordy,
O Lord!
He cried O Lord,
O Lord,
O Lord Lordy Lordy,
O Lord!
He said, and if I had'n my way, (×3)
I'd tear the buildin' down!

Delilah was a woman fine and fair,
A-very pleasant lookin' with coal black hair.
Delilah she gained old Samson's mind
When he saw this woman and she looked so fine.

Oh whether he went to Timothy I can't tell,
But the daughters of Timothy they treated him well.

[g] See The Music, 9.

He supplied to his father to go and see,
Can't you get this beautiful woman for me?
Stop and let me tell you what Samson done,
He looked at the lion and the lion run.
It's written that the lion had killed men with his paw,
But Samson had his hand in the lion's jaw.

Samson burned up a field of corn,
They looked for Samson but he was gone.
A-so many thousand formed a plot,
It wasn't many days 'fore he was caught.

They bound him with ropes, and while walkin' along
He looked on the ground, he saw an old jawbone.
He moved his arms, the rope popped like threads,
When he got through killin', three thousand was dead.

Samson's mother supplied to him,
Can't you find a wife among our kin?
Samson's father said it grieve your mother's mind
To see you marry a woman of the Philistines.[7]

From the Second Book of Kings (2:11) comes the inspiration
for the constantly recurring image of Elijah's chariot: "And it
came to pass, as they still went on, and talked, that, behold, there
appeared a chariot of fire, and horses of fire, and parted them both
asunder; and Elijah went up by a whirlwind into heaven." In
the song "Rock Chariot, I Told You to Rock" there are wedded
symbols of salvation from various portions of the Old and New
Testaments, including Ezekiel and the Revelation of St. John the
Divine. Beginning with Elijah's chariot, the allusions turn to the
gospel wheel of Ezekiel, gospel shoes, and the harps that are to be
played on judgment day.

Rock, chariot, I told you to rock!
    Judgement goin' to find me!
Won't you rock, chariot, in the middle of the air?
    Judgement goin' to find me!
I wonder what chariot comin' after me?
    Judgement goin' to find me!
Rock, chariot, I told you to rock!
    Judgement goin' to find me!
Elijah's chariot comin' after me!
    Judgement goin' to find me!
Rock, chariot, I told you to rock!

Judgement goin' to find me!
Rock, chariot, in the middle of the air!
Judgement goin' to find me!
Wouldn't give you my shoes for your shoes!
Judgement goin' to find me!
Wouldn't give you my robe for your robe!
Judgement goin' to find me!
Wouldn't give you my crown for your crown!
Judgement goin' to find me!
Wouldn't swap my soul for your soul!
Judgement goin' to find me!
Rock, chariot, I told you to rock!
Judgement goin' to find me!
Will you rock, chariot, in the middle of the air?
Judgement goin' to find me!
Rock, chariot in the middle of the air!
Judgement goin' to find me!
Wouldn't give you my wings for your wings!
Judgement goin' to find me!
Wouldn't swap you my grave for your grave!
Judgement goin' to find me!
Rock, chariot, I told you to rock!
Judgement goin' to find me!
Rock, chariot, in the middle of the air!
Judgement goin' to find me!
I wonder what chariot comin' after me!
Judgement goin' to find me!
Elijah's chariot comin' after me!
Judgement goin' to find me!
That must be that gospel wheel!
Judgement goin' to find me!
What wheel children is you talkin' about?
Judgement goin' to find me!
Talkin' about the wheel in Jesus Christ!
Judgement goin' to find me!
Every spoke is a human cry!
Judgement goin' to find me!
Aint you talkin' about the little wheel runnin' in the wheel?
Judgement goin' to find me!
Them folks in Jesus Christ!
Judgement goin' to find me!
Wouldn't swap my wheel for your wheel!
Judgement goin' to find me!
Wouldn't give you my Lord for your Lord!
Judgement goin' to find me!

Aint you got on them gospel shoes?
    Judgement goin' to find me!
I wouldn't swap my shoes for your shoes!
    Judgement goin' to find me!
I wouldn't give you my harp for your harp!
    Judgement goin' to find me! ʰ

The reference to the wheel, syncretized with the chariot in the previous song, comes from one of Ezekiel's visions (1:16): "The appearance of the wheels and their work was like unto the color of beryl; and they four had one likeness; and their appearance and their work was as it were a wheel in the middle of a wheel." This image has been preserved in a well-known spiritual:

Ezekiel saw that wheel
Way up in the middle of the air.
Ezekiel saw that wheel
Way in the middle of the air.

And the big wheel run by faith
And the little wheel run by the Grace of God.
A wheel within a wheel
Way in the middle of the air.

A song usually known as "Job, Job" is one of the outstanding epics of the Negro religious literature. Rarely heard twice the same way because of its length, its scope, and its rich fare, the song alludes to significant scenes scattered throughout the Old and New Testaments. Whether these scenes ever appeared in a more or less chronological order is not evident, but as now heard there is no rigid sequence. In the version given here, the song begins with Job in the first section; goes on in the second to tell about Judas, Pilate, and Pilate's wife; moves back to Joshua and the stopping of the sun in the third; follows in the fourth with scenes from the Revelation of St. John; continues with references to Gabriel in the fifth section; and in the sixth reproduces a vivid picture from the Book of Daniel. The choruses between stanzas vary, no two being exactly alike. They deal with Mt. Zion, the salvation train, judgement day, Elijah's chariot, and, finally, the resurrection. Partly chanted, partly sung, this synthesis of a number of earthly and celestial scenes has a certain poetic grandeur. It would seem that the song originated as a sermon, with the con-

ʰ See The Music, 3.

gregation giving vocal support in the affirmative exclamations
ending each line and singing the short choruses.

Oh Job Job, good Lord,
Tell me how you feel, good Lord,
Oh what you reckon, good Lord,
That old Job supplied, good Lord,
That I'm feelin' good, good Lord,
Oh Job Job, good Lord,
Tell me how you feel, good Lord,
That-a Job supplied, good Lord,
I'm feelin' bad, good Lord,
Well what you reckon, good Lord,
Old Job said, good Lord,
Whilst I'm feelin' bad, good Lord,
I can't sleep at night, good Lord,
I can't eat a bite, good Lord,
And the woman I love, good Lord,
Don't treat me right, good Lord.

Oh Rock Mount Zion,
Rock Mount Zion,
Oh Rock Mount Zion in that morning.
Don't you hear the train comin',
Hear the train comin',
Don't you hear the train comin' in that mornin'.

Oh Pilate's wife, good Lord,
She dreamt a dream, good Lord,
'Bout a innocent man, good Lord,
Said who want to see, good Lord,
Old Pilate's work, good Lord,
Come and seek the man, ahuh,
Said give me water, good Lord,
I want wash my hands, good Lord,
I won't be guilty, good Lord,
'At a innocent man, Lordy,
That Judas was, ahuh,
Not a seasoned man, ahuh,
Forty piece of silver, ahuh,
Go count it out, ahuh,
Go way in the woods, ahuh,
I'm goin' suffer be hung, ahuh,
Before I be guilty, ahuh,
To this innocent man, ahuh,

Don't you want to die easy,
Don't you want to die easy,

Don't you want to die easy in that mornin'.
Don't you want to see Jesus,
Don't you want to see Jesus,
Don't you want to see Jesus in that mornin'.

Joshua was, ahuh,
Son of Nun, ahuh,
Prayed to God, ahuh,
Stop the sun, ahuh,
Lord oh Lord, ahuh,
Got my war cap, ahuh,
On my head, ahuh,
Lord oh Lord, ahuh,
Got my sword, ahuh,
Good and sharp, ahuh,
Lord oh Lord, ahuh,
Got my shoes, ahuh,
Good and tight, ahuh,
Sun stopped steady, ahuh,
Turn the light, ahuh,
Pale the moon, ahuh,
The sun steady, ahuh,
Work was done, ahuh.

Rock Mount Zion,
Rock Mount Zion,
Oh Rock Mount Zion in that mornin'.
Children you better get ready,
You better get ready,
Oh you better get ready in that mornin'.

God send angels, ahuh,
Heaven down, umn-hmn,
Go east angel, umn-hmn,
Veil the sun, umn-hmn,
Go east angel, umn-hmn,
Veil the moon, umn-hmn,
Sail back sun, umn-hmn,
Towards the heavens, umn-hmn,
Done your duty, ahuh,
Sail back moon, umn-hmn,
Drippin' blood, umn-hmn,
Done your duty, ahuh,
Go east angel, umn-hmn,
Hold the wind, ahuh,
God this mornin' umn-hmn,
Rule and chain, ahuh,

Go north angel, umn-hmn,
Hold the wind, umn-hmn,
Don't let it move, ahuh,
God this mornin', umn-hmn,
Rule and chain, umn-hmn,
Go west angel, umn-hmn,
Don't let it move, umn-hmn.

Say Rock Mount Zion,
Rock Mount Zion,
Oh Rock Mount Zion in that mornin'.
Don't you want to die easy,
Don't you want to die easy,
Oh you want to die easy in that mornin'.

God sent Gabriel, umn-hmn,
Go down Gabriel, ahuh,
Tetch the sea, ahuh,
Brace my feet, ahuh,
Water side, ahuh,
Brace my feet, ahuh,
Dry land, ahuh,
Blow loud Gabriel, ahuh,
Seven claps of thunder, umn-hmn,
Other than the one, ahuh,
Spoke to the clouds, umn-hmn,
Sail away clouds, umn-hmn,
Make up in chair, umn-hmn.

Swing low chariot,
Swing low chariot,
Oh swing low chariot in that mornin'.

See God that mornin', ahuh,
Filled up the air, umn-hmn,
Feet be movin', umn-hmn,
Feet be shinin', umn-hmn,
Like polished brass, umn-hmn,
Eyes be movin', umn-hmn,
Zig-zags of lightnin', umn-hmn,
Hair be rollin', umn-hmn,
Like pillars of cloud, umn-hmn,
Hair be shinin', umn-hmn,
Like lamb's wool, ahuh,
God this mornin', umn-hmn,
Rule and chain, umn-hmn.

Over yon comes Jesus,
Yon comes Jesus,
Oh yon comes Jesus in that mornin'.[1]

The story of Jonah and the Whale has inspired many Negro religious songs, most of which have common elements and common lines, suggesting that they may have developed from an early prototype. The song makers exploited to the full all of the dramatic potentials of the tale, condensing where useful, expanding and drawing out where artful. In the case of the Jonah song given here, the singer began with a prose narration of the story, much in the manner that it would be presented in the pulpit, and at the conclusion of the narration launched immediately into the singing.

Where the Bible says simply that "the Lord sent out a great wind into the sea, and there was a mighty tempest unto the sea, so that the ship was like to be broken," this singer-narrator has angels hovering over the ship, fluttering their wings to get the wind down into it. The Bible says with brevity of statement: "Now the Lord had prepared a great fish to swallow up Jonah. And Jonah was in the belly of the fish three days and three nights." But the story teller brings a quality of theater to the event when he says: "And when he struck the water (slap!) a sudden mouth flew open like a ball of fire, and when last seen, Jonah, he was goin' through the water in the bowels of a whale." The story and song, as given by Richard Amerson of Alabama, are as follows:

Jonah was a man, God told him to go over to Nineveh. God called him and spoke to him. And there was a ravine right across a big ocean of water over here. And He told him to go over there amongst them wild men and civilize 'em, preach to 'em. Jonah saw a . . . ship comin' down, and he thought he'd rather go and labor instead of goin' down amongst them men, and he went down there and got him a truck, and helped these people stack this cotton and stuff down there. And whilst bein' down in there amongst all the laborin' men down in the ship he commenced to work a while. Jonah thought he'd stow on that ship, and wouldn't get on the ship they told him to get on. He got on the one he wanted to get on, say he wasn't goin' to preach, and hid down there.

And the captain came on up and locked the hull back up. 'Twas ever so many days, two-three days, and Jonah down there hid. They counted the men and thought the men was all out. But by the captain bein' a forgettin' man—and God was a forgiver, not a forgetter—he forgot Jonah, and God didn't forget him. That shows that you're bound to do what God send you to do. God intend for him to go over and preach gospel to the men and do what he say do. And he couldn't hide it from Him. And God command the ship to run for many miles, and after she run for many miles then she got to rockin'. The captain of the ship supplied to him down here, "What's the matter?" He said, "Let the oars up," and when they let the oars up on the ship it rocked worse. A little windstorm got in it. And the angels drooped their wings down and got the wind in and rocked it worse.

So the spirit of God was revealed in the angels, listen. God say his children can't stay anywhere but where he places 'em to stay. So when the ship began to rock again they got anxious and went down and got to movin' the bales of cotton and found a man, Jonah, lyin' fast asleep. . . . And two caught him by the legs and two by the hands, and before they have this ship destroyed by one man, they throwed him overboard in the water. And when he struck the water (slap!) a sudden mouth flew open like a ball of fire—it was a whale mouth flew open—and when last seen, Jonah, he was goin' through the water in the bowels of the whale. And the whale, you could see so many miles of water bustin' open, he cut the water half in two, he smote the water just like Moses. That was a life-savin' boat God send to save his children anywhere, you know, that's for Jonah. And he struck the open water and when last seen he was cuttin' the sea half in two a-goin'. And when he stop he rest his breastplate over here in Nineveh. He went as far as he could and got on a sand bar. And he opened his mouth and gapped, and Jonah shot out alive. Then the whale turned around and went on back, he had done what God told him to do.

And Jonah lay there so many days. The sun came to shine, the wind and sand, and the sun begin to burn his face. Then come along a raven, came a-flyin' alongside, see a gourd seed, and he picked it up like the birds do, and he flew along and he got even with Jonah's head and the gourd seed dropped right in that wet sand behind the sea. And so God fixed it so . . . he strung up a little vine. And the vine went up [grew] into a tree, and a great big limb of it came right over Jonah to shade him.

And there came along a worm, came a-inchin' down there so many miles, and every weed and stalk he saw, he wouldn't cut there. He inched and he inched till he inched up where that gourd vine growed over Jonah's head. And the inch worm sawed on it and sawed it down. . . . So when it fell in his face it tickled Jonah, and Jonah woke up. When Jonah woke up and came to power, he come up to the city to become a preacher to them wicked men. You know what he do. Well, he did what God told him to do, didn't he? 8

Wake up Jonah, you are the man!
Reelin' and a-rockin' o' the ship so long!

Captain of the ship got trouble in mind!
Reelin' and a-rockin' o' the ship so long!
Let's go way down in the hull o' the ship!
Reelin' and a-rockin' o' the ship so long!
Let's search this ship from bottom to top!
Reelin' and a-rockin' o' the ship so long!
Then they found Brother Jonah lyin' fast asleep!
Reelin' and a-rockin' o' the ship so long!
Layin' way out yonder in the hull o' the ship!
Reelin' and a-rockin' o' the ship so long!
He said wake up Jonah, you are the man!
Reelin' and a-rockin' o' the ship so long!

Well they caught Brother Jonah by hands and feet!
Reelin' and a-rockin' o' the ship so long!
Well they pitched Brother Jonah up overboard!
Reelin' and a-rockin' o' the ship so long!
Well the water whale came along swallowed him whole!
Reelin' and a-rockin' o' the ship so long!
Then he puked Brother Jonah on dry land!
Reelin' and a-rockin' o' the ship so long!
Then the gourd vine growed over Jonah's head!
Reelin' and a-rockin' o' the ship so long!
Then the inch worm come along cut it down!
Reelin' and a-rockin' o' the ship so long!
That made a cross over Jonah's head!
Reelin' and a-rockin' o' the ship so long! [j]

The story of Jesus' birth is told simply and directly, as though
a few clues and allusions are all that are required to establish the
scene and its meanings:

What month was Jesus born in?
Last month in the year.
What month was Jesus born in?
Last month in the year.
Oh Lord, you got January, February, March, oh Lord,
You got April, May, and June Lord,
You got the July, August, September,
October and November,
You got the twenty-fifth day of December,
It's the last month in the year.

He was born in an ox-stall manger,
Last month in the year.
He was born in an ox-stall manger,

[j] See The Music, 1.

Last month in the year.
Oh Lord you got January, etc.

I'm talkin' about Mary's baby,
Last month in the year.
I'm talkin' about Mary's baby,
Last month in the year.
Oh Lord you got January, etc.[k]

The Gospel According to St. John, Chapter 4, tells that Jesus came to a well in Samaria, and engaged in conversation with a woman drawing water there. He spoke to her about the water of everlasting life which he had to offer, and she asked whether she might have some. "Jesus saith unto her, Go call thy husband and come hither. The woman answered and said, I have no husband. Jesus said unto her, Thou has well said, I have no husband; for thou hast had five husbands; and he whom thou now hast is not thy husband: in that saidst thou truly. The woman saith unto him, Sir, I perceive that thou art a prophet." This human, intimate exchange, and the woman's report to the village on the event, is recorded in the following song:

When Jesus met the woman at the well,
Oh she went running to tell,
She said come to see a man at the well,
He told me everything that I done.

She cried oh, oh, he must be a prophet,
She cried oh, oh, he must be a prophet,
She cried oh, oh, he must be a prophet,
He told me everything that I done.

He said woman where is your husband?
She said that I don't have one.
He said woman you done had five,
And the one you got now aint yours.

She cried oh, oh, you must be a prophet,
She cried oh, oh, you must be a prophet,
Oh, oh, you must be a prophet,
You told me everything that I done.

Oh he told that Messiah was coming,
Oh he told me everything that I done.
Oh he told that Messiah was coming,
Oh he told me everything that I done.

She cried oh, oh, etc.[l]

[k] See The Music, 14.   [l] See The Music, 20.

Another version of this song stresses a slightly different point in its choral stanza, and mentions that the people of the village, in response to the woman's report, came to see the man at the well:

Oh listen, don't you hear what he say?
Oh listen, don't you hear what he say?
Oh listen, don't you hear what he say?
He say the truth is the light, and I am the way.

When the people of that city
Came and saw Jesus settin' at the well,
He say I can give water free
That'll save you from a burnin' hell.[9]

The song "Job, Job," which appears earlier in this chapter, refers to the episode of Pilate's washing his hands to symbolize his innocence of the death penalty (Matthew, 27:14). The following song ennumerates the events that followed, according to the gospel:

Look how they done my Lord,
Done my Lord, done my Lord,
Look how they done my Lord,
He never said a mumblin' word,
Not a word, not a word did he say.

Well they whupped him up Calvary,
Calvary, Calvary, Calvary,
They whupped him up Calvary,
He never said a mumblin' word,
Not a word, not a word did he say.

Well they planted him a thorny crown,
Thorny crown, thorny crown, thorny crown,
They planted him a thorny crown.
He never said a mumblin' word,
Not a word, not a word did he say.

Well they placed it on his head,
On his head, on his head, on his head,
They placed it on his head.
He never said a mumblin' word,
Not a word, not a word did he say.

Well they speared him in the side,
In the side, in the side, in the side,
Well they speared him in the side.
He never said a mumblin' word,
Not a word, not a word did he say.

The story of the crucifixion and the resurrection was carried by word of mouth through the countryside, as recalled by the song "Somebody's Talking About Jesus." One stanza and chorus of the song goes:

Everywhere I go,
Everywhere I go my Lord,
Everywhere I go
Somebody's talking about Jesus.

Well my knees been acquainted with the hillside clay,
Somebody's talking about Jesus.
And my head's been wet with the midnight dew,
Somebody's talking about Jesus.[m]

The memory of John the Baptist, who baptized Jesus, preaching in the wilderness, is evoked by this song:

Wonder where is my brother gone?
Wonder where is my brother John?
He is gone to the wilderness,
Aint comin' no more.
Wonder where will I lie down?
Wonder where will I lie down?
In some lonesome place Lord,
Down on the ground.
Wonder where will I lie down?
In some lonesome place Lord,
Down on the ground.[n]

Another song about John the Baptist demonstrates how singing and preaching can merge into an integral form. Except for the choral stanza, which is truly sung, the main body of this piece is Biblical prose chanted with a simple but emotionally charged rhythm, to guitar accompaniment. The words come almost unchanged from the Gospel According to St. Matthew. The rhythmic pauses in the song are a creative device on the part of the preacher-singer. They are suggested here by the way in which the lines are broken down. The story tells about Jesus' baptism by John, and about his forty days of fasting, and his temptation by Satan.

John done saw that number
Way in the middle of the air.
John done saw that number

[m] See The Music, 16.   [n] See The Music, 4.

Way in the middle of the air.
Ee-ay-hay-ay.

In those days came John the Baptist
preachin' in the
wilderness of Judea
and sayin'
re-
pent ye,
for the Kingdom of
Heaven
?
For this is he
that was spoken of
by the prophet Esaias.
Hay-hay-ay.
His voice
the one
cryin' in the
wilderness,
prepare ye
the way
of the Lord and make
his
pathway straight and
the same John had his raiment of
camel hair
and a leather girdle
round his loins.

John done saw that number, etc.

Jesus came from Nazarene
unto
Galilee
to be
baptised
of John
in Jordan
and
John said
unto him
come and talk to me
I need
to be
baptised
of thee and

Jesus said
unto
John
suffer it to be so for
thus it becomes us
to fill all righteousness.

And John done saw that number
Way in the middle of the air.
John done saw that number
Way in the middle of the air.
Cryin' how long, how long, how long, my Lord, oh how long.

Ay
after Jesus was
baptised
of
John
straightway
out of the waters
looked and saw
heavens open
and the spirit
of God
came down and lit
a bow
on him,
and Jesus was
carried up
into the mountain
to be
tempted of the Satan
and when
he had fasted forty days and forty nights
the tempter
came unto him
and said,
If thou be the son of God
cast thy faith
'cause these stones to be
made bread and
Je-eh-he-sus
said unto John (sic),
Get behind me
for it is
written down here

not
tempt the Lord
thy God
but him only
thou shalt serve in faith.
And John done saw that number, etc.[10]

Another song of this type, with a nearly identical chorus, refers
not to John the Baptist but to St. John the Divine. It also has a
preaching style of delivery, with sermonizing and singing interspersed. The various scenes which are depicted come from the
Revelation. One half-sung sermonizing part goes:

There was a beast came out of the sea
Havin' ten horns and ten crowns,
On his horns was a-written blaspheme. . . .

A later section:

God told the angel
Go down see about old John.
Angel flew from the bottom of the pit,
Gathered the sun all in her fist,
Gathered the moon all round her wrist,
Gathered the stars all under her feet,
Gathered the wind all round her waist.[11]

The Revelation of St. John the Divine, with all its spectacular,
visionary, and poetic effects, evidently made a deep impression
on the creators of Negro religious songs. Its free, cosmic, and
often wild and primitive imagery provided rich opportunities for
sermons and for conveying, through musical statements, a spirit
of wonder and awe. Chapter 12 of the Revelation begins: "And
there appeared a great wonder in heaven; a woman clothed with
the sun, and the moon under her feet, and upon her head a crown
of twelve stars." This imagery is the basis of the song given above,
which utilizes the original material in a free, poetic manner.
That identical Biblical passages inspired different song makers
differently is evidenced by another anthem on the same subject:

Wasn't that a wonder in the heaven?
Wasn't that a wonder in the heaven?
Mighty wonder in the heaven?
That woman clothed with the sun,
Moon under her feet!

Read about the wonder in the heaven.
Read about the wonder in the heaven.
Mighty wonder in the heaven.
That woman clothed with the sun,
Moon under her feet.[12]

In chapter 20 of the Revelation, there are numerous references to the book of judgement, such as this: "And I saw the dead, small and great, stand before God; and the books were opened: and another book was opened, which is the book of life: and the dead were judged out of these things which were written in the books according to their works. . . . And whoever was not found written in the book of life was cast into the lake of fire." The song "It's Gettin' Late Over In the Evenin' " draws upon this theme for its substance:

Lord it's gettin' late over in the evenin',
Lord it's gettin' late over in the evenin',
Children, it's gettin' late over in the evenin',
Lord it's gettin' late over in the evenin',
The sun most down.

Don't you seal up your book, John,
Don't you seal up your book, John,
Don't seal up your book, John,
Don't you seal up your book, John,
Till you can sign my name.

Spirit says seal up your book, John,
Spirit says seal up your book, John,
I want you to seal up your book, John,
I want you to seal up your book, John,
Don't write no more.

People, I just keep on tellin' you,
We just keep on a-tellin' you,
We just keeps on a-tellin' you,
Sinner, I just keep on a-tellin' you,
It's a God somewhere.

Children, you can come in my home,
You can come in my home,
Lord, you can come to my home,
You can come to my home,
Lord, and you'll find-a me there.

I'm goin' away to leave you,
I'm goin' away to leave you,

Sinner, I'm goin' away to leave you,
I'm goin' away to leave you,
And I can't stay here.

Lord, we got to make a move,
Lord, we got to make a move,
People, we got to make a move, move,
We got to make a move some day,
And we can't stay here.

Lord, we got to go to judgement,
We got to go into judgement,
People, we got to go into judgement,
We got to go into judgement,
Sister, and we can't tell when.°

Chapter 5 of the Revelation begins: "And I saw in the right
hand of him that sat on the throne a book written within and on
the backside, with seven seals." This passage is the inspiration for
"John the Revelator," which opens with these stanzas:

Well, who's that a-writin'?
John the Revelator.
Who's that a-writin'?
John the Revelator.
Who's that a-writin'?
John the Revelator.
Well, book of the Seven Seals.

Tell me what's John a-writin'?
John the Revelator.
What's John a-writin'?
John the Revelator.
What's John a-writin'?
John the Revelator.
Well, Book of the Seven Seals.[13]

Other stanzas interpolate earlier Biblical events.

One of the most popularized of all spirituals, "Goin' to Shout
All Over God's Heaven," also appears to derive from the Revelation. At various places in the book, there are references to wings,
harps, robes, crowns, and other effects that are present at the
scene of the final judgement, all of which are used to symbolize
salvation:

° See The Music, 8.

Ah you got shoes. I got shoes,
All of God's children got shoes.
And when I get to heaven goin' to try on my shoes,
I'm goin' to shout all over heaven.

Chorus (after every stanza)
Oh heaven, heaven,
Everybody talkin' about heaven aint goin' there,
Heaven, heaven,
I'm goin' to shout all over God's heaven.

Well you got a robe, I got a robe,
All of God's children got a robe,
And when I get to heaven goin' to try on my robe,
Goin' to shout all over God's heaven.

Well you got a crown, I got a crown,
All of God's children got a crown,
And when I get to heaven goin' to try on my crown,
Goin' to shout all over God's heaven.

Well you got a harp, I got a harp,
All of God's children got a harp,
Ah when I get to heaven goin' to play on my harp,
I'm goin' to shout all over God's heaven.

The certainty that those who lead a good Christian life will
pass the test on judgement day runs through many spirituals and
other religious songs, along with warnings to sinners that the time
for repentance is short. How does one know for certain that his
name appears in the list of the saved? The Revelation (21:12)
says that 12,000 people from each of the twelve tribes were chosen,
144,000 in all. An angel shows John the New City, which "had
a wall great and high, and had twelve gates, and at the gates twelve
angels, and names written thereon, which are the names of the
twelve tribes of Israel."

How'd you know your name been written down?
How'd you know your name been written down?
On the wall, oh, it's been written down.
On the wall, oh, it's been written down.
Oh the angel told me, been written down.
Oh the angel told me, been written down.
How'd you know your name been written down?
How'd you know your name been written down?
Well the Lord told me, been written down.
Well the Lord told me, been written down.

Be sure your name been written down.
Be sure your name been written down.
On the wall in heaven been written down.
On the wall in heaven been written down.
I know my name been written down.
I know my name been written down.
On the wall in heaven been written down.
On the wall in heaven been written down.
Aint you glad your name been written down.
Aint you glad your name been written down.[p]

Among the finest of all judgement day songs is "Didn't You Hear?" The responsive part is sung like a clarion trumpet, and the entire scene projects a wildly joyous, cosmic New Year's Eve celebration with bells ringing, doves "moaning," ravens singing, horns blowing, harps playing, thunder rolling, lightning flashing, saints singing, brothers praying, sisters shouting, preachers preaching, and the organ playing. Note that the harp is "blown." To many rural people, as pointed out elsewhere, the heavenly harp is the mouth harp, or harmonica.

Didn't you hear my Lord when he called?
    Yes I heard my Lord when he called!
Didn't you hear my Lord when he called?
    Yes I hear my Lord call!
Didn't you hear my Lord when he called?
    Yes I heard my Lord call!
My Lord callin', in my soul! (×4)

Didn't you hear them angels moan?
    Yes I heard the angels moan!
Didn't you hear them angels moan?
    Yes I heard the angels moan!
Angels moanin', in my soul! (×4)

Didn't you hear them turkle doves moan?
    Yes I heard the turkle doves moan!
Didn't you hear them turkle doves moan?
    Yes I heard the turkle doves moan!
Didn't you hear the heaven bells ring?
    Yes I heard the heaven bells ring!
The turkle doves moanin', my soul! (×6)
The angels moanin', my soul! (×2)

[p] See The Music, 13.

Didn't you hear the harp when it blowed?
  Yes I heard the harp when it blowed!
Didn't you hear them ravens cryin'?
  Yes I heard the ravens cryin'!
Didn't you hear that horn when it blowed?
  Yes I heard the horn when it blowed!
Didn't you hear my Lord callin'?
  Yes I heard my Lord call.
The turkle dove moanin', my soul! (×4)
The harp is blowin', my soul! (×2)
My Lord callin', my soul! (×2)

Didn't you hear that thunder roll?
  Yes I heard the thunder roll!
Didn't you see the lightnin' flashin'?
  Yes I see the lightnin' flash!
Didn't you hear them saints when they singin'?
  Yes I hear the saints when they sing!
Didn't you hear that brother pray?
  Yes I hear the brother pray!
Couldn't you hear them sisters shoutin'?
  Yes I heard the sisters shout!
Didn't you hear them preachers preachin'?
  Yes I heard the preachers preach!
Preachers preachin', my soul! (×2)
Sisters shoutin', my soul! (×2)
Thunder rollin', my soul! (×2)

Didn't you hear them organ playin'?
  Yes I heard the organ playin'!
Didn't you hear them horns blowin'?
  Yes I heard the horn when it blowed!
Didn't you hear them saints singin'?
  Yes I heard the saints all singin'!
Saints all singin', my soul! (×2) q

Among the religious songs, there are, of course, many without direct allusion to Biblical scenes. Their themes are more generalized, or they may deal, for example, with the idea of death (usually accompanied by direct or indirect reference to salvation, or warnings to sinners), or Christian behavior. Inspiration for many of these songs may have been in Biblical passages the identity of which is not readily recognized; or they may have been inspired by a local event or circumstance, or by sermons.

q See The Music, 12.

In the following song, "Got No Travellin' Shoes," the message is for everyone to be prepared for death by seeking salvation, and not to be caught unready:

Death went out to the sinner's house,
(Said) come and go with me.
Sinner cried out, I'm not ready to go,
I aint got no travellin' shoes,
Got no travellin' shoes, got no travellin' shoes,
Sinner cried out, I'm not ready to go,
I aint got no travellin' shoes.

Death went down to the gambler's house,
Called him come and go with me.
The gambler cried out I'm not ready to go,
I aint got no travellin' shoes,
Got no travellin' shoes, got no travellin' shoes,
Gambler cried out, I'm not ready to go,
I aint got no travellin' shoes.

Death went down to the preacher's house,
Called him, come and go with me.
The preacher cried out, I'm a-ready to go,
I got my travellin' shoes,
Got my travellin' shoes, got my travellin' shoes,
The preacher cried out, I'm ready to go,
I've got my travellin' shoes.ʳ

The song "This May Be Your Last Time" consists of a series of brief images dealing with Christian behavior, the unsanctified, the short time left to achieve salvation, and the final judgement:

Chorus (before each stanza, with variations)
This may be your last time, (×3)
May be your last time, I don't know.
Sister, this may be your last time,
This may be your last time, (×2)
May be your last time, I don't know.

Talk about me much as you please,
More you talk, I'll bend my knees.
May be your last time, I don't know.

Way down yonder by Jordan Stream,
Hear God's children tryin' to bend their knees.
May be your last time, I don't know.

ʳ See The Music, 7.

Meet Mr. Hypocrite on the street,
First thing he show you, his tongue in his cheek.
May be your last time, I don't know.

Soon as you can cease from your sins,
Train goin' to stop and take you in.
May be your last time, I don't know.

Jordan deep, Jordan wide,
None don't cross but the sanctified.
May be your last time, I don't know.

If you want to go to heaven when you die,
Stop your tongue from tellin' lies.
May be your last time I don't know.

One of these mornin's, nine o'clock,
This old world begin to reel and rock.
May be your last time, I don't know.

Many souls [that] have never tried to pray,
Got sight of the Lord that day.
May be your last time, I don't know.[8]

Another song, "Israelites Shouting," reflects on the death of various loved ones, all of whom now are "hidden behind God's altar," where they will remain until judgement day. The following stanzas are excerpted:

Oh I wonder where's my sister,
She's gone away to stay.
Got hidden behind God's altar,
She'll be gone till judgement day.

   Chorus (after each stanza, with variations)
   Goodbye, the Israelites shoutin' in the
   Goodbye, the Israelites shoutin' in the heaven
   Goodbye, the Israelites shoutin' in the heaven
   Goodbye, the Israelites shoutin' in the
   This day, the Israelites shoutin' in the heaven
   This day, the Israelites shoutin' in the

Oh I wonder where's my father,
He's gone away to stay.
He left his church this mornin',
And now he can't be found.

Stanzas that follow name the mother and various other relatives, and then:

* See The Music, 5.

God knows I am a Christian,
God knows I'm not ashamed.
Well the Holy Ghost is my witness,
The angels done signed my name.[t]

The song "Low Down the Chariot and Let Me Ride" uses the familiar Elijah's chariot as its central theme:

Let me ride, let me ride,
Oh let me ride, let me ride,
Oh let me ride, let me ride,
Oh low down the chariot and let me ride.

I'm humble to ride, oh let me ride,
I'm humble to ride, oh let me ride,
I'm humble to ride, let me ride,
Oh low down the chariot and let me ride.

Got a right to ride, etc.

Got a ticket to ride, etc.

My mother done rid, etc.

Train comin', etc.

I'm a soldier, etc.

My father done rid, etc.[u]

"The Sun Will Never Go Down," which appears to paint a picture of life after death, has a haunting, slow melody, and the lyrics have a special poetic quality:

Oh the sun will never go down, go down,
Oh the sun will never go down, go down.
The flowers are blooming for evermore,
There the sun will never go down, go down.
Don't you feel like shouting sometimes, sometimes?
The flowers are blooming for evermore,
There the sun will never go down.

Don't you miss your mother sometimes, sometimes?
Don't you miss your mother sometimes, sometimes?
The flowers are blooming for evermore,
There the sun will never go down.[v]

A good many religious songs, as we have noted, stress moral pressures on sinners or straying sheep. The epic-like "King David," a few pages back, has interpolated parts of this kind, such as the lines:

[t] See The Music, 17.   [u] See The Music, 18.   [v] See The Music, 10.

You got a true way to find
Mr. Hypocrite out.
At the first thing [he's] gwine
To church and shout.

Another song notes that sinners, liars, and gamblers need not
expect mercy on judgement day:

This train don't carry no sinners, this train!
This train don't carry no gamblers, this train!
This train don't carry no liars, this train!

The song "My God Aint No Lyin' Man" contains the verse:

I got a home where the gambler can't go,
I got a home where the gambler can't go,
Oh, Jesus, Lord have mercy,
I got a home where the gambler can't go.

Although the content of such songs is religious and the values
specifically those of the church, one cannot help but be aware of
their relationship to the traditional Negro song of social comment and criticism. The main difference is that the religious
social comment usually has a generalized target, while secular
social criticism is more often personalized. Religious social comment is a reflection of community attitudes toward a class or group
of people who behave in a non-approved way, while comparable
secular songs, including blues, have more specific targets, or at
least more specific protagonists. Nevertheless, many of the religious songs which comment on backsliding can be sung at
times which give them a particular relevance. The partly
preached, partly sung "God Don't Like It" concerns itself with
church members that are addicted to corn liquor:

Chorus (×2 after each stanza)
Well God don't like it, no, no!
God don't like it, no, no!
God don't like it, no, no!
It's a-scandalous and a shame!

Some people stay in the churches,
They settin' in a deacon's chair,
They drinkin' beer and whisky,
And they say that they don't care.

Some people say that yellow corn
Can make you the very best kind.

They better turn that yellow corn into bread
And stop that makin' shine.

Some members in the churches
They just send to testify,
But when you come to find out,
They're somewhere drinkin' shine.

Now some people goes to church
Just to speak their soul or mind,
But when you come to find out,
They been somewhere drinkin' shine.[14]

In some versions of this song-sermon, a number of other subjects are commented upon, such as hypocritical preachers, church members who shout but don't put money in the collection box, vanity, loose living, lustful behavior, and people who don't return borrowed money.

Preachments of this kind are not essentially different from comments that turn up frequently in secular songs, both in the United States and the West Indies. The following Calypso-type song from San Andrés in the Caribbean, for example, is a comment on people who have "bad minds" and who are always making unfavorable remarks about others in the community:

In every home that you can find,
There are people who have bad mind.
In every home that you can find,
There are people who have bad mind.

Chorus (after each stanza)
Certain bad mind that sit and lie,
Sit and criticise the people who pass.
Certain bad mind that sit and lie,
Sit and criticise the people who pass.

(Each couplet is repeated to fill out a stanza)
You meek and you lookin' thin,
They say consumption in your skin.

You rosy and you big and fat,
They say dropsy in your skin.

You get up and you go to church,
Instead of gospel you goin' to grind.

You kneel in your home to pray,
They say a hypocrite you did play.[15]

Except for the difference in idiom, this Calypso-type song might easily be taken for a United States Negro anthem. The song preceding it could be sung to exactly the same Calypso beat and melody, and would readily be accepted in this guise as within West Indian tradition. It is only a small step from "Well God Don't Like It" to the following secular song, "Jimmy Bell's In Town," as rendered by a traditional blues singer:

Jimmy Bell's in town,
Lordy, walkin' round.
He got greenbacks enough, sweet babe,
To make a man a suit,
Make a man a suit,
Make a man a suit.
He got greenbacks enough, sweet babe,
To make a man a suit.

Jimmy Bell in the pulpit,
The Bible in his hand.
All them sisters sittin' back in the corner
Cryin' Jimmy Bell my man,
Jimmy Bell my man,
Jimmy Bell my man.
All them sisters sittin' back in the corner
Cryin' Jimmy Bell my man.

Jimmy Bell told the sexton
Go and tone that bell,
Cause some of these old members here
Sure is goin' to hell,
Sure is goin' to hell,
Sure is goin' to hell.
Cause some of these old members here
Sure is goin' to hell.

Etc.[16]

In the theme of this song, one can appreciate how close Negro religious and secular literature can be. The singer includes the tune in his blues repertoire, yet in form it is not true blues; it is much closer to the form of the religious or secular ballad.

Various natural disasters, tragedies, and other events—including fires, floods, and crop failures—have been the inspiration of songs sung by religious street singers. One song of this kind is

based on a windstorm which occurred in Terrebonne Parish,
Louisiana, in the year 1909:

> In the last day of September,
> In the year nineteen nine,
> God Almighty rose in the weather,
> And that troubled everybody's mind.
>
> The storm began on a Sunday,
> And it got in awful rage.
> Not a mortal soul
> In the globe that day
> Didn't have any mind to pray.
> And God was in the windstorm
> And troubled everybody's mind.
>
> God Almighty and his ministers,
> They rode up and down the land.
> All God Almighty did that day
> Was to raise the wind and dust.
>
> God, he is in the windstorm and rain,
> And everybody ought to mind.[17]

Cast in the form of a ballad, the song "God Moves On the
Water" owes its existence to the sinking of the *Titanic* in 1912:

> *Chorus (before each stanza)*
> God moves on the water,
> God moves on the water,
> God moves on the water,
> And the people had to run and pray.
>
> In the year of nineteen and twelve,
> On April the thirteenth day,
> When the great Titanic was sinkin' down,
> Well the people had to run and pray.
>
> When the lifeboat got to the landing,
> The womens turned around
> Cryin', look way cross that ocean, Lordy,
> At my husband drown.
>
> Captain Smith was a-lyin' down,
> Was asleep for he was tired.
> Well he woke up in a great fright,
> As many gunshots were fired.
>
> Well that Jacob Nash was a millionaire,
> Lord, he had plenty money to spare.

When the great *Titanic* was sinkin' down,
Well, he could not pay his fare.[18]

The theme of the sinking *Titanic* seems to have appealed to a number of gospel singers, who invested the event with moral significance. Although the subject was the same, the creative street bard cast it into his own mold, and many of the *Titanic* songs were different enough so that they could not really be considered merely variants. Compare this one, for example, with the one preceding:

On a Monday morning
Just about nine o'clock
The *Titanic*
Begin to reel and rock.
People a-kickin' and cryin'
Guess I'm goin' to die.

Chorus (after each stanza)
Wasn't that sad when that great ship went down,
Sad when that great ship went down,
Sad when that great ship went down.
Husband and wife, children lost their life,
Wasn't that sad when that great ship went down.

When that ship left England
Makin' for that shore
The rich paid their fares,
Would not ride with the poor
Could't get boats a-lowered,
Fightin' at the door.

People on that ship
Long way from home,
There's prayin' all around me,
They know they got to go,
Death came a-ridin' by,
They know they got to die.[19]

The *Titanic* drama was presented in many secular songs also (some of them not for print). The lyrical, non-religious version known by Huddie Ledbetter has as the chief protagonist the Negro prize fighter Jack Johnson, who was refused passage on the ill-fated ship:

It was midnight on the sea,
The band was playing "Nearer My God to Thee,"
Fare thee, *Titanic*, fare thee well.

Titanic when it got here slowed,
Captain he hollered all aboard,
Fare thee, *Titanic,* fare thee well.

Titanic was comin' round the curve
When it run into that great big iceberg,
Fare thee, *Titanic,* fare thee well.

When the *Titanic* was sinkin' down,
They had them life boats all around,
Fare thee, *Titanic,* fare thee well.

They had them life boats all around,
Savin' the women and children and lettin' the men go down,
Fare thee, *Titanic,* fare thee well.

Jack Johnson wanted to get on board,
Captain he said I aint haulin' no coal,
Fare thee, *Titanic,* fare thee well.

When he heard about that mighty shock,
Might o' seen a man doin' the Eagle Rock,
Fare thee, *Titanic,* fare thee well.[20]

A more recent topical event, the Soviet Union's rocket shot at the moon, is the springboard for this street gospel song recorded in New Orleans. Its allusions to modern technology contrast vividly with Biblical references:

Oh Russia, let that moon alone! (×2)
Moon aint worryin' you!
Oh Russia, let that moon alone!
God told you go till the earth,
God didn't tell you to till the moon!
You got to let that moon alone!
Oh Russia, let that moon alone!
You can make your sputnickles
And your satellites,
You can't get God's moon!
Let God's moon alone!
The moon aint worryin' you! (×2)
God told man to till the earth,
God didn't tell you to till the moon!
You better let God's moon alone!
The moon aint worryin' you!
Oh [people] in Russia, get out on your knees and pray!
And let God's moon alone!
The moon aint worryin' you! (×2)

God put the moon up there to give you light by night!
Oh let God's moon alone! ᵂ

Etc.

The Negro musical literature dealing with religious subject matter is rich and panoramic. It encompasses the anthems and spirituals with which we are largely familiar, chanted or half-sung sermons, improvisations by laboring gangs, the songs of itinerant street singers, and the spontaneous cries or hollers that are heard in the open fields. There is great variation among them in music and subject matter, but they all draw upon a common wellspring of inspiration and imagery. They are not all equally good or equally evocative. Each carries the mark of the feeling and genius that created it. Some achieve the level of pure or great poetry, while others contrive to make drama out of prosaic substance, and still others never quite manage to escape being doggerel. But the total picture is one of splendorous vision and a sensitive comprehension of the religious precepts out of which the vision derives.

ᵂ See The Music, 24.

IV. Cries, Calls, Whooping, and Hollering

WHILE WALKING in the open countryside of northern Nigeria some years ago, I heard a cry from a distant hill which was so musical that I thought I was listening to the beginning of a song. But the sound died on a thinning note and the air was silent. After a minute or so it came again, the liquid, melodic line sustained a little longer than before, then dying so gently that it seem audible after it had ended.

I asked an African friend who was with me what it was. He pointed quietly toward another hill, perhaps a thousand yards from the first. From there, a moment later, there was another musical cry, fainter, with hard to describe ornamentations. "What is it?" I asked again. "No word," my African informant answered, "them boys are friends, they say good night."

In Haiti, another time, I heard a lone peasant, working in a mountain field, emit a liquid, quavering sound which slid up and down and suggested something like a melody, and ended abruptly with a "hoooo-ooooo" that echoed across the ravine.

Almost before the sound had died, there was a response from a small thatched hut on the mountainside. In a few moments the peasant shouldered his hoe, picked up his machete, and began to walk home. Again in Matanzas Province, Cuba, I heard Negro workers calling out this way in the cane fields.

These melodic calls, unexpected wordless birds of sound coming out of the stillness of the fields, are also in the tradition of the rural Negroes in our own southland. Although they must have been commonplace in old plantation days, memory of them is slowly fading away. The old people remember them and sometimes use them. So do some of the younger people, but in general they have given them up, and there are some Negroes in the southern states who have never heard them in their natural setting. According to the testimony of a number of older informants, calls and cries were used in the old days in the corn and cotton fields, in the woods, and on the rivers, wherever men and women worked. There were calls to communicate messages of all kinds —to bring people in from the fields, to summon them to work, to attract the attention of a girl in the distance, to signal hunting dogs, or simply to make one's presence known.[1] There were still others, more aptly described as cries, that were simply a form of self-expression, a vocalization of some emotion. A man working under the hot sun might give voice to such a cry on impulse, directing it to the world, or to the fields around him, or perhaps to himself. It might be filled with exuberance or melancholy. It might consist of a long "hoh-hoo," stretched out and embellished with intricate ornamentation of a kind virtually impossible to notate; or it might be a phrase like "I'm hot and hungry," or simply "pickin' cotton, yoh-hoo!" Sometimes this elemental music, carried beyond a single line or phrase, would take on the form of an elemental song.

More than a hundred years ago, in 1853, a correspondent of the New York *Daily Times*, Frederick Olmsted, heard and wrote about what he called "Negro jodling" or "the Carolina yell." The scene was in South Carolina, night time along the railroad tracks: "At midnight I was awakened by loud laughter, and, looking out, saw that the loading gang of negroes [slaves hired out to the railroad] had made a fire and were enjoying a right merry repast. Suddenly one raised such a sound as I had never heard before, a long, loud, musical shout, rising, and falling, and breaking into falsetto, his voice ringing through the woods in the clear, frosty night air, like a bugle call. As he finished, the melody was caught up by another, and then, another, then by several in chorus. When there was silence again, one of them cried out, as if bursting with amusement: 'Did yer see de dog?—when I began eeohing, he turn roun' an' look me straight into der face; ha! ha! ha!' and the whole party broke into the loudest peals of laughter, as if it was the very best joke they had ever heard.

"After a few minutes I could hear one urging the rest to come to work again, and soon he stepped towards the cotton bales, saying, 'Come, bredern, come; let's go at it; come now, eoho! roll away! eeoho-eeoho-weeioho-i!'—and the rest taking it up as before, in a few moments they all had their shoulders to a bale of cotton and were rolling it up the embankment." [2]

The Negro cries and calls of the open spaces are known by different names in different places. Sometimes they are called "cornfield hollers," "cotton field hollers," or just "hollers." In Alabama, the term "whooping" is used, and it sometimes appears in songs ("Don't you hear me whoopin', oh, baby!"). According to one chronicler, some regions refer to the cries as "loud mouthing." [3]

The cry does not have to have a theme, or to fit into any kind of formal structure, or to conform to normal concepts of musical propriety. It is often completely free music in which every sound, line, and phrase is exploited for itself in any fashion that appeals to the crier. It may be short and sharp, with an abrupt end, or like the Nigerian cry previously described it can waver, thin out, and gently disappear into the air. It may consist of a single musical statement or a series of statements, and may reflect any one of a number of moods—homesickness, loneliness, lovesickness, contentment, exuberance. The clue often lies in the words as well as the music. One cry, heard in Alabama, went like this:

Ay-oh-hoh!
I'm goin' up the river!
Oh, couldn't stay here!
For I'm goin' home!

So bad, I'm so far from home!
And I can't get there for walkin'!
I want to go home so bad partner!
I'm goin' up the river, but I can't stay here!
I'm goin' home, woh!
I won't get back till July and August.
I won't get there till fall.
My boat up the river.
But I can't stay here, want to go back!
Oh Lord!

Another cry of similar vintage, heard in the same place, is this one.

Oh I'm goin' away partner!
Aint goin' to be here long!
If I aint got time to tarry here,
Better down the road I'm gone!
I aint got time to wait,
For the times don't get no better here!
Better down the road I'm gone! [4]

An elderly woman of eastern Alabama whose father was born a slave in that area remembered and was able to sing some of the field calls she heard as a child.[5] As distinguished from cries, these calls all had some kind of communicative purpose. They conveyed simple messages, or merely made one's whereabouts known to friends working elsewhere in the fields. According to a number of aged informants, calls of this kind had great importance to slaves who were confined by their work to particular fields, and who were not free to socialize at times of their own choosing with friends in other fields or on neighboring plantations.

Sometimes, just for the comfort of making one's presence known to others, a field hand would give a wordless call such as this one (Example 10).

EXAMPLE 10

And from a distance, in identical musical phrasing, would come the answer: "Yeh-ee-ee, yeh-hee! Yeh-ee-ee, yeh-hee!"

When the father called to his children for assistance in the fields, it sounded like this (Example 11).

EXAMPLE 11

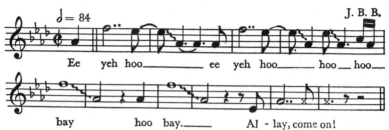

Ee yeh hoo_____ ee yeh hoo_____ hoo__ hoo__
bay   hoo bay._____ AI - lay, come on!

Young people seeking companionship or love might give the following call (Example 12).

EXAMPLE 12

Yeh_____ eh - beh- oo   eh_____ oo eh ____ oo
eh_____ oo__ yeh__ beh-oo yeh - oo   yeh beh beh
beh- oo woh_____   oo woh oh__ yeh__ woh-oo woh - oo
yeh_____ beh-oo eh_____ oo eh_____ oo__ eh beh-oo_____
_____ beh beh_____ beh beh- oo woh_____   oo
beh beh__ beh beh-oo woh ____ oo eh_beh-oo oh___

In slavery days, the field calls doubtless had a special importance that they lacked later. They were a means by which the slaves could keep in touch with one another, and perhaps get around regulations of the overseer that isolated one work party from another. In early slave days, these calls undoubtedly were in African dialects, insofar as actual words were used, and they must have been a source of irritation to white overseers who could not understand them. If one considers the tonal aspects of West and Central African languages, the possibility is that many of the calls and cries were less wordless than they seemed. It is now well understood that African signal drumming is based largely on simulation, through rising and falling inflection, of speech tones. Voice signaling in Africa is sometimes based on this same principle, and signal horns are used in the same manner. In some instances, voice signals are not modeled directly on speech tones, but on the sound of instruments imitating speech.[6] Many of the early day slave calls and cries in the United States may have utilized these communicative devices. In such disguise, seemingly wordless messages could have been quite unintelligible to outsiders.

Many contemporary American Negro cries and calls are far from wordless, however, and, though given in a free form, they closely approximate what we regard as song. The call in Example 13, rudimentary in form though it may be as a song, has a particular melodic beauty.[7] One field hand calls across the open spaces to another, asking where he has been. The other man says he has "been in the jungle," a metaphor that might mean escape into the woods, prison, or some other kind of unhappy experience.

EXAMPLE 13

Hey   Ru - fus,   hey   boy,_____

where in the world____ you been____ so____ long?

Hey   bud - dy,   hey   boy.____   Well__

I been in the jun - gle,——— aint go - in' there no more.—— Well I been in the jun——— gle, aint go - in' there no more.——— Hey Ru - fus, hey——— boy.

In the cotton fields and the cornfields of the present time, as on the old plantations, the water carrier is in constant demand. The call for the water boy (or girl), in one or another of its many variants, is well enough known that it has been interpolated into theater music and used by the concert recitalist. Some water calls such as "Water Boy, Where Are You Hidin'?" have come to be regarded as true songs, and may be heard on phonograph recordings. The water call given here (Example 14) was recorded in Alabama in 1950.[8]

EXAMPLE 14

Wa - ter boy wa - ter boy! Wa - ter boy, wa - ter boy! Wa-ter on the wheel,——— how does——— the sun shine——— that——— I——— feel, lit tle wa - ter time, hey,——— lit tle wa - ter boy.

lit - tle wa - ter time, hey,___ lit - tle wa - ter boy.

Wa - ter on the whee _____ 1   how does the

sun shine_____ that I ___ feel, lit-tle wa - ter boy.

The folk song entertainer Huddie Ledbetter had in his repertoire a water call which he sang to guitar accompaniment:

Bring me a little water, Silvie,
Bring me a little water now.
Bring me a little water, Silvie,
Every little once in a while.

Don't you hear me callin'?
Don't you hear me now?
Don't you hear me callin'
Every little once in a while.[9]

Negro field calls, cries, whoops, and hollers end where the cities
begin, but the cities have calls of their own. In Charleston, Savan-
nah, New Orleans, Shreveport, and almost any other southern
metropolis, one may still hear the calls of the food vendors, floor
sanders, chimney sweeps, fix-it men, ice men, and junk peddlers.
Elsewhere, in the north, in Negro sections of Chicago, Detroit,
New York, and Cleveland, among other places, service and mer-
chandise peddlers advertise their wares in the same fashion. Sometimes sung with elaborate ornamentation, sometimes more nearly
chanted, many of these calls are so distinctively individual that
specific vendors often may be recognized long before they are seen.

Work calls are not the exclusive property of the American Negro
community. In white rural areas of America, cattle calls are commonplace, as they are in Europe. Work and hunting cries and
calls are used by tribal peoples in the Philippines, Africa, and
Southeast Asia. American and European cities since times long
past have heard the calls of knife sharpeners, umbrella menders,

peddlers, and old clothes merchants. And ancient Korea knew the call of the needle and sword mender. Urban calls are an old tradition in many cultures. What the Negro has brought to them is something of his own music and imagery.

Some commentators in the field of jazz or folk music have put forward the idea that calls and cries are a source, even a prime source, of blues and jazz. This notion can only be regarded as part of the romanticism that has attached to the subject of jazz origins. Before the first Negro call or cry was uttered in the New World, Negroes possessed a highly developed and sophisticated music. They were conspicuously knowledgeable in this field, and had well defined concepts of the uses to which the voice could be put. There was no need to begin afresh with a rudimentary, formless cry. Although it is evident that some of the elements heard in the cry are also heard in blues and other Negro songs, these elements are merely part of a general repertoire of musical effects upon which all Negro music draws. The ornamentations and free melodic and rhythmic elements heard in field calls may also be heard in prayers, moans, spirituals, blues, and solo worksongs. While the self-conscious song composer or interpreter may "borrow" call themes to incorporate into a blues piece, for example, the traditional singer already possesses these resources, and, in using them, it would never occur to him that he was taking from one genre to apply to another.

Calls and cries are simply extracted out of the common storehouse of musical tradition.

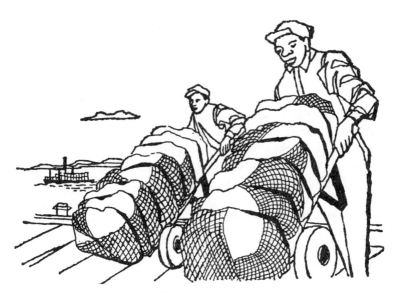

V. Sounds of Work

THE NEGRO WORKSONG, particularly the kind sung by railroad gangs, roustabouts (stevedores), woodcutters, fishermen, and prison road gangs, is in an old and deeply rooted tradition. Few Negro musical activities come closer than gang singing does to what we think of as an African style. The melodies may be essentially European, the rhythms may be simple (dictated by the nature of the work being done), and the harmonic sounds may be no more African than European, but the over-all effect instantly calls to mind the group labor songs of Jamaica, Haiti, and West Africa.[1]

The substance of the gang songs ranges from the ribald to the devout, from the humorous to the sad, from the gentle to the biting, and from the tolerant to the unforgiving. The meanings can be personal or impersonal. The statement can be direct, tangent, or metaphoric. As throughout Negro singing generally, there is an incidence of social criticism, ridicule, gossip, and protest. The men may sing of the work they are doing, women, heroic events, places they have been, good lives or lives gone wrong, preachers and gang bosses, the hard lot of the Negro, or salvation. Some gang songs, or certain portions of them, are taken over from church singing, children's games, or from balladry. But most of them, by far, draw their substance from life on the levies, in the pine forests, in the fishing boats, on the tracks, and from the living scene generally.

The singing leader is as essential to the work gang as the singing leader or preacher is in the church. He must have the feel of the work that is being done, an understanding of the men with whom he is working, and the capacity to evoke both music and motor response. As in the dance, music and motor activity are inseparably joined. Although the prime objective of the gang song is not entertainment, it nevertheless must be more than melody, words, and timing; the song that captures the imagination of the workers, that engages them, will get the work done by keeping the men in a working spirit. For members of work gangs, either on the railroads or in prison battalions, many of the songs they hear are part of an old and familiar repertoire. A good singing leader senses what kind of song is needed at a given time, and how to sing it. Frequently he has a talent for improvisation or new creation. A good many worksongs were heard for the first time only a few moments after the events on which they comment took place. Some action of the boss or "captain," some overheard conversation, a passing woman, a quarrel, or anything else may be turned into a song if the leader can grasp it and distill it into a singing statement. Sometimes a leader improvises on a theme that has personal meaning to him, but in such terms that it can also have personal meaning for the other men in the group.

In its choice of subject matter, its responsive form, its improvisation, its direct relation to work being done, and in the tie between sound and action, the Negro group worksong bears a striking affinity to its counterparts in the African tradition. From northwestern Africa to the Cape, the African tends to think of music as heard action, and of any silent rhythmical activity as an echo of music. Singing, and sometimes percussive effects, customarily accompanies the cutting of trees, the clearing of brush, the hoeing of fields, the hoisting of sails, the hauling of a hawser, the pounding of grain in a mortar, and the winnowing of rice. An individual working alone at such tasks may depend upon singing to complete his physical activity.

I have asked Africans, West Indians, and American Negroes what worksongs meant to them. In Durban, South Africa, I asked a Zulu member of a work gang which was inching a heavy fuel hose along a pier what would happen if the men stopped singing. Wouldn't they have more breath for their labor? After a perplexed silence he answered: "No. If we don't sing we have less breath. Without singing we have no strength." I mentioned that in America men often performed similar work without singing. He replied: "Perhaps in America you have so many men that a man doesn't have to be as strong as here." In Nigeria, a similar question brought forth the answer: "If the trees are to be cut, you must sing. Without a song the bush knife is dull." This comment I later heard cited as a commonplace proverb. In Haiti, I was told that singing and percussion music "encourage" the worker. In Alabama, a track liner said: "Man, singing just naturally makes the work go easier. If you didn't have singing you wouldn't get hardly anything out of these men."

Through identification and experience with work, the singing leader is able to convert song into movement and force. Timing is part of it. He mustn't pace the workers too fast or too slow. He senses when he can "pile it on" and when he must slacken. So valuable is a good leader or caller that in some gangs he is excused from actual work (as is the case in the West Indies and West Africa). Curiously, gangs of Negro prisoners in Alabama have been prohibited (at least at the time of one of my visits there) from singing on the job. This regulation was regarded as (or at least amounted to) additional punishment. Some "captains" have ignored the regulation, knowing that their men would be more content on the job, and would get more done, if they were singing than if they were not.

It is not only in group singing that the American Negro work gang shows similarities with African tradition, but in the patterns of group working as well. Throughout large parts of West and Central Africa, formal and informal labor groups for mutual assistance are commonly observed, and the tradition has survived strongly in Haiti, Jamaica, and other West Indian islands. Even where the institutionalized aspects of gang work have been altered in Africa, as in the instance where men gather to work for pay, the old patterns of work have nevertheless continued. The rhythmic use of tools, the sense of community, and responsive singing have remained significant elements in those patterns.

Under conditions of slavery in the New World, the idea of mutual dilemma and common enterprise was sufficient to sustain work music traditions. Men laboring in groups sang together as a natural consequence of working—not, as has sometimes been said, in spite of hard labor.

The structural patterns of the Negro gang worksongs are varied. Some of those commonly encountered are:

1. Unison singing, leader and chorus singing together note for note, except for accidental harmonies in seconds, thirds, fifths, sometimes in octaves or falsetto.

2. The leader sings his first solo line, follows with the response line, then sings his second solo line, after which the group picks up the indicated response. Each line of the solo part, except for occasional repetition, is different.

```
   leader        chorus
a) _____
b) _____
c) _____
                b) _____
d) _____
                b) _____
e) _____
                b) _____
f) _____
                b) _____
```

3. The chorus repeats in full the solo lines, each of which is different.

```
   leader        chorus
a) _____
                a) _____
b) _____
                b) _____
c) _____
                c) _____
d) _____
                d) _____
```

4. The leader sings every line twice, a fixed choral response following each solo line.

leader   chorus

a) ———
          b) ———
a) ———
          b) ———
c) ———
          b) ———
c) ———
          b) ———
d) ———
          b) ———
d) ———
          b) ———

5. The leader sings a line with one or more repetitions, with the chorus picking up the last word or several words of each line and then singing the responsive part.

leader   chorus
a) ———/———
a) ———/———
a) ———/———
          b) ———
c) ———/———
c) ———/———
c) ———/———
          b) ———

6. The leader sings each line twice, with an alternating choral response between.

leader   chorus

a) ———
          b) ———
a) ———
          c) ———
d) ———
          b) ———
d) ———
          c) ———
e) ———
          b) ———
e) ———
          c) ———

7. Combinations of these patterns.

A number of the forms mentioned above are commonly found in West Indian singing, particularly in the worksongs and ring play songs of the English speaking islands and the worksongs of Haiti.[2]

Peter Seeger, who recorded gang songs in Texas, remarks that the singing he heard there was marked by antiphony, the most casual attention to harmony, and a tendency toward a shifting melody. "Harmonically, most of the songs rarely leave the tonic chord. Only a few have occasional dominant or subdominant feeling. However, any singer able to would readily sing a high tenor part or bass." [3] These observations would appear to hold for Negro gang singing in other areas and settings.

The Negro railroad worker, like any other railroad hand, often followed the tracks in search of work, or moved from one place to another with the section crew. A man who joined up in Georgia might eventually find himself in Arkansas, Louisiana, or Ohio. He might then shift to another railroad line in order to work his way back home. Some of his work expeditions turned into long voyages that lasted a year or more. Many of the songs of the railroad hands reflected their homesickness. The following song (Example 15) expresses the desire of the singers to go back to East Colorado, a place name for which each man can mentally substitute a location of his own choosing.

EXAMPLE 15

Bim! when'd you come here, here, bud-dy when'd you come here?

Cap-tain send me down a cool drink of wa ter.

Bim! Just to heal my side, side, bud-dy just to heal my

side. Ev-a-li-na,—   (*etc. with variations*)

Intermixed among memories of East Colorado are thoughts about some of the women who aren't so far away:

Evalina,
When you goin' to tell me what I asked you? Bim!
I don't know, know, know,
Buddy buddy I don't know.
Captain I want to
Go back East Colorado. Bim!
But they don't allow me, me,
Buddy buddy don't allow me.
Mattie Campbell,
When you comin' back over? Bim!
Mattie Campbell,
When you comin' back over?
I don't know, know, know,
Buddy buddy I don't know. Bim!

In railroad lingo, track liners are called gandy dancers. The foreman gives his orders to his straw boss, the singing leader, who relays them to the gandy dancers and then gives them a song and a rhythm to work by. In the following song, there is a note of good humored bravado in the first stanza, carried to presumptious lengths in the third, in which the singing leader suggests that he would like to marry the foreman's daughter and be his straw boss when the foreman gets his section—that is, his promotion.

Called:
All right, Captain want to line the track. Hoh! Hold em right there!

Get you six bars! Put two bars on this side over here! All right, shake it east!

Sung:
Oh the Captain can't read, the Captain can't write,
Captain can't tell you when the track's lined right.
Mobile, Alabama. [↑↑↑↑↑↑↑] [a]
Mobile, Alabama. [↑↑↑↑↑↑↑]

Called:
Oh, move it, give me j'int ahead, j'ine 'em back behind the j'int ahead! Set two bars in there and hold it east! Three bars, shake it west! Oh, set it down boys!

Sung:
Woh, eat 'em up whiskers, one-eyed shave,
Eat 'em up by the light [. . . . . . .] day.
Big boy, let's line it. [↑↑↑↑↑↑↑]
Big boy, let's line it. [↑↑↑↑↑↑↑]

Called:
Oh, j'ine ahead, j'int back, ahead of the j'int ahead! All right, set 'em down and shake 'em west! Woh, set 'em down boys!

Sung:
Woh, Captain, when you get your section, want to be your straw,
Git your daughter, be your son-in-law.
Mobile, Alabama. [↑↑↑↑↑↑↑]
Mobile, Alabama. [↑↑↑↑↑↑↑]

While the standard and improvisatory verses sung by the callers for track lining are seemingly endless in number, and while they may vary considerably according to the individual callers, there is a common element which runs through many of them, particularly in the part of the song which accompanies the shaking operation. The metallic "rattle-dattle" sounds made by the bars against the track are, in the ears of the workmen, an integral part of the music. Whenever a man sings one of these songs outside the actual work setting, he finds the need of filling in with onomatopoeic sounds to represent the shaking. One singer uses "ratta-datta-datta-datta," another, "yakka-yakka-yakka."

In the following track lining song, into which is woven the image of Moses striking the water with a two-by-four, the action portions have a strong similarity to the comparable parts of "The

[a] This symbol marks the rattle-dattle sound of shaking the rails with the bars to line them up.

Captain Can't Read," even though the two songs were recorded a great distance apart:

> All I hate about linin' track,
> This old bar's 'bout to break my back.
> Big boy, can't you line 'em? [↑↑↑↑↑↑]
> Oh boy, can't you line 'em? [↑↑↑↑↑↑]
> Oh boy, can't you line 'em? [↑↑↑↑↑↑]
> Here we go line them track.
>
> If I could I surely would
> Stand on the rock where Moses stood.
> Big boy, can't you line 'em? [↑↑↑↑↑↑]
> Oh boy, can't you line 'em? [↑↑↑↑↑↑]
> Oh boy, can't you line 'em? [↑↑↑↑↑↑]
> Here we go line them track.
>
> Moses stood on that Red Sea shore,
> Smoten that water with a two-by-four.
> Big boy, can't you line 'em? [↑↑↑↑↑↑]
> Oh boy, can't you line 'em? [↑↑↑↑↑↑]
> Oh boy, can't you line 'em? [↑↑↑↑↑↑]
> Here we go line them track.[4]

The theme of being in trouble with the law is central to a large number of worksongs. In an environment in which minor infractions by a Negro might easily result in arrest and quick conviction, the story of getting out of town quickly found its way into many songs. So commonplace was the threat in some regions that the nature of the offense itself was a secondary element in the saga, and frequently it went unspecified. In the following song, the singer calls on his woman to meet him in the swamp with his shoes, so that he can be on his way:

> Meet me in the bottom with my boots and shoes,
> Whoo Lordy mamma, Great God A'mighty,
> Meet me in the bottom with my boots and shoes,
> Got to leave this town now, got no time to lose.
> The woman I love she got to bring my boots and shoes,
> Whoo Lordy mamma, Great God A'mighty,
> The woman I love, with my boots and shoes,
> Say the woman I loved by, see her every day.
> The woman I love, she got long black curly hair,
> Whoo Lordy mamma, Great God A'mighty,
> The woman I love got long black curly hair,
> Say the woman I hate, I see her every day.

Meet me in the bottom with my boots and shoes,
Whoo Lordy mamma, Great God A'mighty,
Meet me in the bottom with my boots and shoes,
Got to leave this town now, got no time to lose.[b]

In the song "Goin' to Have a Talk With the Chief of Police,"
a man tells the story, largely through allusions that are not self
explanatory, of his pursuit of a woman named Rena who goes to
great lengths to keep out of his way. He goes to the river to scan
the boats that pass, in the hope of seeing her. Then it turns out
that she has taken a train, and the ardent pursuer declares that
he is going to find the chief of police to talk the whole problem
over with him.

I'm goin' uptown have a talk with the chief police,
How my good girl in trouble and I cannot see no peace.
Don't I love you baby, and I just can't take [sic] your place.
Don't I love you, baby, and I tell you that I do,
I hope some day, baby, come to love me too,
And I hope some day, baby, come to love me too.
I went to the river and I looked up it, up and down,
Thought I'd see my good girl when she walkin' cross the town,
I tell my baby why she come back home,
And I had no lovin', babe, since you been gone.
I tell my woman, tell her Lord for me,
Lord she can't quit me and it aint no use of tryin'.
But my baby caught the train and I swore [. . . . . . .]
Singin' to her that she can't quit me, Lord it aint no use of tryin'.
Oh I tear uptown in the mornin' have a talk with the chief police,
Cause Rena in trouble and I cannot see no peace.[c]

The prison camp songs with which we have become more familiar recently through field recordings [5] are worksongs in a
special setting, and do not comprise a completely separate category, though they do contain a higher incidence of reference to
prison camp life, escapes, and other adventures, and an understandable melancholy lurking behind even humorous themes.
Nevertheless, they do have a special character, something that sets
them apart from the main body of worksongs. The continuing
association of the prisoners over long periods of time, their day
by day common experiences, their lack of normal emotional and
intellectual outlets, their shared sense of frustration and, some-

[b] See The Music, 34.   [c] See The Music, 31.

times, injustice, and their practiced familiarity with a large body
of song literature have combined to bring the contemporary Negro
worksong to its highest point. As Alan Lomax remarks: "The
wildest and most beautiful of . . . Negro work songs come from
the penitentiary where the old Southern system of forced labor
reaches its apogee." [6]

In the prison camps, as on the railroads, religious themes appear
frequently in the singing repertoire; the extent to which this is
so depends largely upon the men who are present. In some prison
gangs, there may be men with religious proscriptions against
secular or sinful songs. They may be served by the singing leader
with basically secular songs into which religious motifs have been
woven; this gives the songs an acceptably nonsinful character. A
song starting out as a description of the prisoners' work shifts
into a narration of the Noah story. The thread that binds the two
parts together is the pounding of the hammers, which may be
used for the breaking of stone, the driving of spikes, or some similar operation. The following lines are sung by the leader; after
each of his lines, the gang responds with "Oh don't you hear my
hammer ringing?"

    I says I'm ringing in the bottom, (×2)
    I says I'm ringing for the captain,
    I says I'm ringing for the sergeant,
    I says I'm ringing for the steerer, (×2)
    I believe we ring for everybody. (×2)

This introduction or "dedication" has the character of many West
African songs in that it takes note of the important personages
within earshot. Once the song is properly dedicated, any irony
or criticism contained in later portions presumably will be overlooked by the personages concerned.

    I'm going to tell you 'bout my hammer, (×2)
    Well, 'bout a-killing me, hammer, (×2)
    I says the captain's gone to Houston, (×2)
    He's coming back by Ramsey,[d]
    He's coming back by the Ramsey.
    He's gonna bring my partner, (×2)
    He's gonna give us both a hammer,
    And we're gonna live in the bottom.

[d] Ramsey State Farm.

We're gonna walk to the live oak,
Don't turn and walk away, sir,
We're gonna walk to the gopherwood. (×2)
Now, these words he did say, sir,
He says ring old hammer. (×2)

The scene shifts to the building of the ark, comparing Noah's ordeal with that of the prisoners:

I says God told Norah
About a rainbow sign,
Well, there'll be no more water,
Oh, there'll be no more water
I b'lieve 'fore your next time, sir,
Oh before next time, sir.
Says he destroy this world, sir,
Say he destroy this world, sir.
Well, Norah, Norah,
Oh don't you remember what I hold you
About a rainbow sign, sir.
I'm gonna run and get some water
Oh before your next time, sir.
Well, old Norah got his hammer,
Well, went marching to the bottom,
And you can hear Norah's hammer,
Well, you can hear Norah's hammer,
Well, you can hear many ringing,
Well, all over the land, sir,
He's in the country too, sir.
And then the weaker generation,
Well, he asked old Norah,
Yes he asked old Norah,
Well, what in the world you gonna do, sir.
He's gonna build this-a ark-a.
Oh, tell me where you gonna build it.
Oh, just a mile from the river,
I'm gonna build this old building
So it'll float on the water
And on land, and, too, sir,
That's what I'm gonna do, sir.
Says you can hear Norah hollering,
Won't you ring, old hammer,
Now won't you ring, old hammer,
Why don't you ring in the timber,
Why don't you ring like you used to,
You used to ring like a bell, sir.

There aint nobody's hammer (×2)
Nobody's hammer in the bottom
That ring like-a mine, sir.

The scene then shifts back again to the present, with the prisoners singing about themselves:

I say that's all about the hammer,
'Bout a-killing me, hammer.
We're gonna ring this hammer,
I'm gonna ring it in the bottom.
I said, God got the key
And you can't come in, sir.
Why don't you ring old hammer,
Why don't you ring till your number,
Why don't you ring old hammer,
Old hammer won't you ring.[7]

Some prison camp songs are more unequivocally religious, such as "Mighty Bright Light." In this song, the last word of the leader's lines, "down," is picked up by the chorus, which also sings a responsive refrain every fourth line:

It was a mighty bright light that was shining *down,* (×3)
    Oh a mighty bright light that was shining down.
Oh tell me who was the light that was shining *down,* (×3)
    Oh a mighty bright light that was shining down.
Oh King Jesus was the light that was shining *down,* (×3)
    Oh a mighty bright light that was shining down.
My mother saw the light that was shining *down,* (×3)
    Oh a mighty bright light that was shining down.
Oh everybody saw the light that was shining *down,* (×3)
    Oh a mighty bright light that was shining down.[8]

Sagas of escape from prison or prison camps are a favorite subject for songs of Negro convict laborers. Many of these songs are short lived, but others such as "Old Riley," "Here Rattler Here," and "Lost John" have become "classics" and are found in numerous versions throughout the South wherever Negro convicts work together in the swamps, on the roads, in the turpentine camps, in the gravel pits, and in the forest.

The dramatic "Lost John" rates with the finest of escape songs. Opening with lines reminiscent of the cowboy song that begins, "One morning when I was riding for pleasure," this near-epic tells of a prisoner named Lost John who escaped and outwitted his pursuers by the ruse of placing an extra heel on the front of each shoe. When his footprints were discovered, it was impossible to tell the direction of his flight. As sung responsively, each of the following lines, delivered by the leader, was repeated by the chorus.

One day, one day
I were walking along
And I heard a little voice
Didn't see no one.
It was old Lost John,
He said he was long gone
Like a turkey through the corn
With his long clothes on.
Had a heel in front
And a heel behind,
Well you couldn't hardly tell
Well you couldn't hardly tell
Whichaway he was goin'
Whichaway he was goin'.
One day, one day,
Well I heard him say
Be on my way
Be on my way
'Fore the break of day
By the break of day.
Got a heel in front,
Got a heel behind,
Well you can't hardly tell
Well you can't hardly tell
Whichaway I'm goin'.

At this point the song turns to commentary on the conditions which had driven Lost John to escape:

Oughta come on the river
Long time ago,
You could find a dead man
Right on your row.
Well the dog man killed him
Well the dog man killed him
'Cause the boy couldn't go
'Cause the boy couldn't go.
Wake up dead man,
Help me carry my row,
'Cause the row's so heavy
Can't hardly make it

To the lower turn row
To the lower turn row.
Oughta come on the river
Nineteen and ten,
Well the women was rolling
Just like the men.[e]

Following another rendition of the escape story, there is more comment on prison camp life:

Oughta come on the river
Long time ago,
I don't know partner,
Say, you oughta know,
You'd catch plenty trouble
Everywhere you go
Everywhere you go.
One day, one day,
Heard the captain say
If you boys work
Gonna treat you mighty well,
If you don't go to work,
Says we may give you hell.

And at last a small note of hope:

One day, one day,
I'll be on my way
And you may not never
Ever hear me say
One day, one day,
I'll be on my way.[9]

The hero of the song "Here Rattler Here" is usually a man named Riley. The story recounts how he receives a letter telling him that his woman has died, and Riley tells his friends he is going to escape from the prison camp. Should the captain ask if he was running, they could say he was flying; should the captain ask if he was laughing, they could tell him Riley was crying. Riley takes off with the posse and the dog Rattler on his heels, but they never catch up with him and finally give up the chase. First comes a description of Old Rattler. Each line is followed by the choral response, "Here Rattler Here."

[e] Another version of this stanza, sung as a blues, is to be found in Chapter VI. See pp. 132-33.

Why don't you here, Rattler, here,
Oh, don't you here, Rattler, here.
This Old Rattler was a walker dog,
Says he'll trail you 'cross a live oak log.
Says Old Rattler hit the man's trail,
Says he run and bit him on the heel,
And you oughta heard that man squeal.
You holler, here, here, Rattler,
Hollerin' here, here, Rattler.
Says Old Rattler was a walking dog,
He could trail you 'cross a live oak log.

The story proper begins then with the discovery of Riley's disappearance:

Says the captain come a-riding,
Asking where is that sergeant,
Says I believe there's a man gone.
Says the sergeant come riding,
Popping his whip upon the ground,
And Old Rattler turning round and round.
He said here Old Rattler,
Says Old Rattler, here's a marrow bone,
You can eat it, you can leave it alone.
I don't want no marrow bone,
I just want the man that's long gone.
Says Old Rattler went skipping through the morning dew,
And Old Rattler went to skipping through the morning dew,
And the sergeant pop the whip upon the ground,
And Old Rattler begin to turn round and round.
He cried, here Old Rattler,
Crying, here Old Rattler.

At this point there is a flashback to the scene in which Riley announces his departure:

Says Old Riley got worried,
He come running with a letter,
Says you ought to heard what that letter read.
Says Old Riley says that Irene's dead,
Say come home, pretty papa,
Yes, come home, pretty papa.
Says Old Riley he got worried,
Says to the captain that you was a-running,
You just tell him I was flying.
If he asks you was I laughing,
You can tell him I was crying.

Then follows the chase, but Riley has crossed the Brazos River and disappeared:

And it's here, Old Rattler,
And it's here, Old Rattler,
And Old Rattler got to the Brazos,
Well he left him there a-howling.
Old Rattler hollered, oooh, ooh, ooh, ooh!
He hollered, ooh, ooh, ooh, ooh!
And I heard the sergeant blowing his horn,
Oughta heard that sergeant blowing his horn,
Blowed it doo, doo, doo, doo!
Blowed it oo, oo, oo, oo!
Says I believe he crossed the river,
Believe he crossed the big Brazos.
He gonna give up Old Riley,
Take another day back on the way.
I'm going to call Old Rattler,
Hollering here, Rattler, here,
Won't you here, Rattler, here, here,
Won't you here, Old Rattler.[10]

While there are long term prisoners who contend that Riley was a real prisoner in a specific prison, they place the scene variously at Ramsey, Clements, Parchman, and other sites ranging from Georgia to Texas. The song is found in many forms, some of which suggest that the original Riley could have been a slave in antebellum times.

Other versions of this song have protagonists by different names, including Old Whitey, Red Saunders, and Old Coffee, indicating that the story is a framework into which may be inserted the escape tale of any prisoner. One variant, with a hero named Old Milo, has a sadder ending than the one documented for Riley:

Well its soon one morning (×2)
When I called Old Rattler (×2)
Well it's hooo-ah hooo-ah! (×2)
Well Old Rattler here's a marrow bone (×2)
You can eat it Rattler or leave it alone. (×2)
I done treed Old Milo, (×2)
Well Old Milo's in that sycamore tree. (×2)
Whyn't you sick 'im Old Rattler, whyn't you bite 'im old dog. (×2)
Well there's here here Rattler (×2)
I done losed a trusty. (×2) [11]

A stirring prison camp worksong heard in Texas, about an enigmatic "grizzly bear," appears to be a tangent statement about events that are not clearly spelled out. One informant in another area of the South, who had served time in a Mississippi prison, declared the song to be about a convict who escaped from a work gang and lived in the woods, from where he made forages for food and other necessities. Wild in appearance, he was nicknamed Grizzly (pronounced Grizzaly) Bear, otherwise known as Jack of Diamonds (a term of anonymity), so that his real name does not appear in the song. Nevertheless, some people expressed the opinion that the grizzly bear was really just a bear—a view that doesn't seem to withstand the internal evidence of the song text.

Each of the lines given here, sung by the leader, is repeated with minor variations by the group, which also comes in on the last two words of the leader's lines.

Oh that grizzaly, grizzaly, grizzaly bear,
Tell me who was that grizzaly, grizzaly bear.
Oh Jack o' Diamonds was that grizzaly, grizzaly bear.
He had great long tushes like a grizzaly bear,
He made a track in the bottom like a grizzaly bear.
Well that grizzaly, grizzaly, grizzaly bear,
Tell me who was the grizzaly, grizzaly bear.
Jack o' Diamonds was the grizzaly, grizzaly bear.
He made a noise in the bottom like a grizzaly bear,
Well my mamma was scared of that grizzaly bear,
Well my papa went a-hunting for the grizzaly bear,
Well my brother wasn't scared of that grizzaly bear.
Oh the grizzaly, grizzaly, grizzaly bear,
Well I'm gonna kill that grizzaly bear.
Well the grizzaly, grizzaly, grizzaly bear,
Well I looked in Louisiana for the grizzaly bear.
Etc.[12]

Comments on the long terms being served by the prisoners often find their way into work music. In this song, for example, the singer notes wryly that the captain is in a hurry to get the work done, though the prisoners aren't going anywhere and will be in the vicinity for the foreseeable future.

The captain holler hurry,
Goin' to take my time.
Say captain holler hurry,
Goin' to take my time.

Say he makin' money,
And I'm tryin' to make time.
Say he can lose his job,
But I can't lose mine.
I aint got long to tarry,
Just stop by here.
Boys if you got long
You better move along.
Etc.[f]

Love themes naturally form one of the important categories of prison songs. They are not expressed in our customary romantic idiom, but in tangents and in physical imagery. Words and music nevertheless have a poignancy and strength not often surpassed by traditional Western love clichés. As heard in its natural setting, the following song, recorded by Alan Lomax in Mississippi, was sung by the gang leader, with the group coming in on the last two or three words of each line.

Be my woman, gal, I'll / be your man. (×3)
Every Sunday's dollar / in your hand,
In your hand, Lordy / in your hand,
Every Sunday's dollar / in your hand.
Stick to the promise, gal, 'at / you made me. (×3)
Weren't gonna marry till-a / I go free,
I go free, Lordy / I go free,
Weren't gonna marry till-a / I go free.
Well Rosie / oh Lord gal.
Ah, Rosie / oh Lord gal.
When she walks she reel and / rock behind. (×2)
Aint that enough to worry / convict's mind. (×2) [g]

A similar worksong heard in another state, with melody and timing reminiscent of the previous example, substitutes the name Julie for Rosie.

Says huh Julie,
Hullo gal.
Says huh Julie,
Hullo gal.
Says early in the mornin' baby,
Half past four,
Says early in the mornin' baby,
Half past four,
I come to your window baby,

[f] See The Music, 28.   [g] See The Music, 26.

Knocked on the door.
Says get away from my window baby,
Quit knockin' on my door,
Says got another man baby,
Don't want you no more.
Says huh gal, baby,
Done got ugly,
Says huh Julie,
You done got ugly,
Says oh Lord baby,
Don't want you no more.
Says hey gal now,
Hey rock that baby,
Juh baby,
Oh keep him dry.
Says early in the mornin',
Oh soon one mornin',
The clock strike four baby,
And I knocked on the door.[h]

Among the gnawing fears and anxieties of the long term prisoners is the thought that when they return home they may find
that their women are no longer waiting. One song on this theme,
"Baby Please Don't Go" (Example 16), is known widely, though
in different forms from one prison camp to another. Some versions have an almost endless number of stanzas, while others are
only a few stanzas long. The expression "I'm going to walk your
log," which appears in the last stanza of this version, is a threat
that if the woman goes away the prisoner will kill her.

EXAMPLE 16

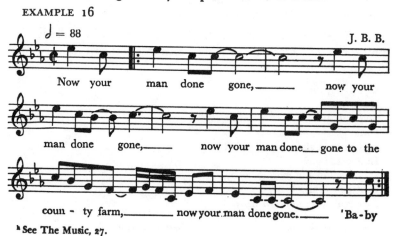

[h] See The Music, 27.

Now your man done gone, (×3)
To the county farm
Now your man done gone.

Baby please don't go, (×3)
Back to Baltimore,
Baby please don't go.

Turn your lamp down low, (×3)
And baby please don't go,
Baby please don't go.

You know I loves you so, (×3)
And baby please don't go,
Baby please don't go.

I beg you all night long, (×3)
And night before,
Baby please don't go.

Now your man done come, (×3)
From the county farm,
Now your man done come.

I'm goin' to walk your log, (×2)
And if you throw me off
I'm goin' to walk your log.

Another variant of this ubiquitous song, heard in a neighboring state, is this one:

Baby please don't go, (×2)
Back to New Orleans,
You know I love you so,
Baby please don't go.

Got me way down here (×3)
By the rollin' fog,
Treat me like a dog,
Baby please don't go.

Oh I be your dog, (×2)
Git you way down here,
Make you walk your log. (×2)

Baby please don't go, (×3)
Back to New Orleans,
Git you cold ice cream,
Baby please don't go.[13]

These versions were recorded within forty miles of each other, and illustrate the facility and ease with which a song can be developed and reformed. Sometimes a singing leader may remember only the melody and a few lines of a song he has heard, but that is usually enough; out of these elements, new variants are born. If there is a single secular song in American Negro tradition that can be safely said to be known on every railroad gang, in every prison camp, in every "jookin' joint," and, probably, in every Negro cabin in the South, it is "John Henry." The song appears in many lengths and forms, and can be heard as a worksong, a field blues, an urban blues, a washboard band tune, a harmonica or guitar theme, a dance melody, and even in prose narrations. So widespread is "John Henry" that it is part of the standard repertoire of many white mountaineer jug bands, white folk singers, and white dance ensembles.

The story is that of a railroad worker of great strength and pride who attempts to prove that the newly imported steam drill cannot replace a hard working hammer man, and who dies of exhaustion as a consequence. John Henry is the epitome of the "natural man." "Steam is only steam," he says in some of the songs, "but I'm John Henry, and I'm a natural man." Some scholars believe that they have established the identity of the original John Henry, a worker on the C. and O. Railroad. But as Guy B. Johnson concluded: "All questions of authenticity of the John Henry tradition fade into insignificance before the incontrovertible fact that for countless admirers John Henry is a reality. To them he will always be a hero. . . ." [14]

Shorter forms of the song only hint at the poetry and grandeur of the story, while some of the longer versions qualify as epic ballads. The story is centered on the dramatic contest between man and machine in the Big Bend Tunnel, but there are stanzas that flash back to his childhood, even to the day of his birth, and forward to scenes that follow his death. As some tell it, John Henry's first words were, "I'm goin' to make a steel drivin' man," and others declare that the day he was born the thunder rolled and the lightning flashed. As Roark Bradford has it in a somewhat literary treatment:

"The night John Henry was born the moon was copper-colored and the sky was black. The stars wouldn't shine and the rain fell hard. Forked lightning cleaved the air and the earth trembled like a leaf. The panthers squalled in the brake like a baby and the Mississippi River ran upstream a thousand miles." [15]

Some versions contend that when John Henry was a baby he had a clear premonition of his life's work and the drama of his end:

John Henry was a little baby,
Settin' on his mamma's knee,
Said the Big Bend Tunnel on the C. and O. Line
Going to be the death of me,
Lord, going to be the death of me.

The details of the momentous struggle against the machine vary a great deal as the story is told, or the song sung, in different places at different times. Individual singers have imparted something of their own visions and dreams to the ballad. The substance of most versions, however, is the tale of the hammer man and spike driver who wielded a nine (or twelve, or twenty) pound hammer as no one else ever did before or since. He could drive from both shoulders (that is, from either side), and he had so much stamina that he wore out his shakers (the men who held the drills for him). It is said that he could hammer all day without turning a stroke (striking a drill off-center).

One rendition has it that two crews of workmen competed in the Big Bend contest, one operating the steam drill, the other "shaking" for John Henry; at the end of thirty-five minutes the machine had drilled a hole nine feet deep, but John Henry had drilled two seven-foot holes, winning for himself a prize of one hundred dollars. But he was so exhausted from the contest that he died that night in bed. Other renditions say that he hammered himself to death right on the job: his eyes went dim, his arms grew weak, and he "died with his hammer in his hand." But the epic does not always end there. John Henry had a woman named, variously, Julie Anne, Mary Magdalene, Pearly Anne, Polly Anne, or Lucy Anne, who could handle a hammer as well as a man could. Hearing of John Henry's death, she went up on the mountain and took his place. And John Henry had a baby who said, "My daddy was a steel drivin' man, he died with his hammer in his hand, I want to die like Papa died."

The version given here is one which I recorded in Alabama in

1950. As with most of the John Henry songs, a migrant theme
from old English balladry enters toward the end—"Who's going
to shoe my feet, who's going to glove my hand?"

John Henry said to the Captain
That a man is not but a man.
Said before I let the steam drill beat me down
I'll hammer my fool self to death.
I'll hammer my fool self to death.

John Henry had a little woman,
Well the dress she wore it's a-red like blood,
And the shoes she wore, it's a-red,
Well the hat she had on, it's a-red,
That woman's eyes they turned red with blood.
Well she come a'screamin' and a-cryin' that day,
Come a-walkin' down that railroad track.
The Captain supplied to the woman,
Said tell me woman, what's troublin' your mind.
Says I'm goin' where my man fell dead,
Says I'm goin' where my man fell dead,
Says I'm goin' where my man fell dead,
Says I'm goin' where my man fell dead.
He done hammered his fool self to death,
He done hammered his fool self to death.

John Henry had another woman,
Well her name was Pearly Anne.
Well Pearly Anne she heard about this man's death,
Well what you reckon she said?
Said before I stand to see my man go down,
Says give me a ten-pound hammer,
Goin' to hook it onto the right of my arm,
Goin' to bring me a nine-pound hammer,
Goin' to hitch it onto the left of my arm.
Before I stand to see my man go down,
I'll go down 'tween-a them mountains,
And before I stand to see (my) man go down,
I'll hammer just like a man,
I'm goin' to hammer just like a man,
I'm goin' to hammer just like a man,
I'm goin' to hammer just like a man
I'm goin' to whup-a this mountain down,
I'm goin' to whup-a this mountain down.
'E says I'll hammer my fool self to death,
I'll hammer my fool self to death.

John Henry had a little baby boy,
You could tote it in the pa'm o' your hand.
Well every time that baby cried,
He looked in his mother's face.
Well his mother looked down at her baby's face,
Said tell me son what you worryin' about?
The last lovin' words she ever heard the boy said,
Mamma I want to make a railroad man,
Mamma I want to make a railroad man.
I'm goin' to die like Papa died,
I'm goin' to die like Papa died.
Son, Papa was a steel-drivin' man,
Son, Papa was a steel-drivin' man
But he hammered his fool self to death,
But he hammered his fool self to death.

John Henry had another little baby boy,
He was lyin' in the cradle kickin' and cryin',
Every time Mamma rocked the cradle bump-de-bump-a-lump,
I want to make a railroad man,
Say I want to make a railroad man.
Goin' to die like Papa died,
I want to die like Papa died.
Son your Daddy was a steel-drivin' man,
Your Daddy was a steel-drivin' man.
But he hammered his fool self to death,
But he hammered his fool self to death.

When Henry was 'tween them mountains
The Captain saw him goin' down.
He supplied to Henry one day,
Tried to pacify his mind,
Says Henry you knows you's a natural man.
Well what you reckon he said?
Says the steam drill drive one hammer by steam,
Says the steam drill drive one by air.
How in the world you expect to beat steam down?
He says how in the world you expect to beat air down?
Henry supplied to the Captain that day,
Steam is steam, I know air is air,
Before I let the steam drill beat me down,
Say I'll die with these hammers in my hand,
I'm goin' to die with these hammers in my hand.
I'm goin' to hammer my fool self to death,
I'm goin' to hammer my fool self to death.

When Henry was 'tween them mountains,
His wife couldn't hear him cryin'.

When she went out 'tween them mountains,
Tried to git him to lay the irons down.
He supplied to his wife that day,
Said my knee bones begin to grow cold.
Said the grip of my hand's givin' out.
My eyes begin to leak water.
Say before I lay these hammers down,
I'll die with these hammers in my hand,
I'm goin' to die with these hammers in my hand.

Take John Henry to the cemetery,
Lay him in his lonesome grave.
While she walked up there to the foot of the grave,
Cast her eyes in her husband's face,
Come a-screamin' and a-cryin' that day.
Preacher looked around in the woman's face,
Tell me woman what you screamin' about?
Last lovin' words that she supplied to him,
'Taint but the one thing troublin' my mind,
That certainly was a true man to me,
That certainly was a true man to me.
But he hammered his fool self to death,
He hammered his fool self to death.

John Henry's wife was sittin' down one day,
Just about the hour of sun,
Come a-screamin' and cryin'.
Papa said, Daughter what's troubin' your mind?
I got three little children here,
Who goin' to help me carry 'em along?
Who goin' to shoe my children's feet?
Who goin' to glove my children's hand?
Who goin' to shoe my lovin' feet?
Who goin' to glove my lovin' hand?
Papa looked around in his daughter's face,
Tried to pacify his daughter's mind.
Daughter I'll shoe your lovin' feet,
Daughter I'll shoe your children's feet,
Daughter I'll glove your children's hands.
Brother he looked in his sister's face,
Tried to pacify his sister's mind,
Sister I'll kiss your rosy cheeks.
But you can't be my lovin' man,
Brother, can't be my lovin' man.
Papa can't be my lovin' man,
Papa can't be my lovin' man.
'Cause you can't file the whole deal down,

Brother can't file the whole deal down,
Papa can't file the whole deal down,
Papa can't file the whole deal down.[1]

Although worksongs today are heard mainly on the railroads, in the prison camps, and among lumberjacks, a generation or two ago group singing was commonplace in planting, harvesting, and other agricultural operations, much as in West Africa. Grain was planted, reaped, threshed, winnowed, and pulverized in mortars to the accompaniment of responsive singing. Though time has altered the social and technological aspects of these operations, many of the songs identified with them have survived.

Rice was one of the important crops of the Sea Islands for many years. When it was harvested it was tied in sheaves. At threshing time, the sheaves were laid on a clean floor, and the grain was beaten out of them with flails. Some flails were constructed of a short stick or wooden knob attached to a wooden handle by a length of cord or rawhide. Usually two people worked on a single sheaf, facing each other and alternating their blows rhythmically. As described by Lydia Parrish:

"When two Negroes 't'rashed' together, they always sang as they faced each other. The short part of the flail which flew in the air in seemingly reckless fashion was called a 'bob,' and it was rather important to have its gyrations rhythmically controlled. As soon as one side of a sheaf was clear of rice it was turned over. . . . By the time the string [which bound the sheaf] was broken, the grain was in a long row in the middle." [16]

According to some informants, a rice threshing party might consist of as many as eight or ten people, half on one side, half on the other. In plantation days, such groups may have been considerably larger. One of the threshing songs taken down by Parrish was this one, with a Biblical allusion:

John say you got to reap what you sow,
John say you got to reap what you sow,
If you sow it in the rain, you got to reap it just the same,
You got to reap in the harvest what you sow.[17]

Husking of rice in the Sea Islands was sometimes done by foot power. The threshed grain was spread out on the floor and trampled with bare feet, and this activity was a natural incentive

[1] See The Music, 40.

to both singing and dancing. Women and children would dance in the rice as though the work were only incidental. One of Parrish's informants recalled a song that accompanied this husking dance:

> Peas and the rice done done!
> High-o, high-o!
> Beaufort boat done come!
> High-o, high-o!
> How do you know? Done heard it blow!
> High-o, high-o! [18]

When rice was husked in wooden mortars, there were generally two people at each mortar wielding long pole-like pestles. The rhythmic pounding provided a percussion rhythm for responsive singing. This pestle song was heard on Sapelo Island:

> Summer comin' again,
> Hard time in Old Virginie!
> Comin' in the rainbow,
> Hard time in Old Virginie!
> Comin' in the cloud,
> Hard time in Old Virginie!
> My old missus promise me,
> Hard time in Old Virginie!
> When she die she set me free,
> Hard time in Old Virginie!
> She live so long
> Hard time in Old Virginie!
> Till her head got bald,
> Hard time in Old Virginie! [19]

Another beating or mortar song from the same area is this one:

> I goin' to beat this rice,
> Goin' to beat 'em so,
> Goin' to beat 'em till the husks come off,
>   Ah hanh hanh!
>   Ah hanh hanh!
>
> Goin' to cook this rice when I get through,
> Goin' to cook 'em so,
>   Ah hanh hanh!
>   Ah hanh hanh!
>
> Goin' to eat my belly full,
>   Ah hanh hanh!
>   Ah hanh hanh! [20]

Even the final operation, the winnowing of the chaff from the grain, was accompanied by singing. This winnowing, or "fanning," was done in a traditional way, by tossing the uncleaned grain into the air from a flat basket, allowing the breeze to carry off the chaff. Another worksong that seems from the internal evidence to date from slavery times is this one:

Missus in the big house,
Mammy in the yard,
Missus holdin' her white hands,
Mammy workin' hard, (×3)
Missus holdin' her white hands,
Mammy workin' hard.

Old Marse ridin' all time,
Niggers workin' round,
Marse sleepin' day time,
Niggers diggin' in the ground, (×3)
Marse sleepin' day time,
Niggers diggin' in the ground.[21]

That group work singing among Negroes remains a living tradition elsewhere than in the deep south is evidenced by chance encounters with Negro construction gangs at work almost anywhere. Negro worksongs may even be heard at sea. Menhaden fishermen hauling nets aboard boats in the Atlantic have been recorded singing rousing worksongs timed to the tempo of their work.[22]

Boat rowing and poling songs sung by Negroes in the early nineteenth century must have had a marked African character, if one may rely on accounts of the period. Frances Anne Kemble's *Journal of a Residence on a Georgia Plantation,* depicting life in the vicinity of the Sea Islands in the late 1830s, contains some impressions of Negro singing which, though limited, help to give us a picture of what it sounded like. To get from one small island to another, her plantation-owner husband was rowed in what must have been a sort of longboat by a crew of slave oarsmen. Miss Kemble described seeing him off on one of his trips:

"As the boat pushed off and the steersman took her into the stream, the men at the oars set up a chorus, which they chanted in unison with each other, and in time with their stroke, till the voices and oars were heard no more from the distance." [23]

In attempting to convey something of what the singing sounded like, she wrote:

"I believe I have mentioned to you before the peculiar characteristics of this veritable Negro minstrelsy—how they all sing in unison, having never, it appears, attempted or heard any thing like part singing. Their voices seem oftener tenor than any other quality, and the tune and time they keep something quite wonderful; such truth of intonation and accent would make any music agreeable. That which I have heard these people sing is often plaintive and pretty, but almost always has some resemblance to tunes with which they must have become acquainted through the instrumentality of the white men; their overseers or masters whistling Scotch or Irish airs, of which they have produced by ear these *rifacciamenti.*"

Miss Kemble commented that the tune to which the rowers took her husband away "was a very distinct descendant of 'Coming Through the Rye.' "

"The words, however, were astonishingly primitive, especially the first line, which, when it burst from their eight throats in high unison, sent me into fits of laughter.

> Jenny shake her toe at me,
> Jenny gone away.
> Jenny shake her toe at me,
> Jenny gone away.
> Hurrah! Miss Susy, oh!
> Jenny gone away.
> Hurrah! Miss Susy, oh!
> Jenny gone away." [24]

This chronicler's assurance that the Negro boat songs were derived, melodically at least, from popular white airs appears to have been undermined in the course of time. At a later date she wrote into her journals:

"I told you formerly that I thought I could trace distinctly some popular national melody with which I was familiar in almost all their songs. But I have been quite at a loss to discover any such foundation for many that I have heard lately, and which have appeared to me extraordinarily wild and unaccountable. The way in which the chorus strikes in with the burden, between each phrase of the melody chanted by a single voice, is very curious and effective, especially with the rhythm of the rowlocks for accompaniment. The high voices all in unison, and the admirable time and true accent with which their responses are made, always makes me wish that some great musical composer could hear these semi-savage performances. With very little skillful adaptation and instrumentation, I think one or two barbaric chants and choruses might be evoked from them that would make the fortune of an opera." [25]

Some of the word texts of the boat songs she heard appear to have perplexed her. She cited as a "peculiar poetical proposition" the lyrics:

God makes man,
Man makes money.[26]

These lines may indeed have been poetic Negro imagery. But they may also have come from an English folk song that went:

The Lord made the bees, the bees made the honey,
The Lord made man and man made money.

Miss Kemble described another piece as "an extremely spirited war song," with the opening lines:

The trumpets blow, the bugles sound,
Oh stand your ground! [27]

Although the slaves urged on her the notion that the main character of the song was Caesar, these few words seem much more appropriate to the saga of Joshua and the Israelites. The fact that plantation owners showed much ambivalence toward, and distrust of, Negro religious activity could well account for the slaves' attribution of the "war song" to Rome rather than to Jericho. One is struck by what appears to be the emergence of Biblical song literature—in this case in a work song—in a hostile environment in the 1830s.

Lafcadio Hearn in his "American Sketches" gives considerable space to the subject of Negro roustabout songs some forty years later. One such song, which he called "one of the most popular roustabout songs . . . on the Ohio," was sung in unison by a Negro boat crew. Called "Molly Was a Good Gal," to Hearn's ears it was a "low and melancholy air." [28]

Molly was a good gal and a bad gal too.
   Oh Molly, row, gal.
Molly was a good gal and a bad gal too.
   Oh Molly, row, gal.
I'll row dis boat and I'll row no more,
   Row, Molly, row, gal.
I'll row dis boat and I'll row no more,
   Row, Molly, row, gal.
Captain on the boiler deck a-heavin' of the lead,
   Oh Molly, row, gal.
Callin' to the pilot to give her turn ahead,
   Oh Molly, row, gal.

Hearn picked up the words of the roustabout song "Shiloh" on the Cincinnati waterfront, and printed about a dozen stanzas in his "American Sketches," leaving out all of those he regarded as "not fit for print." Semi-nonsense verses, satire, and Civil War allusions succeed each other in a way suggesting that many of the stanzas were composed by a singing leader stretching the song to last through a work routine. Though we do not have the music of Hearn's "Shiloh," the lyrics and imagery suggest that Negro worksong style and sea shanty style had blended plausibly. "Shiloh" appears to refer to the Civil War battle of that name. There are other war references, one alluding to Rebel raiding parties, another to General Morgan. Some stanzas, such as the one beginning "Nigger and a white man playing Seven Up," belong to a reservoir of themes and texts drawn upon by various genres of Negro songs. Only a few verses of "Shiloh" are given here:

Nigger and a white man playing Seven Up,
White man played the ace, and the nigger feared to take it up.
White man played ace and nigger played a nine,
White man died and nigger went blind.

   Chorus (after each stanza)
   Limber Jim,
      Shiloh!
   Talk it again,
      Shiloh!
   Walk back in love,
      Shiloh!
   You turtle dove,
      Shiloh!

Jay-bird sittin' on a swingin' limb
Winked at me and I winked at him.
Up with a rock and struck him on the shin,
God damn your soul, don't wink again.

Some folks says that a Rebel can't steal,
I found twenty in my corn field.
Such pullin' of shucks and tearin' of corn,
Never saw the like since I was born.

John Morgan came to Danville and cut a mighty dash,
Last time I saw him he was under whip and lash.
'Long come a Rebel at a sweepin' pace,
Whar 're ye goin', Mr. Rebel? "I'm goin' to Camp Chase."

Eighteen pennies hidden in a fence,
Cynthiana gals aint got no sense.
Every time they go from home
Comb their heads with an old jaw bone.[29]

Hearn describes another song, "Number Ninety-nine" (the address of a source of whisky and perhaps other pleasures), as immensely popular with steamboatmen on the Cincinnati waterfront in the 1870s:

You may talk about your railroads,
Your steamboats and can-el,
If it hadn't been for Liza Jane
There wouldn't been no hell.

  Chorus (after each stanza)
  Oh aint I gone, gone, gone, (×3)
  Way down the river road.

Where do you get your whisky?
Where do you get your rum?
I get it down in bucktown
At Number Ninety-nine.

I went down to Bucktown,
Never was there before.
Great big nigger knocked me down,
But Katy barred the door.

She hugged me, she kissed me,
She told me not to cry;
She said I was the sweetest thing
That ever lived or died.

[Hearn used asterisks here to indicate a stanza he thought too indelicate for print.]

Yonder goes the *Wildwood,*
She's loaded to the guards;
But yonder comes the *Fleetwood,*
And she's the boat for me.[30]

The tie between work and music in Negro tradition in the United States has survived in many places and forms. Even a person working alone may respond to this deeply rooted impulse, especially when his work has a rhythmic character. The professional shoe shiner until recent times often used his polishing cloth as though it were a musical instrument, and produced snapping rhythmic effects almost too complicated for the ear to take in, sometimes to the accompaniment of wordless vocal sounds. Many Negro shoe shiners, particularly those who plied their trade in the streets, had their own special songs or patter to go along with the percussive shining operation. Such songs were sometimes improvised on the spot, though a large number of them were from a standard repertoire, and others were adapted from popular tunes and ring play songs.

This example of traditional shoe-shine patter was recorded in recent years in New Orleans:

Now we shine your shoe like a lookin' glass,
When the water hit that shoe it roll right off!
Shine!

Now we shine that shoe like a lookin' glass,
Make it fly through that natural air!
Shine!

Now we hit that shoe right on the lint,
Where we know that shoe gonna shine gonna glint! [31]

VI. Blues

TOO OFTEN IN RECENT TIMES, folk song performers, innocent by-standers, and casual rustic acquaintances have been called upon to provide definitions, the history, and the philosophy of folk songs. Their answers have ranged from, "Well, man, if you don't know what are we standing here talking for?" to "All those things they call blues come out of spirituals." The value of this "personal interview" approach to problems of analysis and definition is limited if not altogether precarious. Nevertheless, we might take a look at what some folk and blues singers have had to say about blues.

Huddie Ledbetter, Sonny Terry, and Bill Broonzy, among others, have tended to identify blues with melancholy or miserable feelings of one kind or another. As Ledbetter put it—in a pat, theatrical way: "When you lay down at night, turning from one side of the bed all night to the other and can't sleep, what's the matter? Blues got you. . . . When you get up in the morning and sit on the side of your bed, may have father and mother, sister and brother, boyfriend or girlfriend or husband or wife around you, you don't want no talk out of 'em. They aint done you nothing, you aint done them nothing, but what's the matter? Blues got you." [1]

Broonzy may have come a bit closer to talking about the blues song rather than "the blues" when he said: "Blues is a natural fact, something that a fellow lives. If you don't live it, you don't have it." [2] What he meant, I think, is that a real blues song grows out of real life, unlike many other kinds of popular songs. However, blues singers are not likely to be able to tell us much more than this about the blues form or its development. Their role is to sing, not explain how it all came to be, or why it is as it is.

As a form of expression, blues are certainly much more than a statement of personal misery. At its base, the blues song is a sort of exalted or transmuted expression of criticism or complaint, the very creation or singing of which serves as a balm or antidote. The finer the singing or the creative effort, the more effective is the song as a catharsis. A singer in a Louisiana prison declared: "Whenever you sing the blues just right, why you feel like a million, when you may not have a dime. . . . That's the best part of my life, is blues." [3]

Many types of non-Negro folk songs also have the capacity to transform sadness or suffering into more bearable, even ecstatic emotions. Some tragic European ballads fall into this category. But most of those ballads are less personal. They are historical or biographical, memorializing events of tragic proportions. "The Earl of Murray," "Two Sisters," "Lord Randall," "Greensleeves," "The Golden Vanity," and similar familiar Anglo-Scottish songs are movingly sad, but they have a literary character (at least, as we hear them today) and lack the quality of direct statement characteristic of blues. European and American balladry undoubtedly include examples of the more intimate statement, but there are relatively few of them. On the other hand, some white eastern mountain songs have a "me to you" character and a personal imagery with a clear affinity to blues.

As with all music and poetry, the more a song touches the experiences of those who hear it, the more it becomes universal property, despite the author's concern with a seemingly unique set of circumstances. For example, a man sings a blues song about the woman who left him, calling her by name. The circumstances are so generally familiar to others in the same cultural setting that it is easy for them to identify themselves with the situation. If someone "borrows" the song he may find it necessary only to change the woman's name to make the total experience and statement "uniquely" his own.

The blues song is distinguished from most other Negro song forms by both its structure and its content, and it has certain standard—though always variable—musical characteristics. Nevertheless, the blues form is less rigidly conceived by blues singers than by those who have notated the songs. Many songs which are regarded as blues do not have all the elements of the "classical" blues type, but do have enough of them to make classification indisputable. In reality, there are few individual elements found in the blues that may not be found somewhere else, in other kinds of Negro singing—worksongs, gospel songs, field songs, and even in children's game songs. There are times when the distinction between blues and other forms becomes quite blurred.

In discussing blues as folk music, we necessarily concern ourselves with traditional, unwritten music existing primarily in the oral tradition. As blues were taken over by composers and arrangers such as Handy, and later by jazz singers and instrumentalists, they became raw material for processing. The music which resulted was often more elaborate and sophisticated, or, on the contrary, more restricted, confined, and stereotyped. In talking about the origin of his famous "Mr. Crump" (later, with different words, to be known as "Memphis Blues"), Handy declared: "The melody of 'Mr. Crump' was mine throughout. On the other hand, the 12-bar, three line form of the first and last strains, with its three-chord basic harmonic structure (tonic, subdominant, dominant, seventh), was that already used by Negro roustabouts, honky-tonk piano players, wanderers, and other of the underprivileged but undaunted class from Missouri to the Gulf, and had been a common medium through which any such individual might express his personal feelings in a sort of musical soliloquy." [4]

Just what are some of the formal characteristics of the blues? It has been a convention among those whose familiarity with blues has been derived from notated songs and sheet music that it usually is a twelve-bar form, composed of three four-bar lines, as described by Handy. That this conception is over-simplified, and even a distortion, becomes apparent when a large number of blues songs of different singers are examined, and particularly when blues that have never been frozen into notated form are analyzed. As Frederic Ramsey, Jr., notes, "definitions of blues have long had a halting way of catching up with one blues performer or artist, then having to lope off after a new rendition in order to reduce it in its turn to a quintessence of words. The burden of a blues song gets sung or said in the space of twelve or eight bars of music (or sixteen when the eight are repeated). The partly flatted third and seventh notes are known as blue notes and considered the *sine qua non* of a blues performance. Beyond that, the actuality of each performance brings variations on variations." [5]

What seems to be evident is that the blues stanza framework *tends* toward eight or twelve bars. In actual rendition, however, especially of songs that haven't been frozen into notations or popularized by performances on recordings, the blues stanza can be presented in eleven, thirteen, fourteen, fifteen, or seventeen bars. One rural blues heard in the South appeared to have twenty-two bars, and another contained twelve and a half bars. Certain blues songs are done in such free style as to fall into no clear-cut bar pattern at all. A contention that any blues song not cast into a twelve or eight bar form is "primitive" or "undeveloped" does not take into account the basic freedoms of folk music. The only consideration of a blues singer is that his song should sound "right," and there is ample elbow room within the limitations of what is effective for a good many types of things. The eight or twelve bar blues is probably no more traditional, and certainly no more "correct," than other variants. We are on firm ground if we think of the blues as a variable form centering in the neighborhood of twelve bars, with the swinging pendulum of improvisation or variation capable of producing a number of possibilities.

Concerning the lyrics of the blues, a number of characteristics stand out. Often, though not always, there is an original statement which is repeated, possibly with a slight word change or an added expletive, followed by another statement that supplements or rounds out the first. A blues song may consist of a series of stanzas which embellish or develop (or repeat) the theme put forward in the first stanza. They give more details of the story, or reflect upon it with different metaphors and images.

An element of rhyming is present in many, if not most, blues songs. Typical is a four-line stanza in which the second and last lines rhyme, or a six-line stanza in which the fourth and sixth rhyme. Sometimes the rhyme is determined by local speech dialect, and is not readily apparent when written. "Radio" may be rhymed with "more" ("mo' "), and "line" with "cryin'." Occasionally the rhyme is impure enough to be only suggested, and other times the rhyming effect is achieved by repetition of the same word. But there are blues in which other combinations of lines are rhymed, or in which no audible rhyme appears at all. Thus, the concept of rhyming is commonplace, but it is loosely conceived and not indispensable.

Another frequent characteristic of blues singing is the dropping or cutting off of the voice in the middle or near the end of a line, so that the burden of completion lies entirely on the instrumental accompaniment. When I asked one singer whether he had forgotten the words or was resting his voice, or whether he had some other reason for doing this, he replied: "No, I just step aside and let the guitar say it." Using this device to an extreme, a singer may articulate a few words at the beginning of a line or stanza and thereafter rely on humming or wordless open throat sounds, except where he withdraws his voice altogether. In such cases, the voice tends to become, in effect, accompaniment to the instrument. This relationship between voice and instrument has been widely observed in West Africa.

One may reasonably suspect that the partially articulated line of the traditional blues style is a carry over from the responsive form which is so fundamental in Negro tradition. In numerous church and gang songs, for example, the statement of the leader is completed by the second singer or chorus.

Among our earliest blues recordings are those of the much celebrated Blind Lemon Jefferson and Ma Rainey, but these performers were not, any more than was Handy, originators of the blues. The blues probably jelled into something like their present form some time in the nineteenth century, if not earlier, and were sung by lonesome street musicians who accompanied themselves on banjo or guitar, by entertainers in small public places, and by country people off the beaten track. There is no indication that something closely akin to blues was not sung in the towns and on the plantations in antebellum days. The mania for continuous change in popular music today—related to the demand for change in the styles of everything—is likely to infect our view of the history of our culture. Jazz enthusiasts are prone to think of their art form as a kind of high point in evolution. In so doing, they assume that various jazz elements came into being at specific times (and even places), and were then transmuted into higher forms. They speak of blues as belonging primarily to the early twentieth century, possibly acknowledging that they may have been known in the dying days of the nineteenth. Before that, it is often stated, blues must have come from religious songs, work songs, or some other kind of songs. However, the persistence of archaic blues songs in cultural backwashes of the South, along with other Negro songs, religious and secular, that clearly antedate the Civil War, suggests that the blues form may be far older than generally recognized, and that it coexisted for a long time with parallel forms out of which it supposedly developed.

In substance, the blues is a genre utilized to express personal dissatisfaction, remorse, or regret; to tell the world about your misfortune and the way you feel about it; to air a scandal; and perhaps to point the finger of accusation at someone who has caused an injury or misery. Other Negro song forms can, and sometimes do, have the same function. Recrimination and accusation against sinners appear in some religious songs. Misery, hopelessness, weariness, ridicule, and personal allusions—all characteristic of the blues —are part and parcel of prison camp worksongs. But the blues is the everyday medium through which feelings of this kind are aired. Anyone aware of the strong tradition in Africa for songs of recrimination, complaint, or abuse, and the survival of this tradition in other Negro communities in the Americas, will probably sense the special character of blues. They protest or call attention to real or fancied injustices—commenting on such topics as jail, prison camp, the electric chair, bedbugs, discrimination, sickness, poverty, lonesomeness, unfaithfulness, or bad treatment by one's mate.

A certain limited comparison with the word content of Calypso-type songs of the West Indies is possible. But the Calypso song is inclined to be more topical (female photographer, taxi drivers, New York subway, Prince of Wales, etc.), based upon news events, something seen or overheard, or a social development such as the migrations of laborers from one island to another. It has the same risqué potentials as blues, but it is more likely to be funny or satirical in a way that blues never are. Nevertheless, within the limits of the true (as opposed to the imitative or spurious) Calypso form may be found themes of a personalized nature which could easily be translated into blues. For example:

> Oh Lord it is Matilda,
> Believe me friends, it is Matilda,
> What is it at all, Matilda,
> Lord, she take my money and run Venezuela.[6]

Compare this with the "Big Foot Mamma Blues":

> Big foot mamma, and all the neighborhood,
> Big foot mamma, and all the neighborhood,
> After she got all the money I made around,
> Then she moved to the piney wood.[7]

The same type of innuendo and sexual double meanings appears in both Calypso and blues. One old Calypso song goes:

> My donkey want water, hold him Joe,
> Better hold your daughter, hold him Joe,
> For when my donkey want water, hold him Joe,
> My donkey is bad, hold him Joe.[8]

This kind of metaphor is commonplace in blues songs. "I want my sea food, mamma," "I'll jump through the keyhole in your door," and "Who'll stir your gravy when I'm gone" are common examples. One well-known song that employs this type of metaphor is "Custard Pie Blues":

> I'm going to tell you something baby,
> Aint going to tell you no lies,
> I want some of that custard pie.
> You got to give me some of it, (×3)
> Before you give it all away.
>
> Well I don't care if you live across the street,
> When you cut your pie

Please save me a piece.
I want some of it (×2)
Before you give it all away.

I want to tell you baby, it's understood,
You got the best pie
In this neighborhood.
I gotta have some of it (×2)
I want some of it
Before you give it all away.[9]

That this type of double entendre is not a new-fangled device
is supported by documentation of nineteenth-century secular songs.
One Negro song taken down by Lafcadio Hearn in 1875 contains
the following stanza:

Bridle up a rat, sir, saddle up a cat,
Please hand me down my Leghorn hat;
Went to see widow, widow warn't home,
Saw to her daughter—she gave me honeycomb.[10]

Probably the most commonplace of all blues themes is "the
woman problem"—or, conversely, "the man problem." A singer
complains of his woman's behavior, of her disinterest, her lack of
faithfulness, or desertion. The following song, for example, reflects a general discontentment with a woman's deportment:

What do you want with a bad rooster,
Won't crow for the dawn of day.
What do you want with a bad rooster,
Won't crow for the dawn.
What do I want with a woman like my gal,
Won't do nothing I say.[11]

A somewhat related complaint appears again and again in blues
literature:

Yes, a man aint nothing but a stupid fool
To think he got a woman all by himself.
Yes, a man aint nothing but a stupid fool
To think he got a woman all by himself.
Well, I say, soon as his back is turned
You know she cuttin' out with somebody else.
Yes, man aint nothing but a crazy fool
To give one woman all his pay.
Yes, man aint nothing but a crazy fool
To give one woman all his pay.

Well, I say, soon as his back is turned
Yes, you know she get out and throw it all away.[12]

A similar complaint, spiced with double entendre:

I come home last night about half past ten,
I tried to get the key in the lock and couldn't get it in,
'Cause she done changed, well she done changed the lock in the door.

Well she said that key you got won't fit the lock no more,
I looked in through my window to see what I could see,
You know she was kissing another man, and I know it wasn't me.

'Cause she done changed, she done changed the lock in the door.
I called my baby up, honey, what you want me to bring?
She whistled back low and easy, said don't bring a doggone thing.[13]

Another complaint against a successful rival is this one:

Yes, you been digging my potatoes,
Trampling on my vine.
Yes, you been digging my potatoes,
Trampling on my vine.
Well I have a special plant
Resting on my mind.

Well I went out this morning, left my gate unlatched,
When I come back home, I found that boy in my potato patch.[14]

Some blues about women have a more plaintive quality:

Come back baby, please don't go.
The way I love you baby, you'll never know.
Come back baby, please don't go.
The way I love you baby, you'll never know.
Come back baby, please don't go,
Let's talk it over one more time.[15]

In the following example, a man quotes a higher authority in commenting on his woman problem:

Going to tell you something dear God told the Jews (×3)
If you don't want me, what do I want with you? [16]

Sometimes a song simply complains about a woman who should go away but doesn't:

She's a kinky headed woman
And she keeps a-combin' it all the time.
She's a kinky headed woman
And she keeps a-combin' it all the time.

I can't stand nothin' she done,
She keeps good lookin' women on my mind.[17]

Homeless, roaming, lonesome, footloose songs constitute another large thematic category of the blues. The imagery is sometimes generalized and stock phrased, as in this piece:

Well I'm drifting and drifting
Just like a ship out on the sea.
Well I'm drifting and drifting
Just like a ship out on the sea.
Well I aint got nobody
In this whole world who cares for me.[18]

Again:

Nobody want me, nobody seem to care.
Nobody want me, nobody seem to care.
Speaking of bad luck, people,
For you know I've had my share.

I'm gonna pack my suitcase,
Gonna move on down the line.
Gonna pack my suitcase,
Gonna move on down the line.
You know there aint nobody worryin',
Child, it aint nobody cryin'.[19]

Jail and the prison camp are also among the experiences aired in blues songs:

Well I'm sittin' down in jail, down on my knees,
Well I'm down in jail, down here on my knees,
And I aint got nobody to come here and help me please.[20]

Among the blues dealing with prison life, there are some that stand out vividly for their impact, their imagery, and their ability to communicate something of the penitentiary experience. One such piece has transposed a powerful prison gang song, "Aint No More Cane on the Brazos," [21] into a haunting blues rendition.

Ummmmmmmm! Big Brazos, here I come!
Ummmmmmmm! Big Brazos, here I come!
You know I'm gonna do time for another man
When there aint anything this poor boy done!

You ought to been on the Brazos in 1910,
Bud Russel drove pretty women just like he done ugly men.
Ummmmmmmm! Big Brazos, oh Lord yes, here I come.

Figure on doing time for another man
When there aint nothing this poor boy done.

You know my mamma called me, I answered "Mam?"
She said, "Son, you tired of working?" I said, Mamma, yes I am."
My papa called me, I answered, "Sir?"
"If you're tired of working, why the hell you goin' to stay there?"

I couldn't. . . . ummmmmmmmm,
I just couldn't help myself.
You know a man just can't help feelin' bad
When he's doin' time for someone else.[22]

An unusual combination of talking and singing blues recorded at the Louisiana State Penitentiary has all the appearance of having come into being as a deeply felt extemporaneous rendition. It is personal and direct, devoid of the clichés and commonly used metaphors of blues literature. The content is extraordinary, and the phrases of the talking part, at least, are conceived as prose rather than poetry. The delivery is slow, with pauses coming in unexpected places in a way that builds up tension and suspense, a faint ad-lib fingering of a guitar in the background. The story is that of the singer ruminating on his family and his decline in prison.

Lord, I feel so bad sometimes,/ seems like that I'm weakenin' every day./ You know I've begin to get grey since I got here,/ well a whole lot of worry causin' of that./ But I can feel myself weakenin',/ I don't keep well no more,/ I keeps sickly./ I takes a lot of medicine, but it looks like it don't do no good./ All I have to do is pray,/ That's the only thing'll help me here./ One foot in the grave, look like,/ and the other one out./ Sometime look like my best day/ got to be my last day./ Sometime I feel like I never see/ my little old kids any more./ But if I don't never see 'em no more,/ leave 'em in the hands of God./ You know about my sister,/ she like a mother to me./ She do all in the world that she can./ She went all the way along with me in this trouble/ till the end./ In a way/ I was glad my poor mother had 'ceased/ because she suffered with heart trouble,/ and trouble behind me,/ sure would-a went hard with her./ But if she were livin'/ I could call on her sometime./ But my old father dead too./ That make me be motherless and fatherless./ It's six of us sisters,/ three boys./ Family done got small now,/ looks like they're dyin' out fast./ I don't know,/ but God been good to us in a way,/ 'cause old death/ have stayed away a long time now.[23]

At this point, the narrator begins to sing (Example 17):

EXAMPLE 17

Lord, my worry sure carryin' me down.
Lord, my worry sure is carryin' me down.
Sometimes I feel like, baby, committin' suicide.
Yes, sometime I feel, feel like committin' suicide.
I got the nerve if I just had anything to do it with.
I'm goin' down slow, somethin' wrong with me.
Yes, I'm goin' down slow, somethin' wrong with me.
I've got to make a change while that I'm young.
If I don't, I won't ever get old.

Another variety of complaint, heard in numerous forms, sometimes plaintive, sometimes humorous, deals with bedbugs:

My house is full of bedbugs,
And chinches just crawl around.
My house is full of bedbugs,
And chinches just crawl around.
But they bite me so hard at night
I can't hardly stay on the ground.

The bedbugs got a road to my bed,
And man, it's wide open too.
The bedbugs got a road to my bed,
And man, it's wide open too.
That's why you hear me singing
Deep bedbug blues.[24]

The "hard up" theme recurs over and over in blues literature, from simple statements such as "didn't have a thin dime" to more elaborately developed statements such as this one:

Well I went to the pawnshop,
Went down to pawn my radio,
Yeah,
Went down to pawn my radio.
Well the man said you aint got a T.V.,
We don't take radios no more.

The final stanza contrives a special meaning for the three pawnshop balls, in colloquial terms:

I asked the pawnshop man
What was those three balls doing on the wall.
Hey,
What was those three balls doing on the wall.
Well I'll bet you two to one buddy,
You won't get your stuff out of here at all.[25]

The blues have provided a convenient outlet for protest against racial injustice. Songs commenting on this subject are sometimes direct and bitter, sometimes gentle and tolerant, sometimes ironic. Occasionally they are in a humorous, playful mood in which the sting is several layers deep.[a]

One blues song interpolates into a comment on women the following stanza:

Cook's in the kitchen picking over collard greens,
Cook's in the kitchen picking over collard greens,
White folks in the parlor playing cards
And the cook got to pick 'em clean.[26]

Another comment with more edge to it is this one:

They say if you's white, you's all right;
If you's brown, stick around,
But as you're black, mmm mmm, brother git back, git back, git back.[27]

That the blues is not used exclusively for complaint, criticism, and gossip, but can be utilized for social comment of another kind, is indicated in the song "Joe Turner," based on the memory of a local Saint Nicholas. According to one account of the legend, a white man named Turner (but not Joe) had a habit of looking after the Negro people in his region whenever they were in dire need. Sometimes there were bad drouths, when all the cotton and garden crops dried up and people were hungry. They would all go off hunting for nuts, berries, and small game, and when they came home they would find a sack of flour or beans, a tin of lard, and perhaps a smoked ham setting by the door of each cabin. All anyone knew was that it was a gift from a man named Turner, Joe Turner they thought, but they didn't know who Joe Turner was. Around 1892, there was a bad flood and people lost everything they had. When the flood receded and they came back to their houses, they found food waiting for them, wood for fuel, and even axes to cut the wood. Joe Turner had been there. Their benefactor's identity was discovered when a general storekeeper some miles away died, and the kindnesses came to an end. It turned out that Turner's hired man, a Negro named Joe, had carried news of the local disasters to him, and had toted the provisions to the places where they were needed. Out of this human miracle came the song:

[a] See "Limber Jim," Chapter V, pp. 120–21.

They tell me Joe Turner been here and gone.
They tell me Joe Turner been here and gone.
They tell me Joe Turner been here and gone.[28]

Although the song is part of a blues repertoire, it has neither the characteristic content, sound, or point of view of a typical blues. The simplicity of the single line statement, repeated over and over with all its poignant meaning, suggests a relationship to what in American Negro tradition is an archaic form. Many West Indian and West African songs are constructed in the same fashion, with a single line of text repeated over and over, with slight musical variations. What the original "Joe Turner" sounded like, we have no way of knowing, but this blues version manages to stir up thoughts about blues prototypes.

A number of blues of recent vintage comment on wartime experiences. "I Got My Questionnairy," for example, combines the problems of military service and being taken from home:

Well I got my questionnairy,
And it leads me to the war.
Well I got my questionnairy,
And it leads me to the war.
Well I'm leavin', pretty baby,
Child, can't do anything at all.

Uncle Sam aint no woman,
But he sure can take your man.
Uncle Sam aint no woman,
But he sure can take your man.
Boys, they got 'em in the service
Doin' something I can't understand.[29]

In their search for subject matter for their songs, blues singers have not overlooked the possibilities offered by Negro and Anglo-American ballads. Blues molded out of ballads, in whole or in part, sometimes have an atypical form, doubtless because of the continuing impression of the original. One ballad that has had an unusual appeal for blues singers is "John Henry," [b] and innumerable blues versions are known. One of them goes:

Take this hammer and carry it to the captain,
Tell him I'm gone, tell him I'm gone, tell him I'm gone.
Take this hammer and carry it to the captain,
Tell him I'm gone, just tell him I'm gone, I'm sure he's gone.

[b] See Chapter V, pp. 110–15.

This is the hammer that killed John Henry,
But it won't kill me, but it won't kill me, but it won't kill me.
This is the hammer that killed John Henry,
But it won't kill me, but it won't kill me, aint goin' kill me.

It's a long way from me to Colorado,
And it's my home, and it's my home, and it's my home.
It's a long way from me to Colorado,
And it's my home, and it's my home, that's where I'm goin'.

John Henry he left his hammer
Layin' side the road, layin' side the road, layin' side the road.
John Henry he left his hammer
Layin' all in the rain, layin' all in the rain, that's why I'm goin'.

John Henry was a steel drivin' boy,
But he went down, but he went down, but he went down.
John Henry was a steel drivin' boy,
But he went down, but he went down, that's why I'm goin'.[e]

The Anglo-American ballad "Careless Love" (meaning different things to different people) has been a favored springboard for many blues lyrics. Despite the liberties that have been taken with the words, and with the apparent meaning of the original, the melody, with slight modifications, has largely remained intact. The ballad's reference to an apron becomes, in the following blues rendition, an "apron string," with quite different connotations:

Love, oh love, oh careless love,
Can't you see what careless love do to me?
You made me roam, made me lose my happy home,
It was love, oh love, oh careless love.

You tied me to your apron string,
You tied me to your apron string.
You said that you loved me, and it didn't mean a thing,
It was love, oh love, oh careless love.[30]

Among the many blues versions of "Careless Love" there are some which are hard to classify as true blues, and some which are nothing more than pop songs in disguise. The singer Lonnie Johnson, for example, turned "Careless Love" into maudlin doggerel:

Careless love, look how you carried me down, (×2)
You made me lose my mother and she's layin' in six feet of ground.
Careless love, I can't let you carry me down.

[e] See The Music, 42.

Careless love, you drove me through rain and snow, (×2)
You have robbed me out of my silver and out of all my gold.
I'll be damned if you'll rob me out of my soul.

You worried my mother until she died.
You caused my father to lose his mind.
Now damn you I'm going to shoot you and shoot you four or five times,
And stand over you till you finish dying.[31]

Among the atypical blues, or, better, non-blues songs sung as
part of a blues repertoire, is the well-known "One Kind Favor."
The music, mood, and structure of this song are such that if it were
found in a different setting one would have difficulty in assigning
it to the blues genre. Nevertheless, it was sung by Blind Lemon
Jefferson and many other singers who emulated him. It contains
some of the familiar imagery of Anglo-American balladry—"two
white horses in a line," digging a grave with a silver spade, and
lowering the coffin with a golden chain.

Well there's one kind favor I ask of you, (×2)
Just see my grave just kept clean.

Well there's two white horses in a line, (×3)
Goin' carry me to my buryin' ground.

My heart quit beatin' and my hand got cold, (×3)
Weren't long before my eyes was closed.

Did you ever hear a coffin sound? (×3)
You know by now he's in the ground.

You dig a grave with a silver spade, (×3)
You can let her down with a golden chain.

Did you ever hear a church bell tone? (×3)
You know by now he's dead and gone.[32]

A good many, if not all, of the blues songs mentioned so far are
known to contemporary folk singers, and in one form or another
they have appeared in recorded form. Some established blues
singers occasionally hazard a guess about who originally composed them, or at least who first sang them for phonograph records.
But although they are contemporary, they are not necessarily new.
Indeed, most of them are quite old by comparison with pop songs
that go back, say, to the mid-1930s. Discographers who attempt to
date blues songs by reference to the year of their appearance on
recordings might consider that about a century intervened between

the composition of "The Yellow Rose of Texas" and its performance on recordings. The recording of blues songs did help to establish a "standard" version of a given piece. But in time, these
"standard" versions became jumping off places for new, personalized variants.

Some types of blues, usually called "primitive" or "free" forms,
have never been sung for recordings by professional singers. Some
of these types might be called "field blues" or "rural blues" for
want of a better term—not to be confused with what is popularly
known today as "country blues." Sung without instrumental accompaniment, they have a freedom that scorns the notion of com-
pact form. There is considerable improvisation, and no depend-
ence on the background beat of a guitar or banjo. Vocal tones are
drawn out and embellished as desired, and, as in prison camp
songs, new motifs appear whenever the singer conceives them. In
all of these respects, these "field blues" are related to hollers.
They are unhurried, unmeasured. They last as long as the singing
impulse lasts.

One of the most unforgettable of field blues is "Black Woman."
The simplicity of conception, the humming and moaning, the occasional use of falsetto, the rhythmic "ah hmm" heard elsewhere in
Negro preaching, and the impression that the singer is singing to
himself seem to relate it to the field songs that must have been
commonplace in plantation days.

A number of phrases and images that occur in this song are free
currency out of which many blues have been built: "I looked in
my kitchen, mamma, and went all through my dinin' room,"
"Don't your house feel lonesome when your biscuit roller gone?"
and "I want you to tell me where did you stay last night." But
they are woven together into a drama that is persuasive and haunting.

Well I said come here Black Woman,
Ah-hmm, don't you hear me cryin', Oh Lordy!
Ah-hmm, I say run here Black Woman,
I want you to sit on Black Daddy's knee, Lord!
M-hmm, I know your house feel lonesome,
Ah don't you hear me whoopin', Oh Lordy!
Don't your house feel lonesome,
When your biscuit roller gone,
Lord help my cryin' time don't your house feel lonesome

Mamma when your biscuit roller gone!
I say my house feel lonesome,
I know you hear me cryin' oh Baby!
Ah-hmm, ah when I looked in my kitchen Mamma,
And I went all through my dinin' room!
Ah-hmm, when I woke up this mornin',
I found my biscuit roller done gone!
I'm goin' to Texas Mamma,
Just to hear the wild ox moan,
Lord help my cryin' time I'm goin' to Texas
Mamma to hear the wild ox moan!
And if they moan to suit me,
I'm going to bring a wild ox home!
Ah-hmm I say I'm got to go to Texas Black Mamma,
Ah-hmm I know I hear me cryin', oh Lordy!
Ah-hmm I got to go to Texas Black Mamma,
Ah just to hear the white cow I say moan!
Ah-hmm, ah if they moan to suit me Lordy
I b'lieve I'll bring a white cow back home!
Say I feel superstitious Mamma
'Bout my hog and bread Lord help my hungry time,
I feel superstitious, Baby 'bout my hog and bread!
Ah-hmm, Baby I feel superstitious,
I say 'stitious Black Woman!
Ah-hmm, ah you hear me cryin',
About I done got hungry oh Lordy!
Oh Mamma I feel superstitious
About my hog Lord God its my bread.
I want you to tell me Mamma
Ah-hmm I hear me cryin' oh Mamma!
Ah-hmm I want you to tell me Black Woman,
Oh where did you stay last night?
I love you Black Woman,
I tell the whole wide world I do,
Lord help your happy black time I love you Baby,
And I tell the world I do!
Ah-hmm, I love you Black Woman,
I know you hear me whoopin' Black Baby!
Ah-hmm, I love you Black Woman
And I'll tell your Daddy on you, Lord! [d]

As we have seen, there are some songs which we are inclined to
call blues because there is no other category for them. Ballads or
worksongs rendered by singers in blues style become, for the sake
of convenience, blues. But we must recognize that the outer bound-

[d] See The Music, 29.

aries of some song forms overlap other forms. Some of the criteria established for religious songs apply also to certain secular songs. Worksongs sometimes are recast religious songs. Thematic materials of a certain kind may be found in ring play songs, blues, and worksongs. And some musical characteristics are shared by spirituals, gang songs, game songs, and blues. Yet these various forms do have elements which, in general, distinguish them from one another.

The worksongs of the Negro gang, though they often deal with melancholy themes appropriate to blues, tend toward the dramatic. They may excite by building up tension, and entertain or interest the participants because of story content, but only a small portion of them convey what a blues song does. Even though the latter may be stereotyped, and perhaps marked by hardly disguised sentimentality, it is more personal. The complaint of the prison camp worksong, "Go Down Old Hannah," is couched in larger images than is usually found in a blues:

Oh go down Old Hannah [the sun], well well well,
Don't you rise no more, don't you rise no more,
Why don't you go down Old Hannah, don't you rise no more.

Well I looked at Old Hannah, well well well,
She was turning red, she was turning red,
Well I looked at Old Hannah, it was turning red.

Well I looked at my partner, well well well,
He was almost dead, he was almost dead,
Well I looked at my partner, he was almost dead.[33]

It is not difficult to imagine how an experienced blues singer would treat the same idea—perhaps something like this:

Well the sun has got me, and the day aint hardly gone,
Yes the sun has got me, and the day aint hardly gone,
If it shines much longer they can bury me in this hard ground.

A good many of the old gospel songs have the same plaintive qualities characteristic of blues. This is particularly true of songs sung by religious street bards, such as Blind Willie Johnson, who has by now become something of a legend to which various singers have attempted to attach themselves in some fashion as a mark of distinction. In listening to Johnson's "Dark Was the Night," one is not immediately aware that he is hearing an expression of religious feeling.[34] Marked by humming, moaning, foggy voice, and tones resembling those of the accompanying guitar, the rendition fulfills all the requirements of blues singing at its best. Capable of making religious songs sound like blues, Johnson also sang basically secular songs and endowed them with religious feeling. His song "Motherless Children Have a Hard Time" has a text which, emotionally laden though it is, probably would have to be classified as secular. There is only a single explicit reference in it to a religious theme—an unexplained interpolation of "It's no mistake about that Canaan Land." Atypical of the blues approach is the absence of the first person plea. The subject is not "me" but "motherless children."

Well well well,
Ahhhhh,
Well motherless children have a hard time,
Motherless children have a hard time [when] mother's dead.
They don't have anywhere to go,
Wanderin' around from door to door,
Have a hard time.
Nobody on earth can take a mother's place, man,
When mother is dead, Lord,
Nobody on earth take mother's place when mother's dead,
Nobody on earth take mother's place [when she was startin'] fade away,
Nobody'll treat you like mother will, man.
Your wife your husband may be good to you
When mother is dead, Lord,
May be good to you, mother's dead,
But your husband may be good to you,
Better'n nothin' else, true but true,
Nobody treat you like mother will, man,
When mother is dead, Lord.
Lord Lord Lord,
Well ehhhh well,
Ahhhhh,
Well some people say that sister will do
When mother is dead,
That sister will do when mother is dead.
Some people say that sister will do,
But soon as she's married she'll turn her back on you,
Nobody treat you like mother will.
Ehhh, father will do the best he can
When mother is dead, Lord,
Will do the best he can when mother's dead.
Well he'll do the best he can,

It's no mistake about that Canaan Land,
Nobody treat you like mother will.
Ehhh, motherless children have a hard time
When mother is dead, Lord,
Motherless children have a hard time
Mother's dead.
Well they don't have anywhere to go,
Wanderin' around from door to door,
Well, a hard time.[e]

Blues singing has had a deep affect on the white folk music of the United States throughout the South and in the eastern mountain belt, home of the so-called hillbilly songs. Blues-like lyrics are found in many mountain songs, as is the simple blues structure. The repetition of the initial statement, found in blues, is a commonplace characteristic, and Negro tonality and phrasing is used freely. Various mountain songs contain typical Negro imagery, idiom, and metaphors. Similar instrumentation—banjo, guitar, jugs, bones, tubs, and washboards—is frequently encountered. And the term blues is used by mountaineers to designate many songs that have only a remote resemblance, or perhaps none at all, to the Negro blues form. There are strong possibilities that the similarities are the result of a long term, two way fertilization process. In the following mountain song, "I Wish I Was a Mole In the Ground," one detects imagery reminiscent of Negro singing, a blues-like direct presentation of complaint and longing, and a blues-like repetition of the first line of the stanza:

I wish I was a mole in the ground,
Yes I wish I was a mole in the ground.
If I was a mole in the ground I'd root that mountain down,
And I wish I was a mole in the ground.

Kempie wants a nine-dollar shawl,
Yes Kempie wants a nine-dollar shawl.
When I come over the hill with a forty-dollar bill,
'Tis baby, where you been so long.[35]

Despite the mountain-style banjo accompaniment, the galloping rhythm, and a melody deriving out of English tradition, this song would be readily accepted by a good blues singer, who could transpose it into the blues idiom without difficulty.

Some cowboy songs share with mountain songs and blues the

[e] See The Music, 30.

direct, first-person element. Negro blues have incorporated some motifs and themes of western songs, and the latter have apparently taken over, in some cases, Negro themes and musical concepts. We are accustomed to thinking of blues as a *musical* form, and because this form seems so self-evident, and because the music is often haunting and moving, it is easy to overlook the reality that a genuine blues in its natural setting is not primarily conceived as "music" but as a verbalization of deeply felt personal meanings. It is a convention that this verbalization is sung. (The word "sing" has to country people a great deal of the connotation of making a statement. When a preacher exhorts his congregation to "sing it" he is thinking of verbalization rather than what we think of as "music.") Music is the vehicle which carries the statement, but it is not the statement itself, and this applies to spirituals and anthems as well as to blues. A blues singer may take over an old melody, or a style that is standard, when he wishes to make a statement, and he is not very much concerned if the music somewhat resembles "Kansas City Blues." What he is saying is of first importance. If the musical part of the blues statement has a fresh or compelling character, it is because a specially endowed singer has something to say. This reality does not overlook the complex esthetic relationship, in a good song, of text and melody.

As sung in their natural setting, the blues have a social importance which disappears from the popular, second-hand renditions. The originals have the function of verbalizing personal feelings, of calling community attention to one's predicaments or misfortunes. In this respect original blues and original (as opposed to modern) Calypso have much in common. Both have the element of extemporizing and projecting ideas in a musical framework. Behind every blues, as sung for the first time, is a buildup of experience and emotion which needs an outlet. As one blues singer stated the case: "When you make a new blues and it says exactly what you got on your mind, you feel like it's pay day. Some blues, now, they get *towards* it, but if they don't quite get to what you got on your mind, you just got to keep on trying. There have been times when I sang till my throat was hoarse without really putting my difficulties in the song the way I felt them. Other times, it comes out just right on the first try."

VII. Ring Games and Playparty Songs

SONG PLAY AND GAME SONGS seem to be widely dispersed around the world. Indeed, few children anywhere are without them in some form or other. In the Western Hemisphere, they are found in virtually all communities which derive from French, Spanish, Portuguese, Dutch, and other European settlement. In the United States, ring games and playparty songs of British and French origin constitute a large part of the national repertoire. Many other such songs and games, some of them not traceable to Europe or the Anglo-American community, appear to have been Negro developments, or to be in pre-American Negro tradition.

Children's songs, games, and play patterns have considerable tenacity as well as spontaneous and innovative elements. They require no props or equipment. Belonging to the children's world, they have their own rules of inheritance and survival. While adult society now lays great stress on change and newness in recreation and entertainment, tradition is in some ways stronger among chil-

dren. It is they, not the adults, who have preserved the vast reservoir of games, songs, rhymes, and nonsense patter which most grownups once knew but long since put behind them. Whereas many activities are learned by children from adults, traditional street and yard play, with its complex of refinements, is inherited by one generation of children directly from another, with adults rarely intervening. New words, new patter, and new play motifs appear, but all this newness is inadequate to drastically change things. Old games and songs persist in thinly disguised forms and in many variants.

Playparty songs and games are not an exclusive juvenile phenomenon. They were popular in many frontier communities a century or two ago as adult recreation, along with barn dances—or, in settings where dancing was frowned upon, as a substitute for dancing. Adult Negro slaves of the same period must have relied a great deal on playparty activities for social amusement, and there was probably no age barrier to prevent children from participating. One result of this confraternity of the young and the old was the cross-fertilization of youthful and more sophisticated song lyrics which remains evident in Negro children's songs to this day.

Adult playparty traditions remained alive in rural Negro America until quite recent times, perhaps to this very moment in some parts of the country. Some of these activities are not clearly defined as "playparty," however. In the Sea Islands, for example, certain acting-out songs are sometimes identified as "dance" or as shout games.[a] And various social, semi-festival gatherings which sing and clap out spirited religious anthems are playparties in thin disguise.[b]

A great many playparty games and songs in the United States are known to children generally, without regard to cultural background. Such singing games as "Charlie Over the Ocean," "Stoopin' On the Window," "Bluebird, Bluebird," and "Green, Green, Rocky Road," for example, might have been seen almost anywhere a decade or two ago, particularly in the rural South, but also in northern cities. The same games were played by Negro and white children in the South even where they were separated

[a] See "March Around" and "Down In the Mire," Chapter X, p. 201.
[b] See The Music, 6, "Move Members Move."

by segregation. But although the games and songs were common property, there were sometimes considerable differences in treatment. Negro children brought to them musical concepts derived from the mainstream of Negro musical tradition. They endowed the songs with a distinctive imagery, and often gave the postures and motions of the accompanying action some of the characteristics of Negro folk dancing. Responsive singing, to the accompaniment of rhythmic (often syncopated) handclapping, sometimes approximated the effects of adult gang songs or church songs. In other words, Negro children played and sang in Negro style.

Ring play games and songs gradually have been disappearing from their native setting, and they seem to have been going at a faster rate in white communities. They appear to have survived longest where the surroundings have been most insulated from rapid social changes, or where important homogeneous influences act as a stabilizing force in the midst of change. Thus, children's playparty games that were popular in the rural southern countryside are still played on the sidewalks and streets of the northern cities.

The best place to find ring games in the South today is probably in the rural or semi-rural schoolyard where recent innovations in recreation have not yet intruded. But more and more the rural schoolhouse, even in the most isolated region, is stressing "modern" forms of play—athletic competition, "constructive" activities, and "organized" fun—and soft ball, basketball, field hockey, and athletic events are more likely to be seen than ring games. In white communities, generally speaking, more alternatives have been provided, and so the traditional ring games have receded into the past at a more rapid rate.

Although a great portion of the games and associated songs appear to have European or Anglo-American origins, we should note that this type of play is traditional in large parts of Africa. Ring and line games were old hat to Africans in the New World. In taking over various songs and games from the white culture, they were making slight adaptations of familiar ideas. In short, African and Anglo-American ring play were quite compatible. Many such songs were altered, improvised upon, and reshaped to the extent that they lost their European character altogether. And it is most apparent that a large number of game songs, whatever their original source or inspiration, are purely Negro developments.

Much the same thing occurred in the West Indies, where European and African traditions were brought together. Some of the children's games of Haiti—for example, play activity connected with old-style storytelling—strongly resemble games known in West Africa. Other games show strong French influence. But as in the United States, the way in which the songs are sung and the way in which the games are played are outside traditional European style.

In one American ring game, each player has a number; when his number is called by the leader he must respond with an appropriate answer without becoming rattled, and then pass the play on to another individual. If a player gives the wrong response, he is counted out of the game. Thereafter, his number cannot be called, as he is no longer a participant; should someone call his number in the heat of play, he too goes out. The repartee is half-sung—more properly, called, with stylized inflections—to the accompaniment of rhythmic clapping.

All Together: One two three and a zing zing zing.
   Leader: Number one.
Number One: Who, me?
   Leader: Yes, you.
Number One: Couldn't be.
   Leader: Then who?
Number One: Number five.
Number Five: Who, me?
   Leader: Yes, you.
Number Five: Couldn't be.
   Leader: Then who?
Number Five: Number nine.
Number Nine: Who, me?
   Leader: Yes, you.
Number Nine: Couldn't be.
   Leader: Then who?
Number Nine: Number two.
Number Two: Who, me? [1]
    Etc.

Another American variant is this one:

All Together: Who took the cookie from the cookie jar?
      Leader: Number One took the cookie from the cookie jar.
  Number One: Not me took the cookie from the cookie jar.
      Leader: Then who took the cookie from the cookie jar?
  Number One: Number Seven took the cookie from the cookie jar.
 Number Seven: Not me took the cookie from the cookie jar.
      Leader: Then who took the cookie from the cookie jar?
 Number Seven: Number Ten took the cookie from the cookie jar.[2]
        Etc.

A Haitian version of the game, with similar counting-out rules, is known as "Uncle Pierre." Each player is given a name specifying a certain number of sheep—Four Sheep, Ten Sheep, Six Sheep, etc. As translated from the Creole, the repartee goes:

       Leader: Uncle Pierre went to my farm and took seven sheep.
  Seven Sheep: *Tomantor.*
       Leader: How many sheep did he take?
  Seven Sheep: Nineteen sheep.
Nineteen Sheep: *Tomantor.*
       Leader: How many sheep did he take?
Nineteen Sheep: One sheep.
    One Sheep: *Tomantor.*[3]
        Etc.

In the Negro ring game song shown in Example 18, recorded in Alabama, there are the usual fun-inspired lines without any special significance, but there is an interspersed ironic theme about people who migrate north to better themselves, only to find that their lot has not been improved. This type of social allusion is characteristic of adult songs of critical comment, and is found in numerous Negro ring game lyrics. The responsive form of the song is comparable to that of certain kinds of religious or gang singing. The leader sings everything but the last word of each line, which is reserved for the chorus.

EXAMPLE 18

Then:

I'm goin' up north *satisfied!*
And I would tell you, *satisfied!*
Lord I am *satisfied!*
Some peoples up there, *satisfied!*
Goin' bring you back, *satisfied!*
Mamma cooked a chicken, *satisfied!*
Have to get all the girls *satisfied!*
Their bellies full, *satisfied!*

Another ring game song (Example 19) with the same response, "satisfied," deals with another subject, but like the previous song (Example 18) the social complaint has a theme somewhat beyond the experience of the participating children. Beginning with the line "See see rider" (a phrase appearing in a number of blues songs, sometimes written as C. C. Rider), there is a kind of generalized blues statement of discontent, followed by specific criticism.

See see rider, *satisfied!*
What's the matter? *Satisfied!*
I got to work, *satisfied!*
And I am tired, *satisfied!*
And I can't eat, *satisfied!*
Satisfied Lord, *satisfied!*

After other lines of a typical nonsense variety, the song admonishes the older generation, seemingly, for its double standards:

Mamma Mamma, *satisfied!*
Leave me alone. *Satisfied!*
When you were young, *satisfied!*
Were you in the wrong? *Satisfied!*
Papa Papa, *satisfied!*
You the same, *satisfied!*
You the one, *satisfied!*
Give Mamma's name. *Satisfied!*

EXAMPLE 19

A song for the line game "Old Lady Sally Wants to Jump-ty Jump" ridicules the no-longer-young lady who cavorts in unseemly fashion in order to get a man; it finishes with an unconnected bit of ridicule directed at a preacher:

Old Lady Sally want to jump-ty jump,
Jump-ty jump, jump-ty jump,
Old Lady Sally want to jump-ty jump,
And Old Lady Sally want to bow.

Throw that hook in the middle of the pond,
Catch that girl with the red dress on.
Go on, gal, aint you shame'? Shamed of what?
Wearin' your dress in the latest style.

Many fishes in the brook,
Papa caught 'em with a hook,
Mamma fried 'em in a pan,
Baby eat 'em like a man.

Preacher in the pulpit
Preachin' like a man,
Tryin' to get to Heaven on a 'lectric fan.[c]
Do your best, Papa Daddy, do your best.[d]

The foot play and other motions accompanying this song vaguely
echo the type of ballroom dance of earlier days in which the dancers
lined up in two rows facing each other. Here, two lines of children
—standing face to face—sing, clap, and move forward and back.
On the last line of each stanza, the participants jump forward,
feet together, and bow.

A good many of the ring and line games are of the courting
variety. In the ring game "Green, Green, Rocky Road," for example, the children stand in a circle singing and clapping, with
the leader or caller in the center. At the appropriate moment the
leader names a person of his (or her) own choice. This person,
after being kissed, becomes the leader in turn. The leader sings
the first part of each line in the first stanza, with the group coming
in responsively with the words "rocky road." In the second stanza,
the entire group sings while the leader is bringing the person of
his choice to the center of the ring for a kiss.

Green, green, *rocky road,*
Some lady's green *rocky road.*
Tell me who you love, *rocky road,*
Tell me who you love, *rocky road.*

Caller (who has been skipping around inside the circle):

Minnie Town.

*Caller brings Minnie Town to the center of the ring and kisses her while
the group sings:*

Dear Miss Minnie, your name's been called,
Come take a seat beside the wall.
Give her a kiss and let her go,
She'll never sit in that chair no more.[e]

Green, green, *rocky road,* etc.

Minnie Town, in turn, selects a boy, and the play is repeated.

In the game "Amasee" (Example 20), boys and girls face each
other in two lines. The caller sings the directions, and the group

---

[c] Sung in some variants as "Tryin' to get to heaven on borrowed land."
[d] See The Music, 35.   [e] See The Music, 36.

responds with "amasee, amasee." The action patterns suggest that the game is a simplified version of a reel. The boy and girl facing each other at the head of the lines join hands and skip between the rows toward the other end, swinging each other on the leader's command:

EXAMPLE 20

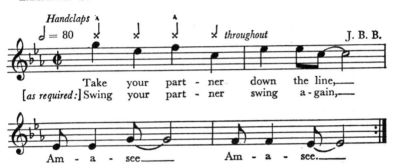

Take your partner down the line,
    Amasee, amasee.
Take your partner down the line,
    Amasee, amasee.
Swing your partner, swing again,
    Amasee, amasee.
Swing your partner, swing again,
    Amasee, amasee.

"Rosie Darling Rosie" (Example 21) is another partner-choosing game. The children form two circles, one within the other. As a partner is chosen, the pair skips around between the two circles; the erstwhile leader then takes his place in the vacated spot, and the one he has chosen becomes the new leader.

Rosie darling Rosie,
    Ha ha Rosie!
Rosie darling Rosie,
    Ha ha Rosie!

Way down yonder in Baltimore,
    Ha ha Rosie!
Need no carpet on my floor,
    Ha ha Rosie!

Grab your partner and follow me,
    Ha ha Rosie!
Let's go down by Galilee,
    Ha ha Rosie!

Rosie darling hurry,
Ha ha Rosie!
If you don't mind you gonna get left,
Ha ha Rosie!

Some folks say preachers won't steal,
Ha ha Rosie!
But I caught two in my cornfield,
Ha ha Rosie! *

One had a bushel and one had a peck,
Ha ha Rosie!
The baby had a roasting ear round her neck,
Ha ha Rosie!

You steal my partner, you won't steal her no more,
Ha ha Rosie!
Better stay from round my door,
Ha ha Rosie!

Stop right still and study yourself,
Ha ha Rosie!
See that fool where she got left,
Ha ha Rosie!

EXAMPLE 21

*This is a passage that crops up in secular songs of many kinds. In Civil War days, the culprits were "Rebels" (and perhaps, further south, "Yankees"). See Chapter V, p. 121.

The song "Little Sally Walker" has sophisticated lyrics which give the appearance of having filtered down from an older age group. The meaning of the first few lines is not readily apparent, but those that follow are geared to postures and dance movements that were frowned upon in straight-laced Negro communities. The game is a partner choosing activity. One person standing in front of the group goes through the motions indicated by the directions (often with an understanding that belies his or her years), "shaking" toward the chosen member of the opposite sex.

Li'l Sally Walker
Sittin' in a saucer, [g]
Cryin' for the old man
To come for the dollar.
Ride Sally ride,
Put your hands on your hips,
Let your backbone slip,
Ah, shake it to the east,
Ah, shake it to the west,
Ah, shake it to the very one
You love the best.[h]

The ring game "Loop de Loo" (or "Loobie Loo") is a dramatization of the Saturday night bath scene:

Chorus (before each stanza)
Here we go loop de loo, (×3)
All on a Saturday night.

I put my right hand in,
I take my right hand out,
I give my right hand a shake, shake, shake,
And turn my body about.

I put my left hand in, etc.

I put my right foot in, etc.

I put my left foot in, etc.

I put my big head in, etc.

I put my big self in, etc.

"Watch That Lady" is a kind of stationary follow-the-leader activity, played in a circle with the leader in the center. To the accompaniment of rhythmic singing and clapping, the leader makes

[g] In some versions, "Sittin' in the parlor."   [h] See The Music, 37.

motions or assumes difficult postures which the other participants must imitate. The movements may represent some familiar action such as washing clothes, combing hair, or pulling weeds, or they may be pure nonsense motions. The game belongs to a genre so widespread that it can't be said to belong to anybody in particular, but it is worth noting, in passing, that it is known in West Africa and among Afro-Americans in the West Indies. In Jamaica, it is called "Gallant Boy," and, in Haiti, "Théatre." [4]

> I been all around my last time, last time, last time,
> I been all around my last time,
>
> Young lady hold the key.
> Just watch that lady how she hold that key,
> Just watch that lady how she hold that key,
> Young lady, hold the key.[1]

The line game song "Mary Mack" is perhaps less noteworthy for the action which accompanies it than for the singing and lyrics:

> Oh Mary Mack, Mack, Mack,
> All dressed in black, black, black,
> With silver buttons, buttons, buttons,
> Up and down her back, back, back.
>
> And I love coffee, coffee, coffee,
> And I love tea, tea, tea,
> And the boys love me, me, me.
>
> I went to the river, river, river,
> And I couldn't get across, 'cross, 'cross,
> And I paid five dollars, dollars, dollars,
> For the old grey horse, horse, horse.
>
> And the horse wouldn't pull, pull, pull,
> I swapped him for a bull, bull, bull,
> And the bull wouldn't holler, holler, holler,
> I swapped him for a dollar, dollar, dollar.
>
> And the dollar wouldn't spend, spend, spend,
> I put it in the grass, grass, grass,
> And the grass wouldn't grow, grow, grow,
> I got my hoe, hoe, hoe.
>
> And the hoe wouldn't chop, chop, chop,
> I took it to the shop, shop, shop,
> And the shop made money, money, money,
> Like the bees made honey, honey, honey.

[1] See The Music, 38.

See that yonder, yonder, yonder,
In the jay-bird town, town, town,
Where the women got to work, work, work,
Till the sun goes down, down, down.

Well I eat my meat, meat, meat,
And I gnaw my bone, bone, bone,
Well goodbye honey, honey, honey,
I'm going on home.[j]

One of the many hiding and finding ring games is "Bob-a Needle," which at least one informant believes was originally "Bobbin Needle." The children form a tight ring, their hands behind them, and rapidly pass an object around the circle. The person standing in the middle, who is "it," tries to locate the moving object. On the lines "Bob-a needle is a-running," the object is in motion. On the lines "Bob-a needle aint a-running," whoever has possession of it must hold it, and the one who is "it" has a chance to guess its whereabouts. When he thinks he has located it, he calls "You got bob-a."

Well oh bob-a needle, bob-a needle,
And oh bob-a needle.

Bob-a needle is a-running,
Bob-a needle aint a-running,
Bob-a needle is a-running,
Bob-a needle aint a-running.

And oh bob-a needle, bob-a needle,
And oh bob-a needle, bob-a needle.
You got bob-a.

"Charlie Over the Ocean" is a drop-the-handkerchief type of game, in which the leader moves around the outside of the ring. He sings each line of the song, which the group repeats responsively. He thrusts a small object, such as a stone, in the hand of a person standing in the ring; the individual so designated chases the leader around the outside of the ring and tries to catch him before he gets to the vacated space. If he fails to accomplish his mission, he, in turn, becomes the leader.

Charlie over the ocean,
  Charlie over the ocean,
Charlie over the sea,
  Charlie over the sea.

[j] See The Music, 39.

Charlie caught a blackbird (or blackfish),
    Charlie caught a blackbird,
    Can't catch me,
Can't catch me,

One song taken from an elderly informant was described as "real grown-up playparty, the kind they don't do any more." Other than that "it was a kind of wild game that could get you thrown out of the church," no information was given about the activity that accompanied the song:

Whoa, mule, can't get the saddle on, (×2)
Stop that mule, I can't get the saddle on, (×2)
Whoa, mule, I can't get the saddle on, (×2)
Run, mule, I can't get the saddle on,
Catch that mule, can't get the saddle on, (×4)
Yon go that mule, can't get the saddle on,
Go that mule, can't get the saddle on.[5]

A play song that had a burst of popularity a decade or so ago as a show tune is "Shortnin' Bread." In its playparty format, it looks like this:

I do love—*shortnin' bread,*
I do love—*shortnin' bread,*
Mamma loves—*shortnin' bread,*
Everybody loves—*shortnin' bread.*

Two little babies layin' in the bed,
One playin' sick and the other playin' dead.

I do love—*shortnin' bread,*
I do love—*shortnin' bread.*

Ever since my dog been dead,
The hog's been rootin' in my 'tatoe bed.

I do love—*shortnin' bread,*
I do love—*shortnin' bread,*
Mamma loves—*shortnin' bread,*
Papa loves—*shortnin' bread,*
Everybody loves—*shortnin' bread.*

All them darlin's sick in the bed,
Sent for the doctor, the doctor said,
All they needs is some shortnin' bread.

I do love (etc.) [6]

As with the theme of the preacher (or rebel) in the corn field, the shortning bread motif has early antecedents in Negro song tradition. One old song from Negro minstrelsy goes:

Put on the skillet,
Pour on the grease,
Don't make a little,
But a great big piece.

    Corn bread, corn bread,
    All lazy niggers loves corn bread.

Sift out the bran and
Drop in the pone,
Lord knowed what he's doin'
When he made that corn.

    Corn bread (etc.) [7]

VIII. Louisiana Creole Songs

THE DEVELOPMENT OF NEGRO MUSIC in southern Louisiana followed a different course than in the English-speaking areas of the United States. Established as a New World colony by the French, Louisiana became a Spanish possession in 1765 and returned to French control in 1803—just as France irrevocably lost her rich colony of Haiti in the West Indies. Although under Spanish domination for nearly forty years, Louisiana's character remained French— in language, culture, and ties with the motherland. When the slave revolts in Haiti became a national liberation movement at the beginning of the nineteenth century, many French planters and their families sought sanctuary in Louisiana. The mainland colony's population, apart from Negro slaves and some Indians, was largely of French origin. Its outlook, its folklore and superstitions, and the music of its salons and ballrooms were French.

Thus, while Negro life in the southeastern states was compounded out of African and, largely, English cultural elements, in Louisiana the components were primarily African and French. The latter mixture produced, as it did in the French West Indies, what we have come to know as the Creole Negro culture.

The term Creole (*Criollo* in Spanish, *Créole* in French) was first applied by the Spaniards to native born Louisianians of European stock who regarded the New World colony as their home. In time, the mulattos and free Negroes of Louisiana also came to be called Creoles. Eventually the hybrid language spoken by the Negroes on the plantations came to be known as Creole.

This language was shared with other New World areas of French settlement which had slave populations. It was spoken in Haiti, Guadeloupe, Martinique, Trinidad, and other West Indian islands. The social and historical developments in those islands, up to a point, were similar to what had occurred in Louisiana. The life and activities of the French élite, whether in the islands or on the mainland, were virtually identical. Many Frenchmen had commercial interests in both places. Some planters shifted their slave workers from the mainland to the islands, or the other way around, as the need arose. It is quite accurate to say that at the beginning of the nineteenth century Louisiana was part of a Caribbean culture.

The Creole songs of Louisiana are of various kinds. Some of them are regional counterparts of Negro song types familiar in English-speaking areas. Among the older songs, particularly, were some which were essentially African in character and with which the Haitians and Martiniquians of that day and this could be completely at ease. Indeed, it is quite likely that a number of these same songs were once sung in Haiti, and even possible that at least a few of them originated there. But as in the islands, there were Creole songs in Louisiana which were much more European in style; their musical concepts were French, their imagery more conventionally European, and their structure conformed at least roughly to traditional songs of Europe.

Songs frequently described, or referred to in passing, by early observers in Louisiana appear to have been those intruding upon white ears at the Place Congo gatherings of slaves and, later, of free Negroes. Most of these songs appear to have had conspicuous African attributes. By the time Cable heard them (first-hand or second-hand) in the 1880s, they were less African in their over-all effects and more Euro-American.

There seems to have been a considerable cultural exchange in some areas between the Negroes and the Cajuns, or Acadians, who were displaced from Nova Scotia during the Seven Years' War. Driven from their northern home, more than a hundred Acadian families found their way to Louisiana, then under Spanish rule. They settled largely in the swamplands and engaged in trapping, fishing, hunting, and the raising of rice and cane. As landless immigrants, the Acadians had a lower social status than the old French settlers; and, as a persecuted minority in their former northern homeland, they were not standoffish with the Negro slaves. Their relations with the Negroes were not tempered by a master-slave attitude. The Cajun dialect of French and the Negro Creole language, though distinct, were mutually understandable. In music, there appears to have been a receptivity on both sides. While reminiscent of Acadian music of Nova Scotia, Louisiana Cajun music today has something different about it. As one specialist on Acadian life noted: "However French they may be in origin, Cajun folksongs have in some cases a definite Negro flavor, to be found in the superimposed elementary rhythms which give them a sort of 'jazzy' atmosphere, nowhere else to be found in folksongs derived from France other than in the Caribbean." [1]

The extent to which Acadian music influenced that of the Negroes is not altogether clear. But it is noteworthy that numerous Negroes in proximity to the Cajuns today sing Cajun songs in Cajun dialect and play Cajun tunes without any suggestion of foreign intrusion. Many Negroes elsewhere in Louisiana sing old French folksongs and ballads in pure style. What, then, are we really discussing when we speak of Negro folk music in this region? We are not immediately concerned with songs that Negroes may happen to sing, but with songs which fall into a category which, because of various components, may be considered a development of Negro culture in this area. For our purposes, this means songs sung in Creole or French patois which derive out of or are part of the experience of the Negro community.

One Creole song taken down toward the end of the nineteenth century has a structure which is familiar in West Indian singing and in United States blues. While the romantic content is not characteristic of blues, it has counterparts in songs of the French Caribbean:

Mo déja roulé tout la côte,
P'encore 'oir pareil belle Layotte.
Mo déja roulé tout la côte,
P'encore 'oir pareil belle Layotte.
Mo roulé tout la colonie
Dipi cé Miché Pierre Sonist,
P'encore 'oir in griffonne com' ça
Comparab' à mo belle Layotte.

I have searched the entire coast
And found no equal to beautiful Layotte.
I have searched the entire coast
And found no equal to beautiful Layotte.
I have searched the entire colony
Since [the time of] Monsieur Pierre Sonist
And not found a griffonne [a] like her,
Comparable to my beautiful Layotte.[2]

In the structure of this piece, we note, first, a repeated couplet which introduces the idea, then, a further development of the theme which does not stray far from the introductory passage. For comparison, here is a Haitian song, "Angelico," in translation:

Angelico, Angelico,
Go home to your mother's house.
Angelico, Angelico,
Go home to your mother's house.
All young girls who don't know how to wash and iron,
Go home to your mother's.[3]

As commented upon previously, this structure is so commonplace as to be virtually basic in blues singing. This blues stanza is typical:

Well I'm drifting and drifting
Just like a ship out on the sea.
Well I'm drifting and drifting
Just like a ship out on the sea.
Well I aint got nobody
In this whole world who cares for me.[4]

Another Creole Negro song (Example 22) taken down by Cable [5] and attributed by him to the repertoire of the Calinda Dance also has a form in which we recognize components characteristic of African and West Indian singing. According to Cable, the tune was recollected from his childhood, when he had heard it sung by

[a] Griffonne: one of the standard gradations of mixed color. In English, griffe.

a street vendor. The fact that it was not set down at the time of hearing, plus the fact that it was sung not by a group but by an individual, probably accounts for its strangely hybridized appearance. It is likely that in its original setting each couplet was sung twice by a singing leader, followed by a short response from the group. And it is just as likely that the words *"bondjoum! bondjoum!"* were given by Cable's singing vendor as a substitute for sounds originally provided by drums.

EXAMPLE 22

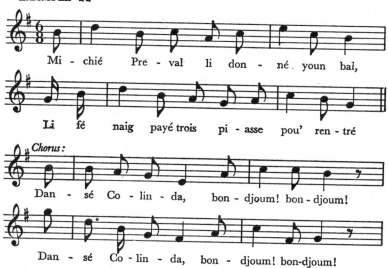

1
Michié Preval li donné youn bal,
Li fé naig payé trois piasse pou' rentré.
Chorus (after every stanza)
Dansé Colinda, bondjoum! bondjoum!
Dansé Colinda, bondjoum! bondjoum!

2
Dans l'equirie la y'avé grand gala,
Mo cré choual la yé té b'en etonné.

3
Michié Preval, li té capitaine bal,
So cocher Louis, té mait' cérémonie.

4
Y'ave de négresses belle passé maîtresses,
Qui volé bel-bel dans l'ormoire momselle.

5
Ala maît' la geôle li trouvé si drole,
Li dit, "moin aussi, mo fé bal ici."

1
Mr. Preval, he gave a ball,
He made people ᵇ pay three dollars ᶜ to come in.

Chorus
Dance the Colinda, bondjoum! bondjoum!
Dance the Colinda, bondjoum! bondjoum!

2
They had the festivities in the stable,
I think the horses were very astonished.

3
Mr. Preval, he was the captain of the ball,
His coachman Louis was master of ceremonies.

4
The Negro women were more beautiful than their mistresses,
They stole ornaments to wear from Madamoiselle's wardrobe.

5
The jail keeper found it all so amusing,
He said, "I also will have a ball here."

Cable also set down the word texts of some old Creole songs for which no music notations were provided. Among them were some fine examples of romantic and historical balladry. One such song is about the battle of Chalmette in 1814. It is basically a personal account of a slave, who tells how he left his master at the scene of the fighting and made his own way to home and safety:

Fizi z'Anglé yé fé bim! bim!
Carabin Kaintock yé fé zim! zim!
Mo di' moin, sauvé to la peau!
Mo zété corps au bord de l'eau;
Quand mo rivé li té fé clair.
Madam' li prend' ein coup d'colère;
Li fé donn' moin ein quat' piquié
Passeque mo pas sivi mouchie;
Mais moin mo vo mie quat' piquie
Passé ein coup d'fizi z'Anglé!

ᵇ Literally, "Negroes," but this word is used, as in the West Indies, to mean "person," "persons," or "people."
ᶜ *Piasse,* from the Spanish, *piastre,* is also used in Haiti to mean dollar.

The English muskets went bim! bim!
Kentucky rifles went zim! zim!
I said to myself, save your skin!
I ran along the water's edge;
When I arrived at home it was day.
Mistress flew into a rage;
She had me whipped at the four stakes
Because I didn't follow master;
But for me the four stakes
Are better than a shot from an English musket.[6]

Another song text taken by Cable came from a former slave. It was a ballad about a Negro insurrectionist named Saint Malo, who was caught and hanged by the colonial authorities. The reference to the *cabildo*—the colonial council that administered Spanish rule of the colony—seems to date the event, if not the song itself, before 1803. As far as one can judge the song on the basis of words alone, it has a marked French character, and is quite similar in style to Creole historical ballads still extant in Haiti. Had it been composed in African tradition, its imagery and treatment would have been quite different. Certain scenes would have been alluded to briefly, there would have been a repetition of certain key lines, and many little observations made in the story would have been left to the imagination. The developing of details, and the tight and logical sequence of events mark the ballad as European in style, but the point of view is that of the Negro slave:

Aie! zein zens, vini fé ouarra
Pou' pôv' St. Malo dans l'embas!
Yé c'assé le avec yé chiens,
Yé tiré li ein coup d' fizi.
Yé halé li la cyprier,
So bras yé 'tassé par derrier,
Yé 'tassé so la main divant;
Yé marré li apé queue choual,
Yé trainein li zouqu'à la ville.
Divant michés là dans Cabil'e
Yé quisé li li fé complot
Pou' coupé cou à tout yé blancs.
Yé 'mandé li qui so compères;
Pôv' St. Malo pas di' a-rien!
Zize là li lir' so la sentence,

Et pis li fé dressé potence,
Yé halé choual—ç'arette parti—
Pôv' St. Malo resté pendi!
Eine hèr soleil deza levée
Quand yé pend li si la levée.
Yé laissé so corps balancé
Pou' carancro gagnion manzé.

Aie! Young men, come to lament
For poor St. Malo out there!
They hunted him with dogs,
They fired guns at him.
They brought him from the cypress swamp,
His arms they tied behind his back,
They tied his hands in front;
They tied him to a horse's tail,
They dragged him to the city
Before the men of the Cabildo.
They accused him of a plot
To cut the throats of all the whites.
They asked him who his comrades were,
But poor St. Malo was silent.
The judge read out the sentence,
And then they prepared the gallows.
They drove the horse—the cart moved off—
And left poor St. Malo hanging there.
The day was an hour old
When they hanged him;
They left his body swinging
For the carrion crows to eat.[7]

Another song (Example 23) of Spanish Colonial days that survived through the nineteenth century is that of a slave escapee, addressed to a member of the Cabildo named General Florido.

Oh General Florido,[d]
It is true, you can't capture me!
Oh General Florido,
It is true, you can't capture me!

There is a ship on the ocean,
It is true, you can't capture me!
There is a ship on the ocean,
It is true, you can't capture me! [8]

[d] Cable suggests that General Florido was the high sheriff Charles Jean Baptiste Fleuriau, who lived in the late eighteenth century.

EXAMPLE 23

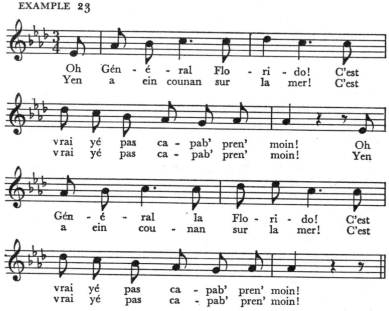

Oh   Gén - é - ral   Flo - ri - do!   C'est
Yen   a   ein   counan   sur   la   mer!   C'est

vrai   yé   pas   ca - pab'   pren'   moin!   Oh
vrai   yé   pas   ca - pab'   pren'   moin!   Yen

Gén - é - ral   la   Flo - ri - do!   C'est
a   ein   cou - nan   sur   la   mer!   C'est

vrai   yé   pas   ca - pab'   pren' moin!
vrai   yé   pas   ca - pab'   pren' moin!

This song, as is evident, has a format which identifies it with Negro rather than French tradition. There is a statement, followed by a choral response, and a repetition. The second stanza, in the same pattern, gives a related allusion suggesting that the runaway slave was escaping by ship. Minute details of the event are regarded as of no importance, contrary to the French ballad's habit of spelling out a story in narrative form.

An unattributed Creole song published in 1945—probably from a nineteenth-century printed source—is of some interest because of its similarity to a number of Creole songs of the French West Indies and Haiti:

Madame Caba, tiyon vous tombé,
Madame Caba, en sortant di bal,
Michiè Zizi, cet in vaillan' nomme,
Michiè Zizi, cet in vaillan' nomme.

    Wa-ya, ya-ya-ya, tiyon vous tombé!
    Wo-wo, wo-wo, tiyon vous tombé!
    Wa-wa, wa-wa, (etc., with variations).[9]

The *tiyon* referred to in the song is the colored kerchief worn by Creole women in Louisiana (French: *tignon*). The statement is of the social comment or gossip variety so commonplace in Caribbean tradition:

> Madame Caba, your headcloth fell down,
> Madame Caba, as you were leaving the dance.
> Mr. Zizi is a handsome man,
> Mr. Zizi is a handsome man.
> Wa-ya, ya-ya-ya, your headcloth fell down!
> Etc.

In Haiti there are a number of songs on the theme of the falling hat, like this one:

> Panama'm tombé,
> Panama'm tombé,
> Ça qui dèyè moin,
> Ramassé li ba mwé.

The setting, like that for Madame Caba, is a dance:

> My hat fell down,
> My hat fell down,
> Whoever is behind me,
> Pick it up for me.[10]

An earlier, ballad-like version of the Haitian "My Hat Fell Down" uses the falling hat as an omen of unfortunate events to come.[11]

Among the Negro Creole songs of Louisiana are many with a marked sentimental character which are close kin to songs still composed and sung in the French-speaking Caribbean islands. When heard in the Creole language, the similarity is striking. One Louisiana song set down on paper around the turn of the century was known as "Zélim." In translation, it went:

> Zélim, you left the valley;
> Ever since, I have missed you.
> My eyes have flowed like a fountain
> Since the last time I saw you.
> At night in my bed
> I dream and remember you.
> In the day, when I am cutting cane,
> It is also you I remember.[12]

The pleasant sentimentality of this piece is reminiscent of the Haitian song, "Paulette," given here in translation:

> Paulette, remember long ago when we were small, our houses facing each other.

When you made mudpies, I was always asking for Paulette.
When you went away you didn't say where you were going, Paulette. (×2)
It was one Saturday morning when I, a farmer, went down to the city,
When I saw Mamma Paulette, tears ran from my eyes.
When you went away you didn't say where you were going, Paulette. (×2) [13]

A goodly portion of old Louisiana Creole songs survive today only in the repertoire of performers who have made an effort to save, and revive, the traditional tunes. Nevertheless, Creole folksongs still are sung in the hinterland, here and there, and some recordings of them have been made within the past few years.

Lullabies are rather plentiful, and most of them seem to be of French derivation. This one is an old favorite in Louisiana and is well known in Haiti and other Creole areas of the West Indies:

Dodo, dodo pitit
Dodo pitit à moin.
Général Le Careau allé la ville,
Pas quit' anyien pou' pitit à moin.
Obligé'm pou' pli jupon moin
Pou'm fai' cassack pou' pitit à moin.
Obligé'm pou' pli jupon moin
Pou'm fai' cassack pou' pitit à moin.

Sleep, sleep little one.
Sleep my little one.
General Le Careau has gone to the city,
He has not left anything for my little one.
I have to cut up my apron
To make a dress for my little one.
I have to cut up my apron
To make a dress for my little one.[14]

French *cantes fables* and African-derived animal tales were prominent in Louisiana folklore until relatively recent times. There was a large repertoire of stories about Boukee (a slow-witted and not always sympathetic character who figures in Haitian and other West Indian lore) and Brother Rabbit (a leading character in animal stories told throughout the South).[15] In many of these tales, little songs were interspersed thoughout the narration. A number of songs originally belonging to folk tales appear to have survived on their own, without the stories to which they once belonged, like this one about Brother Rabbit:

Ai yè ya, Compère Lapin,
C'est ti bête qui conné sauté.
Wai yè ya, Papa Lapin,
C'est ti bête qui conné sauté.

Ai yè ya, Brother Rabbit,
He is a little creature who knows how to jump.
Wai yè ya, Father Rabbit,
He is a little creature who knows how to jump.[16]

There is a temptation to imagine that the Mardi Gras activities in New Orleans and other Gulf communities contain within them interesting survivals of Creole culture. However, this possibility does not appear to apply to music. The New Orleans Mardi Gras has many of the characteristics of Mardi Gras in the French and Spanish speaking areas of the Caribbean. Just as Haiti, for example, has its Mardi Gras bands of "wild men," "cannibals," and "demons," Negro New Orleans has its "Zulus," its "wild men," and its various "Indian tribes"—the Golden Blades, Cheyennes, Blue Eagles, Black Eagles, White Eagles, and Yellow Pocohantas. According to information gathered by the Louisiana Writers' Project, the Zulus seem to have appeared on the scene about 1910, though some of the Indians were evident much earlier. All of the Indians specialize in pantomime, dancing, and war-whooping. Ornate costumes, an elaborate body of protocol between various tribes on the march, feathered scouts or spies roaming the streets to warn of the coming of other bands, and chanting and singing provide a tremendous scene of make believe.

The songs sung by the tribes appear to be largely ad libbed, with a standard choral response—"Tu-way-pa-ka-way"—which is reminiscent of traditional Negro singing. This responsive phrase gives the Indian songs their "authentic" character, though its meaning seems to be unknown. Some informants have vouched that it is "Indian language," though the probability is that it is corrupted Creole.

Among "Tu-way-pa-ka-way" songs taken down about thirty years ago are these fragments:

Get out the dishes,
    Tu-way-pa-ka-way!
Get out the pan,
    Tu-way-pa-ka-way!

Here comes the Indian man,
  Tu-way-pa-ka-way!
Oh, the little Red, White and Blues,
  Tu-way-pa-ka-way!
Bravest Indians in the land,
  Tu-way-pa-ka-way!
They are on the march today,
  Tu-way-pa-ka-way!
If you should get in their way,
  Tu-way-pa-ka-way!
Be prepared to die,
  Tu-way-pa-ka-way!
  Oowa-a-a!
  Oowa-a-a! [17]

A recently recorded Indian song begins this way:

Oh they comin' and a-jumpin',
  Tu-way-pa-ka-way!
Oh they comin' and a-runnin',
  Tu-way-pa-ka-way!
Oh they comin' by the hundreds,
  Tu-way-pa-ka-way!
Oh the chief of the Mardi Grass (sic),
  Tu-way-pa-ka-way!
Oh down on the Bayou,
  Tu-way-pa-ka-way! [18]

On the whole, the Mardi Gras songs do not contain within them the best elements of Negro musical tradition, if recorded materials now available give a fair picture. This reality contrasts vividly with the situation in Haiti and other Creole islands of the West Indies, and in the Spanish speaking islands with their *comparsas*. But there are understandable reasons. Even with its remnants of an earlier day, Louisiana is no longer a Creole culture. Despite the various French dialects still spoken there, the region has been largely absorbed by the mainstream of American life, and New Orleans itself is less French or Creole than sentimental.

IX. Performers' Corner: Ballads and Minstrelsy

ALMOST ANY SYSTEM of organizing Negro folk songs into classifications or types results in overlappings of one kind or another. For one thing, the folk singer is not inclined to think in terms of categories. For another, songs pass with great ease from genre to genre, in whole or in part. Play songs, religious songs, and blues may be sung as worksongs. Worksongs, game songs, and ballads may be recast as blues. Ballads or street songs with moralistic themes may be thought of as religious songs. And archaic plantation-day songs are the inspiration for modern blues, playparty songs, and dance tunes.

Songs sung as performers' or entertainers' art—even though they have connections with other types—appear to constitute a large, if amorphous, category of their own. Most prominent among such songs are the long forms called ballads and a variety of minstrels' songs.

Looking back at examples which have been given in earlier chapters, we note that among the work songs are "John Henry,"

"Number Ninety-Nine," and others which have ballad characteristics. Among the blues, "John Henry" appears again along with "One Kind Favor" (which is certainly ballad-like, and employs familiar stock images from English balladry) and some other songs that we might call "almost-ballads." And the religious songs include such items as "God Moves On the Water" (about the *Titanic*) and "When Jesus Met the Woman at the Well," which have unmistakable ballad character.

It is obvious that Negro song makers in America at a very early date became aware of English, Irish, Scottish, and, in the Louisiana region, French ballad styles. The evidence is widespread in Negro folk songs. Wherever European ballad materials—including the conventional ballad form—were deemed useful or attractive, they were used by Negro song makers. But they were generally absorbed into the main flow of Negro musical tradition, where other concepts dominated, and where a style characterized by allusion and interpolation usually remained supreme. Indirection of statement and selective imagery tended to substitute for unbroken continuity of story line. Story songs sung by blues singers more often than not became compacted into a blues-like format, and, when sung by work gangs, the dictates of the setting, timing, and function altered them into the shape of traditional worksongs.

In popular usage, the term ballad is sometimes loosely applied to varied types of folk songs. In its "classical" form, the ballad is a song which tells a story and which is made up of a series of stanzas (more or less regular), with or without a refrain. There is a progressive, usually chronological, development in the narration, and the musical phrasing is essentially the same, though with decorative variations, for all stanzas.

If this definition is applied to blues songs, we find few true ballads among them. The story projected in a blues song is rarely explicit, chronological, or developed. On the contrary, it is put forward by innuendo, hints, and tangent allusion. Indeed, story as such is not intended so much as personal comment or reaction. Religious songs also, even though they may possess themes which to some extent develop or unfold, rely heavily on repetition and elements of allusion—Biblical scenes, flashes of drama, flashes of revelation, and expressions of faith pegged to unspecified Biblical references. Nevertheless, as we have observed, blues, religious songs, and worksongs include in their repertoires a number of free forms which verge on the ballad, and others which are in a straight line of descent from European balladry. Many of them are to be found in the repertoire of the public entertainer. They are songs which do not require audience participation, only an audience. They are vehicles for expression of the performer's art.

These ballads of the public performer are devoted largely to heroic, sometimes near-epic, actions, to great misfortunes, injustice, and bad men and their deeds. In general, they lack the immediacy of blues and the emotional content and poetic qualities of good religious songs and worksongs. The language often is trite, derivative, or plain doggerel. The drama being depicted is usually seen from a distance. As often as not, the stories are about people in another time and place. Moral judgments and passions are inclined to be stereotyped. Whereas the *Titanic* song of the religious street singers has implicit moral application, "Frankie and Albert" has none. While the "John Henry" work song has warmth about it, "Casey Jones" is cool. And while many blues songs are intimately personal, the story songs seem impersonal. Compare the line from "Frankie and Albert," for example—"He was her man and he done her wrong"—with the poetic statement of a blues "John Henry"—"John Henry left his hammer layin' alongside the road, all out in the rain." These are the generalities, and there are, of course, noteworthy exceptions.

Many ballads known to Negro singers are popular also among whites. Versions of "John Hardy," "John Henry," "Casey Jones," "Railroad Bill," "Stagolee," and "Frankie and Albert," to name but a few, are sung by white mountaineer balladeers and played by mountain jug bands, and there obviously has been a good deal of interplay between white and Negro variants, both in style and content. Some ballads bear an indelible mark of Negro origin. Others, while hybrid, are considered to belong primarily to Negro tradition.

Most of these songs have a sense of continuing action—like the western movie—that is missing in other Negro folk songs. There is a central drama for which the song maker has created a prologue and an epilogue based on fact or fancy, or a combination of both. As in Anglo-American ballads, outlaws are frequently featured.

Of all the bad men who have been immortalized in song, Stagolee (sometimes called Stagalee, Stackalee, Stacker Lee, or Stagerlee) rates as one of the meanest. Whoever the original Stagolee was, and whatever his anti-social acts, to the Stagolee of legend there have been attached a great many tough and heartless actions, a few of them colossal exaggeration. According to one account, Stagolee was responsible for the disaster known as the San Francisco earthquake. Stagolee had gone into a bar for a drink, but the bartender refused to serve him without seeing his money. Stagolee got mad, grabbed hold of the bar and tore it down. All over town buildings collapsed, and a cloud of dust and smoke rose in the air. What had happened was that when Stagolee wrenched out the bar he pulled out the pipes. Since all the water pipes in town were connected, he tore them out too, thus causing the general disaster.

But the central theme of the Stagolee story is an episode that might have been real—the killing of a man named Billy Lyons (or O'Lyons). The crime took place in a barrel house or saloon, where Stagolee accused Lyons of stealing his Stetson hat. Almost all versions recount that Billy Lyons begged for his life, saying that he had three little children and a loving wife. Stagolee's character is stamped on him indelibly by responses such as:

Damn your little children,
And damn your lovin' wife.
You stole my good old Stetson hat,
And now I'm goin' to have your life.

One short version of the ballad summarizes the story in these words:

You remember, you remember
One dark stormy night,
Stagolee and Billy O'Lyons
They had that awful fight.

(After each stanza)
Bad man, Stagolee,
Wasn't he bad, he bad with a gun.

Billy O'Lyons told Stagolee
Please don't take my life,

I got three little children
And a dear little lovin' wife.

Stagolee told Billy O'Lyons
I don't care for your three little children, either your lovin' wife,
You done stole-a my Stetson hat
And I'm bound to take your life.

Stagolee pulled out his forty-four,
It went boom boom boom!
Stagolee saw Billy O'Lyons
Was layin' on the floor.[1]

Other versions dwell on Stagolee's capture by the police, his remorse over his deed, his sentence to seventy-five years in the penitentiary, and even his colloquies with the devil. One song tells that the devil came to get Stagolee's soul, but when next seen, the devil was climbing up the wall and shouting, "Come and get this bad Stagolee before he kills us all." And another one ends:

Them prisoners talkin' together,
Say, what you know about that?
Old Stagolee goin' to hell forever,
Just for an old Stetson hat.

John Hardy was another celebrated murderer. He killed a man at a gambling table, was caught, tried, and hanged. His affinity to Stagolee is affirmed by the lines:

John Hardy had a lovin' little wife,
And of children he had three,
But he didn't care no more for the lot of them
Than he did for the fish in the sea.

Still another outlaw whose deeds are memorialized in song was named Lazarus. Most versions indicate that Lazarus broke into the commissary of a work camp and robbed it, then escaped into the hills. The sheriff and his posse went after Lazarus and shot him down. A good portion of the ballad consists of elaborating the details following the encounter.

Oh, bad man Lazarus,
Oh, bad man Lazarus,
He broke in the commissary,
Lord, he broke in the commissary.

He been paid off,
He been paid off,
Lord, Lord, Lord,
He been paid off.

Commissary man,
Commissary man,
He jump out the commissary window,
Lord, he jump out the commissary window.

Commissary man swore out,
Lord, commissary man swore out,
Lord, commissary man swore out
Warrant for Lazarus.

Oh, bring him back,
Lord, bring him back,
Oh, Lord, Lord, Lord,
Bring Lazarus back.

They begin to wonder,
Lord, they begin to wonder,
Lord, they begin to wonder
Where Lazarus gone.

Where in the world,
Lord, where in the world,
Lord, where in the world
Will they find him?

Well, I don't know,
I don't know,
Well, Lord, Lord,
Well, I don't know.

Well, the sheriff spied poor Lazarus,
Well, the sheriff spied poor Lazarus,
Lord, sheriff spied poor Lazarus
Way between Bald Mountain.

They blowed him down,
Well, they blowed him down,
Well, Lord, Lord,
They blowed him down.

They shot poor Lazarus,
Lord, they shot poor Lazarus,
Lord, they shot poor Lazarus
With a great big number.

Well, a forty-five,
Lord, great big forty-five,
Lord, forty-five,
Turn him round.

They brought poor Lazarus,
And they brought poor Lazarus,
Lord, they brought poor Lazarus
Back to the shanty.

Old friend Lazarus say,
Lord, old Lazarus say,
Lord, old Lazarus say,
Give me a cool drink of water.

Before I die,
Good Lord, 'fore I die,
Give me a cool drink of water,
Lord, 'fore I die.

Lazarus' mother say,
Lord, Lazarus' mother say,
Nobody know the trouble
I had with him.

Since daddy died,
Lord, since daddy been dead,
Nobody know the trouble I had
Since daddy been dead.

They goin' to bury poor Lazarus,
Lord, they goin' to bury old Lazarus,
They goin' to bury poor Lazarus
In the mine.

Me and my buddy,
Lord, me and my buddy,
We goin' over to bury him
Half past nine.

Lazarus' mother say,
Look over yonder,
How they treatin' poor Lazarus,
Lord, Lord, Lord.

They puttin' him away,
Lord, they puttin' him away,
Lord, they puttin' Lazarus away
Half past nine.[2]

The version of "Poor Lazarus" given above is actually a work variant, but it was selected because of its attention to chronological narration, and because it is characteristic of traditional Negro treatment. The form is somewhat free within each four-line stanza, though in general the second and third lines are repeats of the first, with variations, and the fourth concludes the statement. Rhyme is of no significance, the rhyming effect being achieved by the repetition of terminal words. In some instances, two stanzas are used to make a simple statement, creating, as it were, double stanzas. Free and simple as the presentation is, a powerful effect is created by the repetitions and the slow unfolding of the story. Even without an accompanying musical notation, it is readily apparent that this version was produced in a work situation and at work tempo, with the singer feeling his way and shaping his statement and weaving it into the work motions of the men.

The theme of "Frankie and Albert" (also known as "Frankie and Johnnie") has many precedents in English, Scottish, and other European balladry—the revenge of a scorned woman. But the setting for this drama is not a castle, and its characters are not nobility. It is a barrel house, or saloon, and the characters are a sporting man, a jealous woman, and a varied supporting cast from the wrong side of the railroad tracks. There are many versions of the ballad, and few singers have versions in common. Every rendition is an open invitation to improvise. The simple, regular stanzas, with second and fourth lines rhyming, and standard fifth refrain line, are easy to compose, and dead of spirit indeed is the singer who has done the song twice exactly the same way.

Some accounts say Frankie's revenge was carried out with a knife, others with a gun, the exact caliber of which is determined by the rhyme required—twenty-two, forty, forty-one, forty-four, or forty-five. Some singers prefer to have Albert meet his fate on the bar room floor, others in his room with his latest conquest, Alice Fry (or Bly, or Giles, or another similar sounding name).

Frankie was a good girl,
As everybody knows.
She paid a hundred dollars
For Albert's suit of clothes.
He was her man and he done her wrong.

Frankie went down to the corner saloon,
Wasn't goin' to be there long,
Asked the bartender had he seen her Albert,
'Cause he done been home and gone.
He was her man and he done her wrong.

Well, the bartender he told Frankie,
Can't lie to you if I try,
Old Albert been here an hour ago
And gone home with Alice Fry.
He was her man and he done her wrong.

Frankie went down to Albert's house,
Only a couple of blocks away,
Peeped in the keyhole of his door,
Saw Albert lovin' Alice Fry.
He was her man and he done her wrong.

Frankie called out to Albert,
Albert said I don't hear.
If you don't come to the woman you love
Goin' to haul you out of here.
He was her man and he done her wrong.

Frankie she shot old Albert,
And she shot him three or four times.
Said I'll hang around a few minutes
And see if Albert's dyin'.
He was my man and he done me wrong.

An iron-tired wagon
With ribbons all hung in black
Took old Albert to the buryin' ground
And it didn't bring him back.
He was her man and he done her wrong.

Frankie told the sheriff
What goin' to happen to me?
Said looks like from the evidence
Goin' to be murder first degree.
He was your man and he done you wrong.

Judge heard Frankie's story,
Heard Albert's mother testify.
Judge said to Frankie,
You goin' to be justified.
He was your man and he done you wrong.

Dark was the night,
Cold was the ground,

The last words I heard Frankie say,
I done laid old Albert down.
He was my man and he done me wrong.

Last time I heard of Frankie
She was settin' in her cell,
Sayin' Albert done me wrong
And for that I sent him to hell.
He was my man and he done me wrong.

I aint goin' to tell no stories,
I aint goin' to tell no lies.
The woman who stole Frankie's Albert
Was the girl they call Alice Fry.
He was her man and he done her wrong.[3]

The ballad of Casey Jones, the railroad engineer who raced his locomotive against lost time and died in a wreck in the year 1900, is probably the most widely known song about American railroad disasters. The original Casey Jones ballad (to the extent that it was original) is generally attributed to Wallace Saunders, the Negro engine wiper who took care of Jones' locomotive. Popularized versions of the song were widespread in the first decade or so of the century and influenced the development of still other versions. The song "composed" by Saunders was probably compounded, in part, out of a number of railroad disaster songs already current among railroad men, both white and Negro.

While the hero of the song, Casey (John Luther) Jones, was white, the best known variants bear the brand of Negro song makers. There is a curious mixture of Negro idiom and imagery with non-Negro phrases, and sometimes there are interpolations of blues-like stanzas which have no readily apparent relevance to the central theme. Such additions helped the singers to gain time to think of new stanzas, as well as to spin out the yarn to a length befitting an epic subject. Sometimes the inventions of the singers considerably distorted the character of the hero and his family. There is considerable doggerel in most versions, rhyme being required. The following rendition of the ballad has the feel of Negro style and invention. Stanzas such as the one referring to Alice Spratt and the one mentioning the pension appear to be products of fertile imaginations and seem to have caused Mr. Jones' family considerable discomfiture.

I woke up this mornin' four o'clock,
Mr. Casey told the fireman get his boiler hot.
Put on your water, put on your coal,
Put your head out the window, see my drivers roll, see my drivers roll,
Put your head out the window, see my drivers roll.

Lord, some people said Mr. Casey couldn't run,
Let me tell you what Mr. Casey done.
He left Memphis, was quarter to nine,
Got in Newport News it was dinner time, was dinner time,
Got in Newport News it was dinner time.

Lord, people said old Casey he was runnin' overtime,
And I'm nothin' losin' with the 109.
Casey said it aint in line,
I run into glory 'less I make my time.
Said all the passengers better keep themselves hid,
I'm not goin' to shake it like Chaney did, like Chaney did,
I'm not goin' to shake it like Chaney did.

Mr. Casey ran his engine in a mile of the place,
Number Four stabbed him in the face.
The sheriff told Casey, well you must leave town.
For freedom of my soul I'm Alabama bound, Alabama bound,
For freedom of my soul I'm Alabama bound.

Mrs. Casey said she dreamt a dream,
In the night she bought a sewin' machine.
The needle got broke, she could not sew.
She loved Mr. Casey 'cause he told me so, told me so,
She loved Mr. Casey 'cause he told me so.

There was a woman named Miss Alice Spratt,
Said I want to ride with Casey 'fore I die,
I aint good lookin' but I take my time,
I'm a ramblin' woman with a ramblin' mind, got a ramblin' mind.
I'm a ramblin' woman with a ramblin' mind.

Casey looked at his water, water was low,
Looked at his watch, his watch was slow.
On the road again,
Natural born leaf, goin' to roll again.

Lord, people tell 'bout the thought of home,
The manager fired Mr. Casey Jones, Mr. Casey Jones.
Mr. Casey said before he died, one more road that he want to ride.
People tell Casey which road is he?
The Southern Pacific and the Sancta Fee, Sancta Fee.

This morning I heard someone were dyin',
Mrs. Casey's children on the doorstep cryin',
Mamma, Mamma, I can't keep from cryin',
Papa got killed on a certain line, on a certain line,
Papa got killed on a certain line.

Mamma, Mamma, how can it be,
Killed my father in the first degree.
Children, children, won't you hold your breath,
Draw another pension from your father's death, from your father's death.
On the road again,
I'm a natural born leaf and on the road again.

Tuesday morning it look like rain,
Around the curve came a passenger train.
Under the pile laid Casey Jones,
Good old engineer, for he's dead and gone, dead and gone.
On the road again,
I'm a natural born leaf on the road again.[4]

Ballads and other entertainment songs were, as they are today, sung on the streets and in establishments such as barrel houses or saloons, wherever people gathered together. Saturday nights in the Negro sections of southern cities and towns were always festive. People from the countryside who had come in to do their shopping, or selling, lingered on into the evening. They stood or sat in groups along the sidewalk, or in front of the general store, talking, exchanging news and gossip. The drinking establishments were always crowded. In this natural, ready-made setting, the Negro minstrel exploited his talents. Sometimes the "musicianers" appeared in groups of two, three, or more. Their instruments varied— harmonicas, banjos, guitars, jugs. An entertainer sometimes had a whole roster of capabilities. He might be able to sing, jig and buck and wing, play a harmonica, tell stories, and make jokes— a veritable one-man vaudeville show. His songs were of many kinds, including ballads, blues, comic songs, and recent "pop" songs rendered in his own style. In his repertoire, there may have been tunes that had been favorites for a century or more, such as "My old mistress promised me that when she died she'd set me free." His reward for his entertainment was the coins thrown on the sidewalk by his audience. If a minstrel found that he wasn't doing well enough, he would perhaps move on to another town and try his luck there.

Some entertainers found steady employment with traveling medicine shows. Sitting on a platform, or in front of a tent, or on some street corner, they attracted the crowds to which the "doctor" would attempt to sell his various cure-all concoctions. Since the size of the crowd usually depended on the musical pitchman, good entertainers were in great demand in the patent medicine trade, and some of them went from one employer to another according to the inducements offered. Entertainment of this kind must have strongly influenced commercial black-face minstrelsy which for a time was popular throughout the country.

A typical medicine show song that has survived to the present is this one, "Old John Booker." It is pure entertainment, delivered artfully, with change of pace, burlesque humor, clowning, infectious laughing passages, dramatic rendition of lines, and, in this instance, superb banjo playing.[a]

Old John Booker, call that gone!
Old John Booker, call that gone!
Old John Booker, call that gone!

(*banjo passage, then:*)
Mm, now old John Booker, call that gone!
Old John Booker, call that gone!
Old John Booker, call that gone!
(*with emphasis*) I'm goin' down to telephone!

(*in same rhythm as song, half sung, with gleeful effects*)
Ah hah-hah!
Eee hee!
Hah hah!
Wah hah!
Mmm hah!
Eh heh!

Old John Booker, he feel like this!
Old John Booker, call that gone!
Old John Booker, call that gone!
Old John Booker, call that gone?
I'm goin' down—on the farm!

(*spoken*) Now pick it.

(*banjo passage, then:*)
Old John Booker, call that gone now!
(*low voice, staccato delivery, with percussion effects from slapping body of banjo*)

[a] See The Music, 43.

Old John Booker, call that gone!
Old John Booker, call that gone!
Old John Booker, call that gone!
I'm goin' back here on the farm!

Ah-hah ah-hah!
(*half spoken*) Yes yes yes!

(*banjo passage*)
Now old John Booker, call that gone!
Old John Booker, call that gone!
Old John Booker, call that gone?
I'm goin' back down here on the farm!

X. Dances: Calindas, Buzzard Lopes, and Reels

THE CONCEPT of "Negro dancing" can only be an amorphous one if we are thinking in purely contemporary terms, particularly if we try to distinguish traditional dance from popular craze dances. The Charleston and the Black Bottom which emerged in the 1920s, for example—were they ballroom innovations or, on the contrary, popularized developments of Negro dances that had their origins in the deep south? Although some of the characteristics of the Charleston and the Black Bottom were related to traditional Negro dancing, it is hard to escape the impression that they were essentially craze dances which utilized traditional materials indiscriminately with innovation and artifice. They had about the same relationship to traditional forms as did the Rhumba and the Conga in the ballroom. That is to say, very little. It is, of course, possible to perceive in the Charleston certain steps or motifs extracted out of Negro tradition, but over all, it was a synthetic creation, a newly-devised conglomerate tailored for widespread popular appeal. The rhythmic, virtuostic calisthenics that developed around the basic Charleston steps, inspired by acrobatic dancing of the stage, filtered down through the years into Jitterbug. But seen in the perspective of a few decades, the Charleston, along with the Black Bottom, the Rhumba, the Cha-cha-cha, and the Big Apple, appears to belong to a category of short-lived, contrived, popular dance forms that is quite distinct from traditional dance.

We are obliged to limit the field of Negro dance according to the same rules used to delimit Negro folk music. While there is an acknowledged no-man's-land between the traditional and popular, on one side of this ambiguous area are dance activities which belong to unselfconscious Negro tradition. It is with these activities that we are primarily concerned—with what we might call Negro "folk" dances except for the obvious confusion provoked by that term, as well as its redundancy. In speaking of traditional Negro dance in the United States hereinafter, I am referring, first, to dances which were an integral part of Negro culture, whether derived from African or European sources; and, second, to dance activities or patterns preserved and handed on by an unselfconscious process comparable to the process by which folk music is propagated. Neither folk music nor dance are things in themselves; they are related to a complex of activities, attitudes, and customs. When the complex to which they are attached breaks up, their character changes, their meanings change, their importance diminishes, and they become something akin to curious artifacts. Any discussion of traditional Negro dance, as herein defined, must take a good backward look.

Only three-quarters of a century ago, a number of dances were known in Louisiana which have disappeared almost entirely. Cable wrote of having witnessed virtually all of them in Congo Square in New Orleans, and though his descriptions were impressionistic, romantic, or moralistic, and though he failed to understand the full implications of the spectacles he was fortunate enough to see, he did at least set down the names of the dances and something about the instrumental combinations that produced the music. He mentioned the Juba, the Bamboula, the Counjaille, the Babouille, the Cata or Chacta, the Voodoo, the Congo, and the Calinda. All of these dances were then, and are to this day, well-known in the West Indies.

The name Voodoo (more properly Vodoun or Vodun) was particularly well-known in the Caribbean islands on which had been settled African slaves from the region of Dahomey. In a generic sense, it referred to all Dahomean cult activities; a Vodoun dance was any dance related to Dahomean cult worship, and, therefore, Cable's thought that he was referring to a specific dance was inaccurate. The Bamboula is to be found today in, among other places, the Virgin Islands, and the Babouille (Baboule) in Haiti. The Congo—also somewhat of a generic title—is known in Haiti, Cuba, Martinique, and other islands, and the Cata, Counjaille, and Calinda are remembered in scattered areas throughout the Antilles.[1]

The term Counjaille, or Coonjine, is still used in southern United States waterfront areas to mean moving or loading cotton, an activity that once, in all probability, was accompanied by Counjaille-type songs and rhythms. Negro children on the docks and levies sang such songs as:

Throw me a nickel, throw me a dime
If you want to see me do the Coonjine.[2]

The Calinda dance had been reported in the West Indies by Moreau de St Méry in 1798,[3] almost a century before Cable's account, so we are assured of its relative antiquity. In Haiti today, the Calinda has a marked African character, while, in some other areas, it is thoroughly hybridized, or even rather European. Whether the Calinda was at its inception in the New World an African dance with an African name, or a European dance taken over in part and adapted by the slaves, or a European name attached to a number of dances traditional among the slaves is not clear. The fact that there was an old European dance by the name of Colinda, of Rumanian origin, does not help us much. Cajuns of the Louisiana Bayous still have a dance they call the Colinda.[4] Whether it originally came to them as the European Colinda or the Afro-American Calinda is not easy to decide.

The Juba mentioned by Cable was familiar throughout the Negro community in southern United States. In the West Indies— particularly in Haiti, Martinique, Guadaloupe, and other Creole-speaking islands—the Juba was, and remains, an African-type secular dance which is performed on certain special occasions, such as a festival following rites for a deceased person. References to the Juba in the United States sometimes are found in songs like this:

Juba jump, Juba sing,
Juba cut that pigeon wing.
Juba kick off this old shoe,
Juba dance that Jubilo.
Juba whirl them feet about,
Juba blow the candle out.
Juba swing, undo the latch,
Juba do that long dog scratch.[5]

If these words give any clue at all, it is that the Juba was at least on some occasions a kind of reel with a calling leader.

Despite Cable's apparent sympathy for, and romantic interest in, the African activities he witnessed in Congo Square in the 1880s, he vaguely echoed the moralistic views of his community on the dances and revealed his lack of awareness of tradition or meaning in them. His imaginative descriptions were obviously intended to titilate and to evoke images and visions of darkness:

"The ecstacy rises to madness; one—two—three of the dancers fall—*bloucoutoum! boum!*—with the foam on their lips and are dragged out by the arms and legs from under the tumultuous feet of crowding newcomers. The musicians know no fatigue; still the dance rages on. . . .

"It was a frightful triumph of body over mind, even in those early days when the slave was still a genuine pagan; but as his moral education gave him some hint of its enormity, and it became forbidden fruit monopolized by those of reprobate will, it grew everywhere more and more gross. . . ." [6]

Again:

"The contortions of the crowd were strange and terrible, the din was hideous. . . ." [7]

The architect Latrobe saw the dances at Congo Square during a visit to New Orleans in 1819. His reaction was fastidious and impatient:

"A man sung [*sic*] an uncouth song to the dancing which I suppose was in some African language, for it was not French, & the women screamed a detestable burthen on one single note. . . . I have never seen anything more brutally savage, and at the same time dull & stupid, than this whole exhibition." [8]

The dancing seen by Latrobe and Cable at opposite ends of the nineteenth century may have been secular, semi-religious, or religious. There is no clear indication by Latrobe as to exactly what he saw, and part of Cable's description seems to have been constructed out of hearsay and imagination. However, Cable obviously referred to ecstatic seizures or possessions in some of the dances, which would place them in the religious category. That there was a certain amount of what we would regard as uninhibited sexual motifs in some of the dances may be taken for granted. But that these postures and movements represented "abandon" or "orgy" to the participants is doubtful. Such motifs occur frequently in African and New World-African dancing and they are not regarded in their own settings as particularly libidinous. Often, in fact, they represent religious legend or depict the character of deities. In Latrobe's time, the Congo Square dancers were largely slaves—the lowest social class imaginable. It is understandable that their activities—weird and bizarre to the unaccustomed eye and ear—might appear debauched, particularly when measured against Western standards of propriety and the niceties of European music and dance. Cable saw them through a romantic haze, but could not altogether divest himself of the judgment of barbarity articulated by earlier observers. Errors of fact compounded errors of understanding. Cable referred both in articles and stories to the *candio,* which he identified as an African of royal blood. In actuality, the *candio* (pronounced *canzo* in Haiti and West Africa) was a member of an elevated level of the Vodoun cult. A person who was of *canzo* rank had passed through a fire ordeal and had thus risen above the level of the ordinary servitor. At least, Cable found the spectacles entrancing (though darkly savage), whereas Latrobe saw them as a personal affront.

New Orleans was not the only site where African style dancing was done. Certainly, it was part of the cultural inheritance of some Negro communities elsewhere in the deep South. The memory of it survived with older people of the Georgia-South Carolina coastal region still alive close to the halfway mark of the twentieth century,[9] and it would be difficult to believe that a hundred years ago some elements of these dances were not readily seen in Alabama and Mississippi as well.

Even in antebellum days, however, the Negroes were rapidly assimilating the values and social techniques of the white masters. They were appropriating the violin and other such instruments, and taking over the European reels and minuets. As social pressures against old-style African dancing increased, European dance forms were resorted to more and more, though often they became hybrid adaptations in which African concepts of music and dance motion persisted.

By the time that the easily-recognizable African forms had seemingly disappeared, the Negroes had produced new-style dances and new-style music which, if not strictly European, were certainly American. Often there persisted African elements which gave a special character to motion and motor responses, rhythm, and the relationship between sound and movement and between dancing and community purpose or meaning.

One particularly interesting example of hybridized but recognizable African survival is the ring shout, which until recent decades, at least, could be found in almost any rural area of the South. The shout is not, as the name might suggest, merely a loud vocalization of religious experience, but a religious or semi-religious activity combining music, devotion, and movement. It is a cluster of thinly disguised and diluted elements of West African religious practices. It may take place in the church, in some semi-religious setting such as the "praise house," or in the open.

In its customary form, the ring shout consists of a circle of people moving single file (usually counter-clockwise) around a central point, to the accompaniment of singing, stamping, and heel clicking. In some instances, the participants tap (in effect, drum) on the floor rhythmically with sticks to produce percussion effects. The steps are akin to a shuffle, with free foot movement prohibited, and little versatility permitted. Sometimes, the clearly defined single file circle gives way to a sort of amorphous crowd moving around a central point. The tempo may build up gradually, singing interspersed with exclamations characteristic of some other Negro church services, until it reaches a tense peak close to an ecstatic breaking point. At the high point of the excitement, such exclamations as "Oh Lord!" and "Yes, Lord!" turn into nonsense sounds and cries; seemingly wild emotional responses, they nevertheless are related to the music as a whole, and no notation which omits them can give a fair picture of what is heard.

The tension generated in the course of the shout has certain approved outlets, such as ecstatic seizures or possessions, but the feet are required to be kept under control. A person who violates this commonly understood proscription by "crossing his feet"—that is to say, by "dancing"—is admonished or evicted from the service. One elderly man described his own unfortunate experience this way: "Well, don't you know, them folks all shouting, rockin', and reelin', and me in the middle; and I ask you if it wasn't the Holy Ghost that come into me, who was it? Those feet of mine wouldn't stay on the ground in no manner, they jumped around and crossed over, back and forth, and the next thing I know they turned me out of the church."

The shout is a fusion of two seemingly irreconcilable attitudes toward religious behavior. In most of Africa, dance, like singing and drumming, is an integral part of supplication. Not all religious rites in West Africa include dancing, but most of them do; certainly at some stage of supplication dancing plays an essential role. Among West Africans, dancing in combination with other elements is regarded as a form of appeal to supernatural forces, and this tradition remains alive in New World African cults in Haiti, Jamaica, Trinidad, and other West Indian islands.[10] In the Euro-Christian tradition, however, dancing in church is generally regarded as a profane act. The ring shout in the United States provides a scheme which reconciles both principles. The circular movement, shuffling steps, and stamping conform to African traditions of supplication, while by definition this activity is not recognized as a "dance." However, if one violates the compromise by going too far, he has committed an irreverent act.

Anyone who sees a ring shout performed by older people is impressed by the motion patterns. Postures and gestures, the manner of standing, the bent knees, the feet flat on the floor or ground, the way the arms are held out for balance or pressed against the sides, the movements of the shoulders, all are African in conception and derivation. Some of the photographs published by Lydia Parrish in her book on the music of the Sea Islands, as well as her descriptions, reveal the extent to which some of the African dance motifs have been retained.[11] They show also that among the children most, if not all, of these motifs have disappeared. For the older people of the Sea Islands, there was a continuity of relatively undisturbed tradition once the original accommodation had been made between Euro-Christian and African elements. But the outer world has pressed in on the younger generations, and, although life has not changed as rapidly in the islands as it has in the towns and cities, the more archaic traditions are slipping away into the past.

It appears that emphasis on the more dramatic aspects of the ring shout by many writers has tended to obscure its essential meanings. While it is dance (contrary to the premise of the participants), it is not dance brought into religious activity from the secular world, either as a manifestation of revolt against the strictness of Christian concepts or as a means of retaining a pleasurable profane institution in disguise. When a congregation sings, "I'm going to shout all over God's Heaven," the allusion is not to disturbing the peace but to devotional activity including singing, rhythmic sound, patterned movement, and intense emotional expression—elements traditionally associated with worship.

Some of the choreographic aspects (as well as the sounds) of the shout are similar to those of the Revivalist cults of Jamaica, where, also, traditional elements are present. George E. Simpson describes a religious service in Kingston in a way that leaves little doubt of the similarity:

"Halfway through the service the leader may begin to circle counterclockwise the altar, or a table inside the church, or the 'seal' in the yard outside the church. The officers and leading members of the church, often up to twenty people, fall in behind him as all of them 'labor in the spirit.' . . . This 'spiritual' dancing is believed to increase the religious understanding of the participants."[12] As in the shouts, ecstatic seizures or possessions take place. The Jamaican revivalists have overlaid and disguised the African elements in their worship, and hold themselves aloof from the so-called African cults such as the Cumina. Nevertheless, they form a bridge between the ring shout in the United States and the openly acknowledged African-style cult activities of the West Indies and, of course, Africa itself.

Songs used in the shout are of various kinds, some of them clearly religious in content, others drawing largely upon secular experience and imagery but given religious character by interpolations, responses, and underlying attitudes. As with other Negro songs, the statement or idea may be tangent or metaphoric. As the tempo and the emotions heighten, words may be improvised. Some of these songs are reputed to last more than an hour (some observers said as long as three hours), and the words may dissolve into expletives and unrecognizable syllables. Sometimes a second singing leader moves in to relieve the exhausted starting leader. Different leaders employ different styles. Some use a kind of rhythmic preaching style, some a kind of semi-musical call, and others "sing" in the usual sense of the term.

One of the most exciting recorded examples of a ring shout is "Run Old Jeremiah" (Example 24), recorded by John and Alan Lomax in Louisiana in 1934 for the Library of Congress. The recording obviously begins long after the shout is under way and ends before the shouters have finished. This example has an over-

EXAMPLE 24

all character more "African" than many known African performances. Hand clapping and heel stamping produce powerful, driving rhythmic effects, with the short vocal responses sometimes tending more toward musical sounds than words. The words of "Run Old Jeremiah" are partly narrative and partly dramatic sound, with apparent improvisation as the singer strives to maintain his command of the situation, and repetition as he poises himself for a new thought or line. Part way through, a second leader takes over. Early in the recording, the responsive part consists of the words "Good Lord," sung in a growl-like timbre. A little later, as the fervor and tempo increase, the words are replaced by less intelligible sounds, with slight pitch variations. These change briefly to moan-like sounds, and, shortly after the second leader has replaced the first, the chorus responds with a bark-like "Yeah!" This again changes, with the mounting tension, to groans and high-pitched or falsetto yells and yelps. This is the text, minus only the responsive sounds:

Good Lord, by myself. (×5)
You know I've got to go.
You got to run.
I've got to run.
You got to run.
By myself. (×3)
I got a letter. (×2)
Ol' brownskin.
Tell you what she say.
"Leavin' tomorrow,
Tell you goodbye."
Oh my Lordy. (×6)
Well well well. (×2)
Oh my Lord. (×2)
Oh my Lordy. (×2)
Well well well. (×2)
I've got a rock.
You got a rock.
Rock is death.
Oh my Lordy.
Oh my Lord.
Well well well.
Run here Jeremiah. (×2)
I must go.

On my way (×4)
Who's that ridin' the chariot? (×2)
Well well well.

(Second leader takes over)
One mornin'
Before the evening
Sun was going down (×3)
Behind them western hills. (×3)
Old Number Twelve
Comin' down the track. (×3)
See that black smoke.
See that old engineer. (×2)
Tol' that old fireman
Ring his old bell
With his hand.
Rung his engine bell. (×2)
Well well well. (×2)
Jesus tell the man,
Say, I got your life
In my hand.
I got your life
In my hand. (×2)
Well well well.
Ol' fireman told
Told that engineer
Ring your black bell
Ding ding ding.
Ding ding ding ding.
Ol' fireman say
. . .ᵇ
That mornin'.
Well well well. (×2)
Ol' fireman say,
Well well,
I'm gonna grab my
Old whistle too.
Wah wah ho!
Wah wah wah wah ho!
Wah wah ho!
Wah wah wah ho!
(Etc.)
Mmmmmmmmmmmmm.

ᵇ Three lines of lyrics are indistinguishable in recording.

Soon soon soon.
Wah oh!
Well well well.
Ol' engineer,
I've got your life
In my hands. (×2)
Told your father. (×2)
Well well well.
I was travellin', (×2)
I was ridin' (×3)
Over there. (×2)
Ol' engineer.
This is the chariot. (×2)
Etc.

Dancing of the religious or semi-religious kind appears to have been known up to the turn of the century elsewhere than in the church or praise house. Recollections of numerous older people, documented in the 1930s, indicate that dancing was done at harvest festivals, and that something that at least approximated dancing occurred at funerals. There were of course the funeral processions to the beating of drums—out of which, probably, developed the brass band funeral processions of New Orleans—and, it seems, circle dances at the burial site. As one informant described it, "Everybody march round the grave in a circle and shout and pray." [13] Another person recalled: "When the body is put in the grave, everybody shout around the grave in a circle, singing and praying." [14] If there remains any doubt that the "shouting" was in reality dancing, it can be put to rest by the testimony of an informant on Saint Simons Island: "We dance around in a circle and then we dances for prayin'." And again: "They go in a long procession to the buryin' ground, and they beat the drums along the way and submit the body to the ground. Then they dance round in a ring and they motion with the hands." [15]

Old secular dances known or remembered by name along the east coast are many. Among them are such image-laden titles as the Buzzard Lope, Juba, Mobile Buck, Mosquito Dance, Ball the Jack, Snake Hip, Fish Tail, Fish Bone, Camel Walk, and Come Down to the Mire.[16]

The Buzzard Lope as seen in the Sea Islands by Parrish is an animal mimicry dance with obvious connections to African tradition, and to animal mimicry dances of the West Indies, such as the Malfini (the Hawk) of Haiti. The Sea Islands Buzzard Lope is a solo performance which takes place in the center of a ring of people who clap or pat out a rhythmic accompaniment. One person lies down on the ground inside the circle to represent a dead cow, and the dancer moves around him impersonating the scavenger buzzard. A caller sings out the directions to the dancer:

> March aroun'!
> Jump across!
> Get the eye!
> So glad!
> Get the guts!
> Go to eatin'!
> All right! Cow mos' gone!
> Dog comin'!
> Scare the dog!
> Look aroun' for more meat!
> All right! Belly full!
> Goin' to tell the rest! [17]

Some elderly informants recalled that the Buzzard Lope was a favorite dance at the harvest festivals.[18]

The dance Down to the Mire was described by one informant this way: "We dance round and shake the hand and fiddle the feet. One of us kneel down in the middle of the circle. Then we all call out and rise and shout around, and we all fling the foot again." [19] Parrish identifies Down to the Mire as a ring shout activity: "In the center of the ring, one member gets down on his knees and, with head touching the floor, rotates with the group as it moves around the circle. The different shouters, as they pass, push the head 'down to the mire.' " The song accompanying this dance-play was in call and response pattern:

> Sister Emma, oh you mus' come down to de mire. (×2)
> Jesus been down *to de mire* (×2)
> You must bow low *to de mire* (×2)
> Honor Jesus *to de mire* (×2)
> Lower, lower, *to de mire* (×3)
> Jesus been down *to de mire.*
> Sister Josie, etc.[20]

It is possible to add to the dances already mentioned a long list of names, such as Cake Walk, Turkey Strut, Turkey Trot, Swamp

Shimmy, Texas Twist, Georgia Crawl, Eagle Rock, Shuffle, Sukey Jump, Bunny Hug, Walkin' the Dog, and so on. Some of these names, such as Turkey Strut, Shuffle, Twist, etc., are descriptive, referring to steps, postures, and motifs; in their original settings, they probably were not the names of dances as such but rather the names of particular elements of the dance. Any dance might have contained struts, twists, and shuffles. It is of some interest that a number of the motifs thus described (shimmy, crawl, shuffle, strut, and jump, for example) are drawn from Negro and not European tradition. In them, one can see concepts of posture and motion which are related, even if distantly, to those of the African dancer. This observer has seen secular dances in South Africa, Ghana, and Nigeria in which certain passages occurred which were virtually indistinguishable from what in this country go by the name of Cake Walk, Shuffle, and Strut.

In ante-bellum days, the New World Negro slaves must have observed a great many Old World social dances in the homes of the white masters. In the West Indies, slaves were already dancing their own versions of the Minuet, Quadrille, and Mazurka long before their day of freedom, often to music made by African-type instruments, but commonly with violin accompaniment. Remnants of many of these old European dances still survive in isolated regions of Haiti which have little contact with the coastal cities; their presence in these remote spots suggests antiquity rather than recent influence. In the United States, the Negro slaves, particularly those employed around the "big houses," must have witnessed many gala social gatherings of the whites and absorbed a good deal from them, both of manners and ballroom steps. It probably did not take very long for the dances of the salon to travel from the master's house to the slave quarters. In a city like New Orleans, there were numerous free Negroes and mulattoes who held their own social events in the Creole style. Even in the rustic back country, white settlers had their simple barn dances. If we consider the speed with which modern dance crazes can sweep over a large area, or even the manner in which European continental dances made their way from one capital to another, we may surmise safely that the dances popular among the white masters in America had been adopted, in some form or other, by the slaves long before African-style dances had become obsolete. One investi-

gator, Willis James, holds, however, that the square dance that we
know today did not become truly popular among Negroes until
fairly late in the nineteenth century—that is, until some time after
the Civil War.[21]

Based on traditional European steps and figures, the square
dances and reels, as danced by Negroes, still had something in
them carried over from Negro country dances. Movements and
postures characteristic of the Mobile Buck and the Cake Walk,
while subdued, tempered, and disguised, were doubtless present,
just as they are in certain dances of our own time. Negro set callers,
many of them professionals, brought to the square dances an element of spontaneity and improvision characteristic of Negro secular music in general, along with an imagery and idiom that made
the calls unique. Speaking of these callers, Willis James notes:

"There were scores of Negroes throughout the South who
achieved lasting reputations as 'set callers.' In fact, their popularity
rose to such heights that they were in many cases professionals,
being paid a fee to bring color and entertainment to the dance.
They invented an entirely new system of 'callin' sets.' As they
would call the figures, frequently they would dance very original
solo steps and give out their calls in a musical phrase pattern." [22]

Often a set caller had his own unique, fun-inspiring calls, reminiscent more of Negro playparty songs than of the American
frontier's "do-si-do." One call went:

If you like the way she look
Hand the lady your pocketbook.
Swing her fancy,
Come to the middle,
But be careful, don't bust the fiddle.[23]

Another call, anticipating radio and television commercials by
three-quarters of a century, was this one:

Sody water fine
Wid de cakes just brown.
Better buy your gal some
'Fore she put you down.
Lemonade cool
And de glasses tall.
You better buy your gal some
'Fore de others get it all.[24]

XI. Instruments: Drums, Gutbuckets, and Horns

PEOPLE LONG AGO EXPLORED and exploited most of the principles of sound-making utilized in the musical instruments of today. Every so often a newly devised instrument comes along, but, with few exceptions, such devices are improvisations on, or adaptations of, instruments used for centuries or millennia. Certain forms or versions of these instruments are peculiar to certain regions of the earth, and, because of our knowledge of their whereabouts, we are able to follow the migrations of musical cultures. The distribution of the bagpipe, for example, gives us some notion of the path by which this instrument penetrated into southern and western Europe from the Middle East. But musical concepts may travel on their own, without musical instruments. And a migrant instrument does not necessarily take with it the musical conceptions of any specific culture. Thus the music played on a bagpipe in Ireland or Scotland is quite different from that played on bagpipes in Serbia, except, perhaps, to people who recoil at the sound of all bagpipes. On the other hand, except for the drum, no known

African instruments are to be found in Jamaica today, but Jamaican "digging" songs or worksongs still retain the character of African singing. Yet, wherever the instruments or musical conceptions of one specific culture are found in another, one may, ordinarily, assume there has been some kind of cultural continuity or influence.

Folk music instruments in the United States are largely of the simpler kind. This does not necessarily mean that they are "primitive." A rustic homemade fiddle, even with a single string, is only a variation of an instrument with a sophisticated history. Instruments employed in Negro folk music, as we have defined it, include forms that are well developed and others that are elemental. But elemental instruments do not, in themselves, mean elemental music. Wood-block percussion devices are certainly "primitive" in a historic sense, but they are commonly used in symphony orchestras. If we happen to think of brass horns and trumpets as a category of highly developed instruments to which the African was exposed in America during colonial days, it is worth remembering that horns and trumpets of many kinds were widespread in Africa before the first slave cargoes sailed to the New World.

The components that go to make up any musical tradition are many. It is not only musical scales and rhythm that are involved but also sound in a basic sense. It would appear that the range of instruments in a particular community is delimited in part, at least, by traditional concepts of what sounds are appropriate to music. In the West Indies and parts of Latin America, for example, scraping or scratching sounds are regarded as musical, and scraping instruments made of gourds, calabashes, bones, and burros' jawbones are commonly seen. In United States Negro folk music, certain sound qualities are valued, and as in other cultures, instruments capable of producing those sounds have precedence over others, regardless of whether they are "primitive" or highly developed.

It has been customary to regard various Negro folk instruments as makeshift devices inspired by irrepressible instincts to bang or twang on something. This easy view is far from reality. Virtually every device used by the Negro in his folk music had its origin in European or African tradition, and very little was invented in the

United States. What did happen is that substitutes were found for traditional instruments not easy, or impossible, to obtain. In this sense, the folk musician was "inventive."

A typical itinerant Negro street band, as seen almost anywhere in the South and in large urban communities of the North, might be equipped with such devices as frying pans, lard tins, a washboard, a washtub bass, a harmonica, a kazoo, a guitar, and clacking sticks or bones. As makeshift as these instruments may seem, they are anything but haphazard. Certain specific sound qualities are demanded of each piece of "hardware." There is a standard of what is a good sound and what is a bad one which can only be explained by the existence of a tradition.

The washtub bass—known also as a tub, sometimes as a gutbucket —is used to provide the bass tones for the group. It is an inverted washtub (or an appropriate substitute), to the center of which is attached a cord; the other end of the cord is attached to a broomstick, the free end of which is braced against the lip of the inverted tub so that the string is taut. Plucking or slapping the string produces a musical tone, with the tub acting as a resonating chamber. Pressure against the stick varies the tautness of the cord and produces different tones. The tub player usually stands with one foot on its edge to keep it firmly on the ground. Sometimes a second player beats a rhythm on the metal "drum head."

This instrument is an improvisation only in the sense that available modern materials have been adapted to an old use. The ancestor of the washtub bass is found not only in West and Central Africa but also in Afro-American communities in the West Indies. The African device was an apparent development of the spring snare, used for capturing small game. In its more primitive form, the resulting instrument was an earth bow, constructed in the following manner. A hole was dug in the earth next to a small green sapling, or a green stick was imbedded in the ground next to the hole. The hole was then covered with a bark or hide membrane, which was pegged down at the edges. The sapling was bent over the hole and fastened by a cord to the center of the membrane covering. The taut cord was played by rubbing, plucking, and tapping, and a second player sometimes beat a rhythm on the membrane with sticks. A portable variant used a wooden box instead of a hole in the ground for a resonating chamber. Both of these forms have survived in Haiti, with pails or large tins substituting for the wooden box.

The morphology of the American washtub bass leaves little doubt of its African ancestry. Not only is the basic structure of the instrument noteworthy, so is its manner of playing, which is virtually identical with the African technique. Add to this the frequently seen second player beating on the drumhead with sticks, and it is very difficult indeed to conclude anything but that the "makeshift" tub is in reality an instrument with a long history.[1]

The emergence of the double bass viol in jazz band settings as a slapping and plucking instrument is in the view of this writer an associated musical phenomenon. The method of playing on the strings is closely related to that of playing the tub, and the instrument has the same role in relation to the other instruments —that of providing varying bass tones. The plucking of the bass viol and the cello is certainly nothing new, but the concept of the bass viol as an instrument which is not bowed at all is not in the European tradition.

The washboard companion piece to the washtub is sometimes held by the arm, sometimes mounted on a standing frame. It is played by scraping its surface with a wire, a nail, a thimble, or with the bare finger. When the finger is used, tone variations are produced by using the fingernail and the soft part of the finger at will. As noted earlier, scraping instruments are found everywhere in New World Negro cultures. Different forms of the scraper are found in Cuba, Haiti, Jamaica, Martinique, Puerto Rico, and on the South American mainland. The Cuban *guiro* is a notched gourd which is scraped with a piece of wire or bamboo. In that country and elsewhere in the Caribbean, the jawbone of a donkey is sometimes used for the same purpose, the scraping tool being drawn over the teeth. The jawbone device has also been reported in the United States.[2] In the Bahamas, an iron object such as a nail is drawn along the teeth of a saw. Haiti's most common scraping instrument is a kitchen grater or piece of perforated sheet metal scraped with a wire. The idea of scraping devices, so widespread in Negro America, is undoubtedly of African origin. Though scrapers were used by Indians in the Americas, there is no reason to assume that the Negro tradition is derived from that source.

Although the connection between the street band's steel frying pans and metal percussion devices that preceded them is not obvious, it is not difficult to detect that modern hardware is employed within the framework of a tradition. For one thing, frying pans and similar metal objects used as gongs or bells were known in the United States a century or more ago. Secondly, metal percussion is important in much West African music as well as in African cultures of the Caribbean and the South American mainland. Among peoples of the Guinea Coast, the Ivory Coast, and other West African regions, forged iron bells have been commonly used as an element of percussion accompaniment to singing. A single bell, played by striking with a stick or metal rod, might produce two or three distinct tones in the hand of a skillful player, and double—and even triple—bells were frequently used. Where bells were not available, bits of resonant metal were employed, and, in recent times, even bottles have been substituted.

The tradition of metal percussion devices has survived beyond dispute in Haiti, Cuba, other West Indian islands, and, among mainland Negro communities, in Brazil and Venezuela.[3] The classical African-style bell is found in Haiti, Brazil, and Cuba, and, in Cuba, there appears to have developed a wide variety of specially designed metal percussion devices designated by an apparently African name, *agogo*. The ordinary cowbell, stripped of its internal clapper, is used in the same manner by Cuban dance bands, and a set of mounted frying pans for percussion is known as *las sartenes*. Almost anywhere in the West Indies, the metal hoe blade may be used as a percussion instrument.

Negro music in the United States took a different turn from that of the West Indies, but the tradition of metal percussion survived in certain kinds of musical activities. Seen in this light, the frying pan, used singly or in groups of twos or threes, in combination with other instruments, can be considered a descendant of earlier instruments rather than as a makeshift sound-maker. Although the pitch of the pans may not be "true," the musician is nevertheless concerned with their tone qualities. In a small country store in eastern Alabama, I saw a man making a purchase of two iron frying pans for use as musical instruments. He took a great deal of time tapping them with his fingernail until he found two that satisfied him, to the evident amusement (and misunderstanding) of the storekeeper, who commented: "I don't know why they're always doing that. They seem to think you can tell how good a pan is by whacking it."

Small street bands, no less than the large brass bands that came to be so familiar in New Orleans and other cities, found the European cymbals and triangle very congenial to the kind of music they were making. The triangle percussion effects were not strange to the tradition. In the rural countryside, music makers had employed hoe blades, spring-teeth from harrows, and wagon clevises to produce the same effects.[4] Some of these devices produced sounds which closely approximated that of the African bell, and they certainly were not less effective than similar bell substitutes used by Africans. But the forged bell and its substitutes did not have the sonorous quality of the triangle and the cymbals whose tones linger in the air. It seems evident that this obvious fact was enough to induce the Negro musician to use the triangle and cymbals differently than he had used iron percussion. The lingering tones of these devices came to be employed as part of a general melange of effects rather than for a rhythmic background pulse or a figure embroidering upon basic drum patterns. Triangle percussion became popular not only in the Negro instrumental ensembles in the United States but in the West Indies as well. Triangles are used as essential musical devices in the Zion churches of Jamaica, for example, and as occasional instruments in Cuban country music.

Although cymbals were not commonly employed among a majority of African peoples south of the Sahara, they were, and are, well known in the region of the Western Sudan, Senegambia, and adjacent areas. Some itinerant dancers and entertainers in this region used cymbals exclusively. Forged cymbals, sometimes in double or quadruple form, have been observed as far north as Casa Blanca and as far east as Khartoum.[5] Strictly speaking, therefore, the cymbals were no more European than African and probably were not novel, at least in concept, to early Negro musicians in the United States.

Except in brass bands and jazz bands, and to a limited degree in skiffle bands, drumming has ceased to have the importance it once did in American Negro folk music. Remnants of the art are heard in the percussive motifs of one man bands and possibly in the virtuoso performances of jazz drummers, though the latter do not seem to this observer to be closely related to early Negro drum music in the United States. It is a little curious that the drum, usually regarded as the nucleus of West African instrumentation, has lost so much of its importance in folk music here. In the West Indies and South America, the drum, along with a host of other instruments of African inspiration, has survived in an important way to the present day.

The African-style drum and the gourd rattle persisted in the United States until approximately the end of the nineteenth century, along with traditional West African concepts with which they were associated. Both ceased to be significant in folk music as the old cultural concepts withered away. Testimony of elderly Negroes in the Sea Islands in the late 1930s indicates that African-style drums and rattles were used there for dances and rituals not more than fifty or sixty years ago. What is apparent is that these instruments persisted only while African-style dances were still danced, and African-derived custom still practiced. One informant recalled:

"When we was young we used to have big frolics and dance in a ring and shout to [the] drum. Sometimes we have rattle made out of a dry gourd and we rattle 'em and make good music." [6]

Another informant declared:

"We aint have what you call a proper dance today. We aint have much music in those days, but they used a drum to call the people together when they going to have games or meetings." [7]

An old Sea Islander declared he had heard of the custom of beating drums to give notice of a death:

"They always use to beat the drum or blow the horn when somebody die. They beat two licks on the drum, then they stop, then they beat three licks. When you beat that you know somebody done die." [8]

Made of hollowed logs in the African fashion, the drums also were used at wakes.

"There was three sizes of drums. There was the big barrel drum.

It was higher than it was across. Then there was the little drum from twelve to fifteen inches wide and about eighteen inches high. The other drum was the medium size, kind of between the other two. The big drum was the one they beat at the wake." [9]

Drums were also used in the funeral processions: "We beat a drum at the church and we beat a drum on the way to the graveyard to bury 'em. We walks in a long line moaning and we beats the drum all the way." [10]

As we have seen, the drums were often grouped in sets or families of three, as is common in West Africa, and as they are found today in African cults in Haiti, Cuba, Brazil, and elsewhere in Negro America. One informant remembered that the drums were made of hollow logs covered at one end by sheep hide, and that some of them were as tall as three feet. Drums used by the Sea Islanders appear to have been of the type on which pegs are used to fasten the skin heads, and also of the kind on which the heads are fastened by ropes and hoops, both widely known in Africa. In the town of Darien, it was recalled that a man in the community had been making drums "up to two years ago," [11] and, in Brownville, a man was found who still made them. [12]

That African drums and drumming were familiar in the New Orleans area late in the nineteenth century was attested by George Cable. [13] He described long drums hollowed from logs with sheepskin or goatskin heads, played in a horizontal position with the drummer sitting astride and using his heel on the skin as a damper. A second player sometimes played sticks on the body of the drum. Drumming of this type is still to be observed in Haiti, where it is employed for the Juba, Martinique, and Baboule dances, in the Virgin Islands for the Bamboula, and elsewhere in the Caribbean. [14]

Small finger drums, made of sections of gourds covered with sheepskin, also were reported to be used in African religious rites in Louisiana in the 1880s. [15]

Tambourines, of apparent European design (though of course known throughout the world), are now as they were in the nineteenth century extremely popular in the Sanctified churches and among religious street singers.

We have no reason to assume that drums, the core of African instrumentation, were not likewise known and used in the late nineteenth century in other areas between the Mississippi River and the Atlantic Coast. The writer saw the battered remains of a peg-type log drum in western Alabama in 1950, in a Negro cabin where it was being used as a storage receptacle for grain.

Thus, it is known that in relatively recent times the log drum, of African parentage, was used for a variety of purposes, as in West Africa: for calling and signaling, announcing a death, social dances, harvest rites, wakes, and funerals. This knowledge throws some light on the more recent employment of drums (and of music generally) for funerals; on the use of tambourines and other instruments in the Sanctified churches; and on the rhythmic essence of a wide assortment of Negro musical activities.

One of the few stringed instruments in the New World of almost certain African provenience is the banjo. Other African stringed devices in the Americas are the musical bow, in the form of a belly harp (known in Brazil under the name *birimbao*), and a form of the West African zither (known in Negro communities of Venezuela as the *carangano*).[16] An instrument seen by Latrobe in New Orleans in 1818 was described as "a stringed instrument which no doubt was imported from Africa. . . . On top of the rude fingerboard was the rude figure of a man in a sitting posture, and two pegs behind him to which the strings were fastened. The body was a calabash." [17] Competent sketches by this chronicler reveal the instrument to be a three-stringed lute (despite the reference to two pegs) with a bridge, and with a decorative motif clearly in African style. The body, as stated, was made from a section of calabash, and the open side was covered with some kind of membrane, probably skin. A small cut-out in the skin, beneath the strings, acted as a sound aperture. Although the instrument was equipped with a bridge and a skin membrane, its connections with the banjo are not readily apparent. If the latter device was not developed in the United States, it must have stemmed from another line of descent.

The banjo's existence in slave times among Negroes in the United States was documented by a number of nineteenth century observers, including Thomas Jefferson, who put it down as a *banjor;* [18] some accounts referred to it as a *banja*. It is worth noting, in passing, that in the West Indies the word *banza* was used for other types of stringed instruments.[19] The structure of the banjo as we know it today, with a skin stretched over an open rim or hoop, gives support to the probabilities of its African origin, inasmuch as a number of African instruments were made in this way. It is quite possible that the early Afro-American instrument makers used a small tambourine or finger drum for a body, adding to it a neck. Use of the bridge is not regarded as commonplace in African tradition, and some authorities have gone so far as to say it is completely alien to African Negro musical life. The banjo's bridge thus might well have occurred as a Western element adapted to a non-European instrument. Nevertheless, the bridge is found on various forms of the lyre in northeast Africa, on the single-string spike fiddles throughout North and East Africa, on other instruments of Islamic northwest Africa, and in rudimentary form in the West and Central African bamboo zithers. In addition, there is a kind of "reverse" bridge on some African plucked instruments, a cord which pulls the strings down toward the skin head instead of holding them away. The effect on the skin membrane, however, is similar. Whatever its genealogy, the banjo was widely known as an instrument for Negro secular music and for blackface minstrelsy. In the Georgia coastal area, it was played as accompaniment to ridicule or criticism songs directed against erring members of the community—an institution known locally as "putting on the banjo." [20] In his much-quoted article on Congo Square, Cable declared that the banjo was not the favorite musical instrument of Negroes in the region, the favored instrument being the fiddle. However, he said, in the African dances of New Orleans there was wanted "the dark inspiration . . . of the banjo's thump and strum." [21] The instrument was taken over widely by white folk musicians in the eastern mountain communities, where it was used for accompaniment to singing and dancing. In the Tennessee mountain region, the banjo has been reported in various forms, with from two to six strings, and some printed sources say as many as nine strings have been noted elsewhere.[22] Its appearance in jug bands and street bands, both white and Negro, was commonplace until fairly recent times.

Like the fiddle, the banjo used in rural folk music was often home made, constructed out of available materials. As a child in

Indiana, I saw Negro performers with banjos having skin heads mounted on hoops made of orangewood fruit crates. Even a cigar box or a metal basin was used for a banjo body. One blues singer from Tennessee acknowledged that the first such instrument he owned, made for him by an uncle, had for its body a round marshmallow tin and for its neck a crude board.[23] Such devices were not considered to be toys, however, but authentic instruments.

Negro banjo style does not appear to differ greatly from that of, for example, white musicians of the eastern mountains. There are various techniques of playing which have to do mainly with the way in which the strings are stroked or "picked." In general, the banjo is played in a fast, frenetic manner as an accompanying instrument, with emphasis on chords and melodic lines which support a vocal part. Frequently the player plays a short passage between stanzas of a song. On rare occasions, in the hands of gifted banjoists, the instrument can take on a fluid, concert-like quality which suggests classical guitar more than banjo picking. One such performer, Gus Cannon, played banjo passages that resembled in pitch, pattern, rhythm, and tempo the sounds produced on West African lutes.[24]

As noted by Cable and other early observers, the fiddle was once one of the most popular of all instruments in Negro folk music. Large numbers of old tunes that survive today are called fiddle tunes, even though not played on a fiddle, and, in many rural regions, informants testify that the fiddle was once the essential requirement for a good-time dance. Because they were associated with secular occasions, fiddles were in some straight laced communities associated with sinful activity and regarded as creations of the devil. Like the banjo, the fiddle appeared in various makeshift forms, often with a cigar box for a body, sometimes with two strings, or even one.

In recent times, the guitar has largely superseded the banjo as an instrument to accompany solo singing. It is probably the most popular stringed instrument employed in Negro folk music. As with the banjo, there are many playing styles and techniques. A number of blues singers, for example, favor fretting the strings with an object—perhaps a jackknife—which they slide up and down to create chords; this technique produces tones and effects reminiscent of Hawaiian guitar playing, especially when metal strings are used. Some performers, among them Huddie Ledbetter, found the twelve-string guitar most attractive. In more commercial settings, the electric guitar sometimes makes an appearance. Fortunately for folk music, it can be used only where electric power is readily available.

One of the instruments described by Cable in 1886 was the "marimba brett": "A single strand of wire ran lengthwise of a bit of wooden board, sometimes a shallow box of thin wood, some eight inches long by four or five in width, across which, under the wire, were several joints [i.e., strips] of reed. . . . The performer, sitting cross-legged, held the board in both hands and plucked the ends of the reeds with his thumb nails." [25] This device is easily recognized as the African *sansa* or *lukembe,* popularly termed a "thumb piano." It survived until recent years in something like its African form and size in Cuba.[26] In the Caribbean generally, however, the *sansa* grew eventually into the large sized *marimbula* (Haiti, Cuba) or rhumba box (Jamaica), which is employed today mainly for modern country social dancing, though also in combination with other instruments for rhumba-type music in the cities.[27] Although the small *marimba* described by Cable disappeared from the United States musical scene, the enlarged version, nourished in the Caribbean, has been taken in, along with Latin American dance music, by many United States Negro and white dance orchestras. In particular, the influx of Puerto Ricans and Cubans in recent decades has made the *marimbula* a familiar sight and sound in New York and other large cities.

A large variety of other musical instruments, some of only incidental consequence, are known to Negro folk music makers as well as white. Blowing jugs, popular in white mountain music, have been frequently observed in Negro street bands as well, where they are regarded as devices to produce bass tones. Usually, they are not found in combinations where some other kind of bass instrument—such as the washtub—is used.

The kazoo and harmonica (also called a mouth harp or simply a "harp") are widely employed by street performers, but they are also popular in rural settings. The simple buzzing effects of the kazoo make any singer an instrumentalist with a minimum of technique. Inventive improvements on the kazoo include large saxophone-like horns affixed to the end, as well as deep tin cans which, moved forward and back over the opening, produce acoustical and tonal variations.

The harmonica, more difficult to play well, is probably the most ubiquitous of Negro folk instruments. There is probably not a single large Negro work gang in the South in which some member does not carry a mouth harp. It is used not only for playing familiar airs and for supplementing instrumental combinations but also for reproducing mechanical and natural sounds. Harmonica virtuosos are able to play the sounds of animals—goats, sheep, cows, dogs, cats, chickens, and birds—and of crying babies, electric pumps and railroads. There are few experienced country Negro harmonica players who do not take pride in their railroad tunes, which reproduce the puff and surge of engines, the clacking of wheels over the track joints, and the locomotive's whistle. Each player gives the name of some railroad line or famous express train to his individual composition—Cannon Ball, Old Ninety-Nine, Yellow Dog, Southern Pacific, and so on. One popular exercise is the fox chase, in which the harmonica is called upon to imitate the panting and baying of the hounds, their yelps as they approach their quarry, and the fading of the sounds as the pack disappears in the distance. The fox chase motif has also been a favorite among white harmonica players.

In combination with other instruments, the harmonica is sometimes found in religious settings, such as the Sanctified church. Its sanction there—if sanction is needed—may well come from identification of the mouth harp with the harp of David. Several country people indicated that they thought the spiritual "I Got a Harp" referred to the harmonica.

Other musical devices used currently, or at least until recent times, in Negro folk music are the jew's harp, the quills, bone or wood clackers, and musical glasses. The clackers are a pair of flat sticks or bones held between the fingers of one hand, with one or two fingers between them. Skillful manipulation can produce a continuous staccato brittle clacking sound, with rhythmic variations as desired. The effect is similar to that of rapidly played castanets. Sometimes a pair of spoons is used in the same way.

The quills are elementary panpipes, usually made of reeds, though the name suggests that in early days in the United States the quills of large feathers may actually have been used. The various reeds are not joined, but are held together in the hand in playing position. From various reports that are available, it would appear that three or four reeds were used, with the player hooting an occasional tone beyond their range. A few recordings of quill music have been made, but on the whole it has been poorly documented.[28] George Cable included some quill tunes of his time in his "The Dance in Place Congo." One of these tunes, notated by Krehbiel, is shown in Example 25.[29] According to Cable's description, the notes on the staff are those of the quills, while the notes below it are hooted by the player.

EXAMPLE 25

The tuned musical glasses (technically called a harmonica though obviously having no connection with the mouth organ), known for some centuries in Europe, seem to have appealed to a number of Negro street musicians looking for novelty to attract an audience. A series of thin glasses, up to thirteen in number, and perhaps more, were tuned by partially filling them with water, the amount of water determining the pitch. When arranged in the proper sequence, the glasses could provide the approximate tones of an octave (or more) of the piano. They were played by tapping with two light sticks. "Musicianers" playing glasses were seen not infrequently in the larger cities, both North and South, only a generation or two ago.

One rather curious instrument reported in the South only a short while ago is the mouth-bow. It is curious in that it is a device of probable African origin, though played by non-Negroes who claim to have "invented" it. The mouth bow is simply a bowed piece of wood held between the teeth, played by plucking the string, with the mouth cavity acting as a sound chamber. Though a commonplace musical device in West and Central Africa, it has never been noted by observers as part of the Negro musical scene in the United States.[30]

It would perhaps be useful to take a quick look at a number of additional musical devices that were known to Negro musicians of an earlier day, but which are no longer used. In addition to the gourd rattle, already mentioned, the large calabash rattle with a network of external strikers, of African design, was reported early in the nineteenth century. Cable, in the 1880s, noted the presence of the "belt of bells," sometimes replaced by small tin vials of shot.[31] The belt of bells is readily recognizable as of African origin. Such belts are used in Cuba to this day in rites of the Lucumi (Yoruba) cult and the Abakwa (Ibo) secret society.[32] Cable further testified that wooden horns were played in New Orleans. In his early nineteenth-century account, Latrobe reported and sketched an instrument readily identified as a West African hand gong,[33] and he noted also the presence of a "square drum looking like a stool." [34] From his revealing sketch, one sees that the simile was accurate. Furthermore, the device closely resembles the square skin-covered stools which are sometimes used for drums in central Cuba. A square drum was reported in the Maroon country of Jamaica not long ago, used for Coromanti dances. The idea of the square drum almost certainly was of African origin, square drums having been found in Ghana and other parts of West Africa. In her *Journals,* written some years before the Civil War, Frances Kemble recorded that the conch shell trumpet was employed as a signal horn along the Georgia coast,[35] as it is today in Haiti and other West Indian islands and in coastal regions of Africa.

Virtually all of the European-derived musical instruments

known in popular American music have been utilized by Negro musicians—reeds, horns, plucked and bowed strings, piano, and so on. In some settings, they have helped to produce folk music; in others, they steered the music makers away from traditional forms. Few such instruments have failed to interest Negro music makers, but many of them have had only secondary importance in the development of what we mean by the term Negro folk music. Thus, some instruments of African derivation and some of European derivation have played a part in the shaping of the folk music of Negro America. Some instruments were shared with the non-Negro elements of the country. Since Negro music does have a character which distinguishes it from the mainstream, however, the presence of instruments of non-European beginnings must be taken into consideration in evaluating the forces that have gone into the creation of the American Negro musical idiom.

To better visualize the connections between the traditional musical instruments of the United States Negro community and the Negro communities of the Caribbean, we can juxtapose the comparisons in this fashion:

The United States	*West Indies*
Hollow log drums (until recent date); drums made of kegs; boxes and large tins used as drums; European style drums.	Hollow log drums; drums made of kegs; boxes and tins used as drums; European style drums.
Washtub bass (gutbucket).	Earthbow, and portable musical bow with large sound chamber.
Frying pans, cowbells, harrow teeth, clevises used as iron percussion, bottles used as substitute.	Frying pans, forged bells, gongs, hoe blades, etc., used as iron percussion, bottles used as substitute.
Washboards used as scrapers.	Scrapers made of wood, metal, and gourds; saws; and kitchen graters.
Banjo.	Banjo and earlier *banza*.
Blowing jugs.	Blowing jugs.
Wood or bone clappers ("bones").	Wood or bone clappers.
Tambourines.	Tambourines.
Fiddles.	Fiddles.

The United States (Cont.)	*West Indies* (Cont.)
Sansa or marimba, reported in New Orleans. West Indian marimbula returned to the United States with popular West Indian music.	Marimbula or rhumba box.
Gourd rattles, until recently.	Gourd rattles.
Calabash rattles (early nineteenth century) with external strikers.	Calabash rattles with external strikers.
Conch trumpets for signaling (nineteenth century).	Conch trumpets for signaling.
Kazoos.	Kazoos; singing horns.
Hand-gongs (reported in early literature) and contemporary substitutes such as wooden boxes.	Slit hand gongs and improvised substitutes.
Guitars.	Guitars; quatros; seis; mandolins.
European brass instruments in popular and religious music.	European brass instruments in popular and religious music.
Hand clapping.	Hand clapping.

From these and other examples, we can see that there have been European and African influences on the instrumental aspects of United States Negro and West Indian folk music, and that, at least at an early stage, these influences were similar in both areas.

The Music

1. Wake Up Jonah

Wake up Jo - nah, you are the man!__

Reel - in' and a - rock - in' o' the ship so long!__

Wake up Jo - nah, you are the man!__

Reel - in' and a - rock - in' o' the ship so long!__

Cap - tain of the ship got trou - ble in mind,__

Reel - in' and a - rock - in' o' the ship so long!__

Cap - tain of the ship got trou - ble in mind,__

Reel - in' and a - rock-in' o' the ship so long!__ Let's

go way down__ in the hull of the ship!__

Reel - in' and a - rock - in' o' the ship so long!__ Let's

2. Job, Job

J. B. B.

Oh Job__ Job,__ , [tell] me how you feel,__ good Lord,

[*Responsive:*] __ good Lord,__ oh what you reck-on good Lord,__

__ that old Job sup-plied,__ good Lord,

said I'm feel-in' good,__ good Lord,__

oh Job Job__ good Lord,__

tell me how you feel,__ good Lord,__

that Job sup-plied__ good Lord,__

I'm feel-in' bad,__ good Lord,__

well what you reck-on__ good Lord,__

old Job said,_____ good Lord,__

whilst I'm feel - in' bad,_____ good Lord,__

I can't sleep at night,____ good Lord,__

I can't eat a bite,____ good Lord,__

said the wom - an I love,____ good Lord,__

don't treat me right,____ good Lord,____ Oh

Rock Mount Zi - on, Rock Mount Zi - on, oh__

Rock Mount Zi - on in that mor - ning.____

3. Rock Chariot

4. Wonder Where Is My Brother Gone

Won-der where_____ is___ my bro - ther gone?

_____ Won-der where_____ is my___ bro-ther

John?_____ He is gone to the wil-der-ness,___ aint com-in' no more.

_____ Won -der where_____ will I___ lie down?

_____ Won- der where_____ will I lie

down?_____ In some lonesome_place Lord_down on_the ground.

_____ Won-der where_____ will __ I lie

down?_____ In some lone - some place Lord_

___ down___ on___ the ___ ground.___

5. This May Be Your Last Time

This may___ be your last time, this, may___ be your
last time, this, may___ be your last time,
may be your last time,___ I don't know. Sis - ter,
talk a - bout me much as you please,___
more you talk I'll bend my knees.___
May be your last___ time, I don't know. Sis - ter,
this may___ be your last time, this may be your
last___ time,___ this may___ be your last time,
may be your last time___ I don't know.___
Way down yon - der by Jor - dan___ stream,

hear God's chil-dren tryin' to   be   re - deemed.__

May   be   your   last   time,___   I don't know.__

Chorus

Meet Mis - ter Hy - po -crite___   on   the   street,_____

first   thing   he   show   you   his   tongue   in   his   cheek,

etc.

may   be   your   last   time,   I   don't   know.

6. Move, Members, Move

M. K.

Move   mem - bers   move Dan - iel!   Move   mem - bers

Dan - i - el!
move Dan - iel!   Move   mem-bers   move Dan-iel!___

simile

Move members move Daniel! (x4)
Move till I get {there / home} Daniel! (x4)
Got on my Little John shoes!
Got on my little John shoes Daniel! (x3)
Shoes gonna rocka me home Daniel! (x4)

Move members move!
Move members move Daniel! (x3)
Who want to buy this land Daniel? (x6)
Who want to buy this land?
Who want to buy this land Daniel? } (x3)
Move members move Daniel! (x2)
Move till I get {there / home} Daniel! (x2)
Move till I get there Daniel! (x4)
Move till I get home Daniel!
Got on my little John shoes!
Got on my little John shoes Daniel! } (x2)
Shoes gonna rocka me home Daniel! (x6)

7. Traveling Shoes

J. B. B.

♩ = 88

Death went out___ to the sin-ner's house,

come and___ go with me.___

Sin-ner cried out,___ I aint rea-dy to go,___ I aint

got no trav-lin' shoes.___ Got no trav-lin' shoes,___

got no trav-lin' shoes,___ sin-ner cried out,___ I aint

etc.

rea-dy to go,___ I aint got no trav-lin' shoes.___

8. It's Getting Late in the Evening

J. B. B.

Lord, it's get - tin' late over in the eve - nin',___

___ Lord it's get - in' late over in the

eve - - - nin',___

children___ it's get - in' late over in the eve - nin',

Lord it's get - in' late over in the eve ___

nin',___ the sun most down.___

Don't you seal up your book, John,___

don't you seal up your book, John,___

don't_seal_ up_ your book, John, ___

don't_you seal up your book, John,___

till   you   can   sign   my   name.___

Spir - it says seal up your — book, John, ————————

spir - it says seal up your — book, John, ————————

I want you to seal — up your book, — John, ——

——————— I want you to seal up your

book, John, ——————————— don't write — no ——

more. ——— Peo - ple, I just keep on — a

tell - in' you, ——————— we — just keep on a — a

tell - in' you, ——————————————

we just keeps on a — a tell - in' you, ——————

——— sin - ner I just keep on a ——

tell - in you ————————— it's a God some - where.

9. King David

$\quad$ = 96 $\qquad$ J. B. B.

King Da - vid was___ (good Lord___) that shep-herd boy___ (good Lord___). Did - n't he kill Go - li - ath (good Lord___), and he shout for joy___ (good Lord___). Well the tall - est tree___ (good Lord___) in Par - a - dise___ (good Lord___), them Christ - ians called it (good Lord___) their tree of life___ (good Lord___). Lit-tle Da- vid play__ on__ your harp, hal - le - lu___ (hal - le - lu___), lit-tle Da-vid play on ___ your harp, hal - le - lu. Didn't ___ you prom - ise to play on___ your harp, hal - le -

10. The Sun Will Never Go Down

Oh the sun___ will nev-er___ go___ down,___ go down, oh the sun___ will nev-er___ go down,___ go down.___ The flow-ers___ are bloom-in'___ for-ev-er___ more, then the sun___ will nev-er___ go down.

11. When You Feel Like Moaning

When you feel like__ moan-in', it aint noth-in' but love. Ah when you feel like moa-nin', that aint noth-in' but love.___ It must be the Ho-ly Gho-st com-in' down__ from a-bove.___ When you hear me pray-in',___

that aint noth-in' but love.   When you hear me

pray - in', ___   that aint noth-in' but love. ___

If you hear me pray - in', ___

that aint noth-in' but love. ___ That must ___ be the

Ho - ly Gho ___ st ___ com-in' down from a - bove.

Do you love ev - ery - bo - dy, ___

taint noth-in' but love. When you love ev-ery -bod -

___ y, ___ taint noth-in' but love. ___

When you love ev- ery - bo - dy, ___

taint noth-in' but love. ___ That must be the

etc.

Ho - ly Ghost ___   com- in' down from a-bove.

When you feel like moanin',
It ain't nothin' but love.
When you feel like moanin',
That ain't nothin' but love.
It must be the Holy Ghost
Comin' down from above.
When you hear me prayin',
That ain't nothin' but love.
When you hear me prayin',
It ain't nothin' but love.
If you hear me prayin',
That ain't nothin' but love.
That must be the Holy Ghost
Comin' down from above.
Do you love everybody,
Taint nothin' but love.
When you love everybody,
Taint nothin' but love.
That must be the Holy Ghost
Comin' down from above.
When you feel like groanin', $\left.\right\}$ (x3)
It ain't nothin' but love.
Children, that must be the Holy Ghost
Comin' down from above.
Do you love your preacher,
Taint nothin' but love.
When you love your preacher, $\left.\right\}$ (x2)
It ain't nothin' but love.
That must be the Holy Ghost
Comin' down from above.

12. Didn't You Hear

(II) Did - n't you____ hear them an - gels moan?____

Yes   I   heard   the   an - gels   moan.

Did - n't you____ hear them   an - gels moan?____

Yes   I   heard   the   an - gels   moan.

An - gels moan - in'   in   my   soul,____

an - gels   moan - in'   in   my   soul,____

an - gels moan - in'   in   my   soul,____

an - gels   moan - in'   in   my   soul.____

(III) Did - n't you____ hear them   tur - kle doves moan?

Yes   I   heard   the   tur - kle doves moan.

Did -n't   you____ hear them   tur - kle doves____ moan?__

Yes I heard the tur - kle doves moan.

Did- n't You____ hear the heav - en bells____ ring?__

Yes I heard the heav - en bells ring.

Tur - kle doves moan - in' in my soul,____

tur - kle doves moan - in' in my soul,____

tur - kle doves moan - in' in my soul,____

tur - kle doves moan - in' in my soul,____

tur - kle doves moan - in' in my soul,____

tur - kle doves moan - in' in my soul,____ the

an - gels moan - in' in my soul,____ the

an - gels moan - in' in my soul.____

13. My Name's Been Written Down

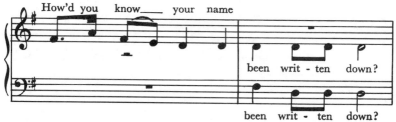

On the wall,—— oh, writ - ten / been writ - ten down? / been writ-ten down?——

On the wall,—— oh, been writ - ten / been writ - ten down? / On the wall —— / been writ -ten down?

(six similar measures, then :)
On the wall, / been writ - ten / been writ - ten down?——

On the wall, / etc. / been writ - ten down?

14. What Month Was Jesus Born in

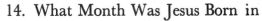

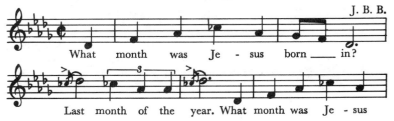

J. B. B.

What month was Je - sus born —— in?

Last month of the year. What month was Je - sus

born_____ in? Last_____ month of the

year._____ Oh Lord____ you got Jan - u - ar - y,_____

Feb - ru - a - ry,_____ March, oh Lo_____ rd. _____

_____ You got Ap - ril, May and June,__ Lord. You got the

Ju - ly, Aug - ust, Sep - tem - ber, Oc - to - ber and No -

vem - ber.____ You got the twen- ty fifth day of De-

cem - ber. It's the last month of the year.____

15. Noah, Noah

J. B. B.

No - ah, No - ah,____ who built____ this ark?____

No - ah, No - ah,_____ who built ___ this ark?__ Now who__

built__ this ark?____ No -ah, No -ah,____ built this ark,

built this ark out of_____ hick'-ry bark. Oh Lord,_

_____ who built_this ark?_____ No-ah, No-ah,_____ *etc.*

who built_this ark?_____ Who built_this ark?_____

16. Everywhere I Go My Lord

J. B. B.

Eve-ry-where I go, eve-ry-where I

go my Lord, eve-ry-where I go,

some-bod-y's talk-in' 'bout Je-sus. Well my

knees__ been a-quaint-ed with the hill-side clay,_____

some-bod-y's talk-in' 'bout Je-sus, and my

head's__ been wet with the mid-night dew,

some-bod-y's talk-in' 'bout Je-sus._____
(well sing__ it then__)

17. Israelites Shouting

Oh___ I won - der where___ is my sis - ter, she is gone a way to stay. She is hid - den be - hind God's al - tar,___ she'll be___ gone___ ___ till jud - ge - ment day.___ One born, the Is - rael - ites a - shout - in' in the, one born, the Is - rael - ites a - shout - in' in the, one born,___ the Is - rael - ites a - shout - in' in the, one born, the Is - rael - ites a - shout - in' in the, let's groan,__ the Is - rael - ites a - shout - in' in the, let's groan,__ the Is - rael - ites a - shout - in' in the,

um - hmm, — the Is - rael - ites a - shout - in' in the,

um - hmm, — the Is - rael - ites a - shout - in' in the.

Oh I won - der where — is my sis - ter, she's

gone a - way to stay. She's hid - den be - hind God's

al - tar, she'll be — gone till judge - ment day. —

— Good bye, the Is - rael - ites shout in' in the,

good bye, the Is - rael - ites a - shout - in' in the

hea - ven, good bye, the Is - rael - ites a - shout - in' in the

hea - ven, good bye, the Is - rael - ites a - shout - in' in the,

this day, the Is - rael - ites a - shout - in' in the

etc.

hea - ven, this day, the Is - rael - ites a - shout - in' in the

18. Let Me Ride

J. B. B.

Let   me ride___ (oh   let   me ride),   oh

let   me ride___ (let   me ride),   oh

let ___ me ride ___ (let   me ride),   oh

low down   the cha - ri - ot and   let   me ride.__ I'm

hum - ble   to ride___ (oh   let   me ride),   I'm

hum - ble to ride,___   let   me ride,___   oh

let___   me ri___ de.   (Let   me ride),   oh

low down   the char - i - ot and   let   me ride.___

19. Dark Was the Night

(3 times with variants)

20. When Jesus Met the Woman at the Well
(notation of second rendition)

♩ = 92 Orig.-1 st.

M. K.

When Je - sus met the wo - man at the well, oh,____ she went run - ning to tell.____ She said come and see a man ___ at the well,____ He told me ev' - ry thing____ that I done.____ She cried oh,____ oh,____ he must be____ a proph - et, she cried oh, oh,___ well, he must be____ a proph - et, she cried oh,____ well,____ he must (be) be a proph - et, He

etc.

told me ev' - ry thing____ that I done.____

21. Way Bye and Bye

♩ = 132 Orig. + 6 st.

M. K.

Way bye___ and bye.___ way bye___ and bye,___

w'e goin' a have a good time, ___ way bye___ and bye.___

Way bye and bye,___ way bye and bye,

w'ay bye and bye,___ way bye and bye,

w'e goin' a have a good time,___ way bye___ and bye.

Way bye and bye,___ way bye and bye,

etc.

we goin' a have a good time,___ way bye and bye.

4th and 5th stanza

(6th stanza)
Meet my moth'r ov'r there,

I'll meet my moth'r ov'r there. ___

etc.

we goin' a have a good time,___ way___ bye and bye.___

(Note opposition between b♮ (3d measure) and b♭ (last measure))

Way bye and bye,
Way bye and bye,
We goin' a have a good time } (x3)
Way bye and bye.

Way in Beulah Land,
Way in Beulah Land,
We goin'a have a good time
Way bye and bye.

Meet my mother over there,
Meet my mother ever there,
We goin'a have a good time
Way bye and bye.

(In next stanza, one voice sings
words of first stanza, while
other voice sings as follows)

Oh oh-o,
Oh ay-y,
Oh Lord,
Oh oh.

(Etc. with variations, then later)

Oh one mornin' soon,
One mornin' soon,
We goin' a have a good time
Way bye and bye.

22. Precious Lord, Take My Hand

M. K.

Note opposition between 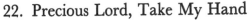 and between ... and ...

23. I'm Crossing Jordan River

Note opposition between

Well I'm crossing
Jordan River,
Lord I want my crown,
Lord I want my crown.

Oh when I'm crossing
Jordan River
I want my crown,
Lord I want my crown.

Jordan River
Chilly and cold,
The love of Jesus
Is in my soul.

Oh when I'm crossing
Jordan River,
Lord I want my crown,
Well I want my crown.

Oh when I'm crossing
Crossing Jordan River,
Lord I want my crown,
Lord I want my crown.

Oh when I'm crossing
Crossing over Jordan,
Lord I want my crown.

Well well, Jordan River
Chilly and cold,
Love of Jesus
Is in my soul.

Oh when I'm crossing
Hey, Jordan,
I want my crown,
Lord I want my crown.

I had a hard time,
Hard time crossing Jordan,
Lord I want my crown,
Well I want my crown.

I had a hard time,
Hey, hey,
I want my crown,
Lord God.

Jordan River
Deep and wide,
None can cross
But the sanctified.

Etc.

24. Russia, Let That Moon Alone
(last section)

Get out on___ your knees and pray and
let God's moon a-lone.___ The moon ain't wor-ryin'
you, the moon ain't wor-ryin' you. God
put the moon up there to give you light by night, Oh
-let God's moon a-lone,___ the moon ain't wor-ryin'
you then let that moon a-lone,___ the
moon won't wor-ry you Oh Rus-sia, get out on___ your
knees and pray, let that moon a-lone.___

Note opposition between b ♮ and b ♭

25. Long John
(fourth stanza)

26. Rosie

♩ = 76 ◁ 80 Orig. pitch + 8 st.

M. K.

Solo
Be my wo-man, gal,— I'll— be your— man.

Solo
Be my wo-man, gal, I'll— be your— man.

Solo
Be my— wo-man, gal, I'll— be your— man.—

— Ev' - ry Sun - day's dol - lar— in your hand,—

— in your hand, Lor-dy,— in your— hand,—

— ev' - ry Sun-day's dol - lar in your— hand.

— Stick to the pro - mise,— gal, that— you made me.

Stick to the pro - mise,— gal, that— you made me.

Stick to the pro - mise,— gal, that— you made me.

Weren't gon - na mar - ry till— a — I go free,

I go— free, Lor - dy,——— I go free,

weren't gon - na mar - ry till— a — I go free.

Well——— Ro - sie O Lord, gal,

ah——— Ro - sie — O Lord, gal.

27. She Done Got Ugly

Says huh Ju - lie,——— hul-lo gal.— Says

huh Ju - lie,——— hul - lo gal.— Says

ear - ly in the mor - nin' ba - by,— half past four.—

Says ear - ly in the mor - nin' ba - by,— oh

half past four.— I come to your win - dow

ba - by, knocked on the door.— Says get

28. Captain Holler Hurry

The Cap-tain hol-ler hur-ry,_____ goin' to take my time._____ Say the Cap-tain hol-ler hur-ry,_____ goin' to take my time.____ Say he mak-in' mon-ey____ and I'm tryin' to make time. Say he can lose his job____ but I can't lose mine.____ I ain't got long to tar-ry,_____ just stop by here.____ I ain't got long to tar-ry,____ just stop by here.____ Boys if___ you got___ long_____ you bet-ter move a-long.____

Say Cap-tain hol-ler hur-ry,_____

_____ I'm goin' to take my time._____ Say the

Cap-tain hol-ler hur-ry,_____

_____ I'm goin' to take my time.____ Say he__ mak-in'

mon-ey,___ and I'm tryin' to make time._____

29. Black Woman

♩ = 108   J. B. B.

Well I said come here__ Black Wo-man,____ Ah-

hmm!   Ah-hmm!   don't you

hear me cryin' oh__ Lor-dy!_____   Ah,-

hmm,   I say run here Black Wo-man____

I want you to sit on Black Dad-dy's____

knee, Lord!   Ah-hmm,   I know your

bis - cuit rol -ler done ___ gone! _____   I'm

goin' to Tex - as Mam - ma, just to hear the wild ___ ox

moan, Lord help my cry - in' time I'm goin' to Tex - as ___

___ Mam - ma do you hear the wild ox moan!

And if they moan to suit me, I'm goin' to

bring a wild ___ ox ___ home! Ah - hmm, I say I've

got to go to Tex - as Black Mam- ma, ah

hmm, I know I hear me cry - in', oh ___

Lor - dy! _____ Ah hmm I've got to

go to Tex- as Black ___ Mam-ma, ___ etc.

ah just to hear the white cow ___ I say moan! ___

30. Motherless Children

♩ = 192 Orig. pitch + 2 st.

Second stanza   **3**   M. K.

Well eh____ well,____   ah.____

3

Well,____ some peo - ple say that____ sis - ter will

do,____   when moth - er is dead,____

that sis - ter will do when____ moth - er is dead.

Some peo - ple say that____   sis - ter will

do, but as soon as she's mar - ried she'll turn

her back on you.____   No bo - dy treat you like

moth - er will.____   Eh,   fa - ther will

do the best he can.____   when moth - er is

31. I'm Going Uptown

I'm goin' up-town____ have a talk____ with the chief po - lice,____ how my good girl in trou - ble____ and I can not____ see____ no peace.____ Don't I love you ba - by, and I just____ can't____ take____ your place,____ don't I love you ba - by, and I tell you that____ I do.____ I ____ hope____ some day____ ba - by come____ to love____ me too,____ and I hope____ some day____ ba - by come____ to____ love____ me____ too.____ I ____

went___ to the ri - ver and I looked___ it___

up___ and down,_____ thought I'd see my

good girl when she walk ___ in' cross the___

town,_____ I ___ tell___ my

ba ___ by why___ she come___ back

home,___ and I had___ no ___

lov ___ in'___ babe___ since ___ you been

gone.___

32. Careless Love

♩. = 104   M. K.

Love, ___ oh love___ oh___ care - less

love. Can't you see what

can love___ do_____ to me?_____

You___ made____ me roam,____

made me lose my_____ hap - py home,

it was love,_____ oh love,

oh care - less love.___

33. Look Down

♩ = 152 Orig.-3 st.   M. K.

Look down, look down that lone - some

road___ be - fore you car - ry

on. Euh,___ look down look

down___ that lone ___ some road be -

etc.

fore you car ___ ry on.

34. Meet Me in the Bottoms

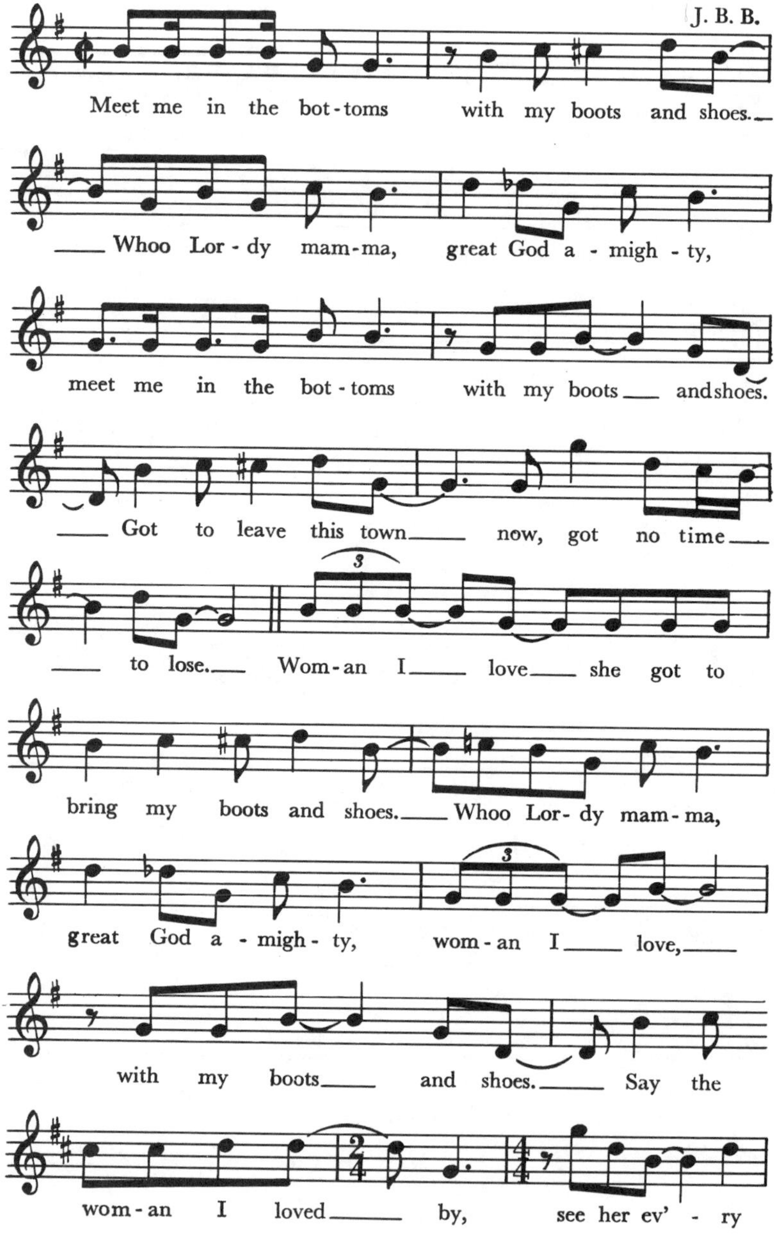

day.___ Wom - an I___ love___ she got

long black cur - ly hair.___ Whoo Lor - dy mam - ma,

great God a - migh - ty, the wom - an I___ love___

got long black cur - ly hair.___ Say the wom-an I hate,

___ I see___ her ev' ___ ry day.___

35. Old Lady Sally Wants to Jump

Handclaps throughout   ♩ = 176   J. B. B.

Old la - dy Sal - ly wants to jump - ty jump,___

jump - ty jump,___ jump - ty jump,___ old la - dy

Sal - ly wants to jump - ty jump,___ and old la - dy

Sal - ly wants to bow. Throw that hook___ in the

mid -dle of the **pond,** catch that girl___ with the red - dress on. Go on gal,___ aint you a shame?___ Shamed of what?___ Wear - ing your dress in the lat - est style.___ Man - y fish - es in the brook, **Pa** - pa caught 'em with a hook. Mam - ma fried 'em in a pan, ba- by eat 'em like a man. Preach- er in the pul - pit, preach - ing like a man, trying to get to Heav - en on a 'lec - tric -fan. ___ Do your best **Pa** - pa **Dad** - dy do your best.

36. Green Green Rocky Road

Green, green, rock-y road, some la-dy's green rock-y road. Tell___ me who you love,___ rock-y road, tell___ me who you love, rock-y road. Min-nie Town.

Dear Miss Min-nie your name's been called, come take a seat be-side the wall, give her a kiss and let her go,___ she'll nev-er sit in that chair no more.___

37. Little Sally Walker

Little Sal - ly Walk - er   sit - tin' in a sauc - er

cry - in' for the old man to come for the dol - lar.

Ride Sal - ly ride, put your hands on your hips,

——— ah let your back - bone slip, ah

shake it to the east, ah shake it to the west, ah

shake it to the ve - ry one you love the best.

38. Just Watch That Lady

I been all a - round my last_____ time,

last_____ time, last_____ time, I been all a -

round my last_____ time, young la - dy hold the

key. Just watch that la - dy how she hold the

key,_____ just watch that la - dy how she hold the

key,_____ young la - dy hold the key, I

39. Mary Mack

Handclaps ♩ = 84 *throughout* J. B. B.

Oh Ma - ry, Mack Mack Mack,_____ all

dressed in black black black,_____ with sil - ver but -

tons but - tons but - tons, up and down her back

back back._____ And I love cof - fee

cof - fee cof - fee, and I love tea tea tea,_____

etc.

_____ and the boys love me me me_____ I

40. John Henry
(Version I)

she came a-scream-in' and a-cry-in' that day,___

come a-walk-in' down___ to that rail-road track.___

The Cap-tain sup-plied___ to the wo-man,___ Said___ tell me wom-an what's

troublin'___ your mind.___ Says I'm go-in' where my

man fell___ dead, says I'm go-in' where my

man fell___ dead, says I'm go-in' where my

man fell___ dead, says I'm go-in' where my

man___ fell___ dead. He done ham-me red his

fool self to death,___ he done

ham-mered his fool self to death.

41. John Henry
(Version II)

J. B. B.

John Hen - ry went up on the moun - tain,___ and he looked down and heaved a___ sigh, said the moun - tain was___ so___ big___ and wide,___ John___ Hen - ry___ was___ so___ small, un - til he fell on his knees___ and he cried and he cried,___ said he fell on his knees___ and he cried. He said___ Cap - tain, Cap - tain,___ you don't know, but the last ham - mer I___ had,___ be -

42. John Henry
(Version III)

♩ = 96⟵100 Orig. — 6 st.

M. K.

Take this ham - mer and car - ry't to the cap - tain, tell him I'm gone, tell him I'm gone, tell him I'm___ gone. — Take this ham - mer___ and car - ry't to my cap - tain, Tell him I'm___ gone, You tell him I'm gone, I'm sure he is gone.

Take this hammer and carry it to the captain,
Tell him I'm gone,
Tell him I'm gone,
Tell him I'm gone.
Take this hammer and carry it to the captain,
Tell him I'm gone,
You tell him I'm gone,
I'm sure he is gone.

This is the hammer that killed John Henry,
But it won't kill me,
But it won't kill me,
But it won't kill me.
This is the hammer that killed John Henry,
But it won't kill me,
But it won't kill me,
Aint goin' kill me.

It's a long way from East Colorado,
But it's to my home,
But it's to my home,
But it's to my home.
It's a long ways to East Colorado,
But it's to my home,
But it's to my home,
That's where I'm goin'.

John Henry left this hammer
Layin' side the road,
Layin' side the road,
Layin' side the road.
John Henry he left his hammer
All over in the rain,
All over in the rain,
That's why I'm gone.

John Henry's a steel-drivin' boy,
But he went down,
But he went down,
But he went down.
John Henry was a steel-drivin' boy,
But he went down,
But he went down,
That's why I'm gone.

43. Old John Booker

♩ = 168 Orig. + 5 st. (2d stanza increasing until ♩ = 192)   M. K.

Old___ John Boo-ker, call that gone?___

Old___ John Boo-ker, call___that gone? Old___

___ John Boo-ker, call that___ gone?___

·Um,___ now old John Boo-ker, call that

gone? Old___ John Boo-ker, call that gone?

Old___ John Boo-ker call that gone?

I'm go-ing down to Ca.-li-forn'

falsetto

Ah, hah, hah, eee, hee, hah, hah,

hah, hah, .hee, hah, hee, hee.

with variations·

Old___ John___ Boo-ker he feel like this.

Notes

I. THE SETTING

1. Melville J. Herskovits, *The Myth of the Negro Past*, New York, 1941.
2. *Ibid.*, pp. 146–47.
3. *Ibid.*, p. 147. Herskovits, at that time, was not aware of the mortar's existence outside of the Sea Islands. Subsequently it was reported in Alabama and elsewhere.
4. Lydia Parrish, *Slave Songs of the Georgia Sea Islands*, photo plates 7 and 8.
5. Herskovits, *op. cit.*, pp. 150–51. 6. *Ibid.*, pp. 161–67.
7. Guy B. Johnson, "St. Helena Songs and Stories," in T. J. Woofter, Jr., *Black Yeomanry, Life on St. Helena Island*, p. 49.
8. Herskovits, *op. cit.*, p. 276. 9. *Ibid.*, pp. 191–92.
10. *Ibid.*, p. 291.
11. The Uncle Remus books of Joel Chandler Harris offer a rich repertoire of U.S. Negro folk tales, among which are a large number with West African precedents. See also Richard M. Dorson, *American Folklore;* Courlander, *Terrapin's Pot of Sense;* and various issues of the *Journal of American Folklore.*
12. See Courlander, *The Drum and the Hoe*, pp. 69–71; and Herskovits, *op. cit.*, p. 233.
13. Robert Tallant, *Voodoo in New Orleans*, pp. 223–24; Herskovits, *op. cit.*, pp. 236, 250.
14. For examples of Cajun folk music, see record album, *Cajun Songs from Louisiana*, Ethnic Folkways Library, FE 4438.
15. Herzog, "African Influences in North American Indian Music," paper read at International Congress of Musicology, New York, 1939. Published 1944.
16. See Courlander, "Abakwa Meeting in Guanabacoa," *Journal of Negro History*, October, 1944.

II. NEGRO FOLK MUSIC IN THE UNITED STATES

1. See *The Oxford Companion to Music,* Oxford University Press, London and New York, 1938, p. 973.

2. *Afro-American Folksongs,* New York, 1914.

3. G. B. Johnson, "St Helena Songs and Stories," in T. J. Woofter, Jr., *Black Yeomanry, Life on St. Helena Island,* pp. 67–73.

4. Richard A. Waterman, "African Influences on the Music of the Americas," in *Acculturation in the Americas,* edited by Sol Tax, p. 208.

5. *Ibid.,* p. 209.   6. Marshall Stearns, *The Story of Jazz,* p. 7.

7. *Ibid.*   8. Stated in conversation with the author.

9. Stearns, *op. cit.,* p. 278.

10. Stated in conversation with the author.

11. Correspondence with the author.

12. From Courlander, *Negro Songs from Alabama,* pp. 20–23.

13. From the recording *Negro Prison Songs,* recorded by Alan Lomax, Tradition Records TLP 1020.

14. Leonard Feather, *The Book of Jazz,* p. 152.

15. See the recording *Folk Music of Haiti,* recorded by the author, Ethnic Folkways Library FE 4407, side I, band 2, "M'pas Bwè M'pas Mangé."

16. John Jacob Niles.

17. Introduction by George Eaton Simpson to the recording *Cult Music of Jamaica,* Ethnic Folkways Library FE 4461.

18. Introduction to the recording *Prison Camp Work Songs,* recorded by Peter Seeger and others, Ethnic Folkways Library FE 4475.

19. Notes in introduction to the record album *Tribal, Folk and Café Music of West Africa,* recorded by Arthur S. Alberts.

20. "Characteristics of African Music," *Journal of the International Folk Music Council,* Vol. XI, 1959, p. 15.

21. Stearns, *op. cit.,* p. 282.   22. Correspondence with the author.

23. Correspondence with the author.

24. From an unpublished manuscript, "Can Jazz Be Defined?"

III. ANTHEMS AND SPIRITUALS AS ORAL LITERATURE

1. "Little Black Train," Library of Congress recording no. 1394. A musical notation of this song appears in Lomax and Lomax, *Our Singing Country.*

2. Lydia Parrish, *Slave Songs of the Georgia Sea Islands*, p. 188.

3. See Irwin Silber, *Songs of the Civil War*, p. 270.

4. There undoubtedly were some songs which served the slaves in their efforts to escape. For example, "Follow the Drinking Gourd" is thought to have been a kind of oral map leading out of slave territory. The "drinking gourd" presumably was the Big Dipper, by which one readily locates the North Star:

When the sun comes back and the first quail calls,
Follow the drinking gourd.
For the old man is waiting for to carry you to freedom
If you follow the drinking gourd.

The river bank will make a very good road,
The dead trees show you the way.
Left foot, peg foot, travelling on,
Follow the drinking gourd.

These and other stanzas are found in Silber, *ibid.*, pp. 278–80. Making due allowance for rearrangements that may have been made in the lyrics since the song was first sung, a careful reading nevertheless gives the impression that the song is not couched in traditional Negro images or vernacular and that the entire effect is literary and contrived. The legend attributed to it says, in fact, that it was taught to the slaves by a peg-leg ex-sailor who wandered around the countryside telling them how to escape to the North.

5. Parrish, *op. cit.*, p. 86, states that this song was used in the Georgia Sea Islands as a ring shout tune. Another version appears in Lomax and Lomax, *op. cit.*, pp. 4–5.

6. Parrish, *op. cit.*, p. 134.

7. Library of Congress recording no. 2659. A similar version with some additional stanzas is to be found in the Folkways album, *Blind Willie Johnson*, FG 3585. See also Lomax and Lomax, *op. cit.*, pp. 6–8.

8. This prose introduction and the song that follows were recorded by Courlander in Alabama in 1950. The story and song, as recorded, may be heard in Ethnic Folkways Library album FE 4418, *Negro Folk Music of Alabama, Religious.*

9. Saxon, Dreyer, and Tallant, *Gumbo Ya-Ya*, p. 470.

10. Sung by the Rev. Moses Mason. Originally recorded by Paramount, no. 12702A, reissued by Folkways on no. FA 2952, *American Folk Music*, Vol. II.

11. Library of Congress recording no. 1335. See Lomax and Lomax, *op. cit.*, pp. 16–21.

12. Parrish, *op. cit.*, p. 139.

13. As sung by Blind Willie Johnson, originally recorded on Colum-

bia label in 1930. Reissued by Folkways in album *American Folk Music,* Vol. II, no. FA 2952.

14. Library of Congress recording no. 1026. See also Lomax and Lomax, *op. cit.*

15. Recorded by Thomas J. Price, Jr. Text taken from Folkways record no. FW 8811.

16. Sung by Cat Iron, recorded by Frederic Ramsey, Jr. There are other stanzas to this song which are not given here. Text taken from Folkways recording no. FA 2389.

17. Saxon, Dreyer, and Tallant, *op cit.,* pp. 476–77.

18. Library of Congress recording no. 188.

19. Sung by William and Versey Smith, "When that Great Ship Went Down," with tambourine, washboard. Text from Folkways Records FA 2951. Original issue Paramount 125058.

20. Recorded by Frederic Ramsey, Jr. *Leadbelly's Last Sessions, Vol. I,* Folkways Records FA 2941.

IV. CRIES, CALLS, WHOOPING, AND HOLLERING

1. Informants: Rich Amerson and Sarah Amerson of Halsel, Alabama; Earthy Anne Coleman of Livingston, Alabama; Rev. M. J. Glover and Simon Agree of Bogue Chitto, Alabama; and others.

2. Frederick Olmsted, "Journey in the Seaboard Slave States," in *The Slave States before the Civil War,* edited by Harvey Wish, pp. 114–15.

3. Willis James, "The Romance of the Negro Folk Cry in America," in *Phylon,* First Quarter, 1955, p. 16.

4. Given by Enoch Brown, Livingston, Alabama, recorded in 1950 by the author.

5. Annie Grace Horn Dodson, Sumter County, Alabama. Her father was Josh Horn, born a slave, who took the name of the plantation owner, Ike Horn. The three field calls that follow the reference were given by Mrs. Dodson and recorded by the author in 1950. They can be heard on the Ethnic Folkways Library album FE 4417, *Negro Folk Music of Alabama, Vol. I.*

6. Rev. J. Camps, in booklet introducing the record album, *The Topoke People of the Congo,* Ethnic Folkways Library FE 4477, p. 6.

7. Given by Annie Grace Horn Dodson, recorded by the author in 1950. May be heard in Ethnic Folkways Library FE 4417, *Negro Folk Music of Alabama, Vol. I.*

8. Given by Mrs. Dodson, as above. May be heard in Ethnic Folkways Library album FE 4474, *Negro Folk Music of Alabama*, Vol. VI.

9. Disc Record No. 3001-A.

V. SOUNDS OF WORK

1. See *Folk Music of Jamaica*, recordings made by Edward Seaga, Ethnic Folkways Library FE 4453, side I, bands 5 and 6; "Haiti Worksong," recorded by Harold Courlander, in *Negro Folk Music of Africa and America*, Ethnic Folkways Library FE 4500, band 13; *Folk Music of Liberia*, recordings made by Packard L. Oakie, Ethnic Folkways Library FE 4465, side I, band 2; and *Folk Music of the Western Congo*, recordings made by Leo A. Verwilghen, Ethnic Folkways Library FE 4427, side I, band 2.

2. See for example the record album *Folk Music of Jamaica, op. cit.*, bands 5–8 of side I.

3. From the introduction to the record album, *Negro Prison Camp Work Songs*, recorded by Peter Seeger and others, Ethnic Folkways Library FE 4475.

4. Disc record 3001-A, as sung by Leadbelly.

5. See: *Negro Prison Songs*, recorded by Alan Lomax, Tradition Records; *Negro Prison Camp Work Songs, op. cit.*; and various Library of Congress record issues.

6. Introductory notes to *Negro Prison Songs, op. cit.*

7. From the record album *Negro Prison Camp Work Songs, op. cit.*

8. *Ibid.*   9. *Ibid.*   10. *Ibid.*

11. From a tape recorded by Peter Seeger and others in Texas.

12. From *Negro Prison Camp Work Songs, op. cit.*

13. Recorded by the author in Mississippi.

14. Guy B. Johnson, *John Henry: Tracking Down a Negro Legend*, pp. 142–46.

15. Roark Bradford, *John Henry*, p. 1ff.

16. Lydia Parrish, *Slave Songs of the Georgia Sea Islands*, p. 225.

17. *Ibid.*, p. 225.   18. *Ibid.*, p. 226.   19. *Ibid.*, p. 234.

20. *Ibid.*, p. 236.

21. Howard Odum and Guy B. Johnson, *Negro Workaday Songs*, p. 117.

22. See *If He Asks You Was I Laughin'*, privately pressed recordings made by Tony Schwartz, manufactured by Legend Recordings, Inc.

23. *Journal of a Residence on a Georgia Plantation*, p. 127.

24. *Ibid.*, pp. 127–28.   25. *Ibid.*, p. 218.   26. *Ibid.*, p. 219.
27. *Ibid.*, p. 219.
28. Lafcadio Hearn, "American Sketches," in *Selected Writings of Lafcadio Hearn*, edited by Henry Goodman, pp. 218–19.
29. *Ibid.*, p. 224ff.   30. *Ibid.*, p. 218.
31. From *The Music of New Orleans*, recorded by Sam Charters, Folkways FA 2461.

VI. BLUES

1. Leadbelly, *Take This Hammer*, Folkways FA 2004.
2. *The Blues, with Studs Terkel Interviewing Big Bill Broonzy, Sonny Terry, and Brownie McGhee*, Folkways 3817.
3. *Angola Prisoners' Blues*, recorded by Harry Oster and Richard Allen, issued by Louisiana Folklore Society.
4. Leonard Feather, *The Book of Jazz*, p. 149.
5. Introduction to the record album *Jazz, Vol. II*, Folkways FJ 2802.
6. *Calypso and Meringues*, Folkways FW 6808.
7. Recorded by the author in Alabama, 1950.
8. *Calypso and Meringues, op. cit.*
9. *Sonny Terry's Washboard Band*, Folkways FA 2006.
10. From Lafcadio Hearn's "American Sketches" in *The Selected Writings of Lafcadio Hearn*, p. 224.
11. Recorded by the author in Alabama, 1950.
12. *Sonny Terry's Washboard Band, op. cit.*
13. *Ibid.*   14. *Ibid.*
15. Recorded in Alabama by the author. For a version on records, see *Snooks Eaglin*, Folkways FA 2476.
16. Recorded by the author in Alabama, 1950.   17. *Ibid.*
18. *Snooks Eaglin, op. cit.*   19. *Ibid.*
20. Recorded in Alabama by the author, 1950.
21. See Library of Congress record no. 13-A-1, recorded by John and Alan Lomax in Texas. See also "Lost John" in Chap. V, pp. 101–3.
22. Text as sung by Sam Lightnin' Hopkins, Folkways FS 3822, except for substitution of the words "this poor boy" for Hopkins' name. The insertion by a singer of his name into a song appears to be a latter day device for putting one's brand on a song that may have originated elsewhere.
23. As transcribed from the album *Angola Prisoners' Blues, op. cit.*
24. Recorded in Alabama by the author, 1950.

25. As sung by Brownie McGhee, Folkways FA 2030.

26. Recorded by the author in Alabama, 1950.

27. See *Big Bill Blues*, Cassel, London, 1955, p. 56; and *Big Bill Broonzy Interviewed by Studs Terkel*, Folkways FG 3586.

28. Broonzy, Folkways, *ibid.*

29. *Snooks Eaglin, op. cit.*

30. *Snooks Eaglin, op. cit.*

31. See RBF label No. 1, *Country Blues.*

32. Recorded by the author in Alabama, 1950. Blind Lemon Jefferson's rendition, called "See That My Grave Is Kept Clean," was originally issued on Paramount 126088, reissued on Folkways FA 2953.

33. *Negro Prison Camp Worksongs*, Ethnic Folkways Library FE 4475.

34. Columbia label 14303 (145320). Reissued in Ethnic Folkways Library FE 4530.

35. As sung by Bascom Lunsford, recorded by Ralph Auf der Heide, Ethnic Folkways Library FE 4530.

VII. RING GAMES AND PLAYPARTY SONGS

1. Folkways, *Street Songs and Games*, FC 7003.   2. *Ibid.*

3. Courlander, *The Drum and the Hoe*, p. 188.

4. *Ibid.*, pp. 186–87.

5. Recorded by the author in Alabama, 1950.

6. Library of Congress record AAFS-20A.

7. Howard Odum and Guy B. Johnson, *Negro Workaday Songs*, p. 180.

VIII. LOUISIANA CREOLE SONGS

1. Lucie de Vienne in introduction to the record album *Cajun Songs from Louisiana*, Ethnic Folkways Library FE 4438.

2. George Cable, *Creoles and Cajuns*, pp. 384–85. This section originally appeared in the *Century Magazine* in February, 1886, under the title, "The Dance in Place Congo." Translation revised by the author.

3. Courlander, *Haiti Singing*, University of North Carolina Press, Chapel Hill, 1939, p. 176. Melody appears as example 126 following

p. 183. See also Folkways album FW 6811, *Haitian Folk Songs*, sung by Lolita Cuevas.

4. Sung by Snooks Eaglin, Folkways FA 2476.

5. Cable, *op. cit.*, p. 389. Translation revised by the author.

6. *Ibid.*, pp. 420–21. Translation revised by the author.

7. *Ibid.*, pp. 418–19. Translation revised by the author.

8. *Ibid.*, p. 430. Translation by the author.

9. Saxon, Dreyer, and Tallant, *Gumbo Ya-Ya*, p. 435.

10. See Courlander, *The Drum and the Hoe*, p. 152.

11. *Ibid.*, pp. 151–52.

12. Translated by the author from *Creole Songs from New Orleans In the Negro Dialect*, by C. G. Peterson, Gruenwald Publishers, 1902.

13. May be heard in the album *Folk Music of Haiti*, recorded by the author, Ethnic Folkways Library FE 4403.

14. A Haitian version with an almost identical melody can be heard on Folkways FW 6811.

15. See Alcée Fortier, *Louisiana Folk-Tales*.

16. Recorded by Harry Oster.

17. Saxon, Dreyer, and Tallant, *op. cit.*

18. Folkways record FA 2461.

IX. PERFORMERS' CORNER: BALLADS AND MINSTRELSY

1. Recorded by the author in Alabama.

2. Odum and Johnson, *Negro Workaday Songs*, pp. 50–51.

3. A somewhat composite version based largely on that of Mississippi John Hurt, originally recorded in 1928, Okeh Record 8560 (w400221), reissued on Folkways FA 2951.

4. As sung by Mississippi John Hurt, Victor 21664 A and B, reissued on Folkways FA 2951.

X. DANCES: CALINDAS, BUZZARD LOPES, AND REELS

1. See Courlander, *The Drum and the Hoe*, p. 126ff.

2. *Ibid.*, p. 352.   3. Moreau de Saint-Méry, *De la danse*.

4. See "Allons Danser Colinda," Side I, Band 6, of the record album *Cajun Songs from Louisiana*, recorded by I. Bonstein, Ethnic Folkways Library FE 4438.

5. A slightly different version of this verse appears in W. C. Handy's

book, *Blues: An Anthology*. Note that each line of the song describes a dance figure.

6. George Cable, *Creoles and Cajuns*, p. 378. This portion of the book originally appeared in the *Century Magazine* in February, 1886, under the title, "The Dance in Place Congo."

7. *Ibid.*, p. 388.

8. Latrobe, *Impressions Respecting New Orleans*, p. 51.

9. See Georgia Writers' Project, *Drums and Shadows*.

10. See Courlander, *The Drum and the Hoe*, p. 130.

11. Lydia Parrish, *Slave Songs of the Georgia Sea Islands*, plates 22, 23, 24, facing pages 128, 129, and 144.

12. George E. Simpson, introduction to the record album, *Jamaican Cult Music*, Ethnic Folkways Library FE 4461.

13. *Drums and Shadows*, p. 127.

14. *Ibid.*, p. 141.   15. *Ibid.*, p. 180.

16. Parrish, *op. cit.*, pp. 13–14; *Drums and Shadows*, *op. cit.*, p. 115.

17. Parrish, *op. cit.*, p. 110.

18. *Drums and Shadows*, pp. 131, 174, 179.

19. *Ibid.*, p. 141.   20. Parrish, *op. cit.*, p. 71.

21. Willis James, "The Romance of the Negro Folk Cry in America," *Phylon*, first quarter, 1955, p. 18.

22. *Ibid.*, p. 18.   23. *Ibid.*, p. 18.   24. *Ibid.*, p. 18.

XI. INSTRUMENTS: DRUMS, GUTBUCKETS, AND HORNS

1. See Courlander, introduction to record albums *Negro Folk Music of Alabama*, Ethnic Folkways Library, 1956, pp. 6–7; introduction to the record *Sonny Terry's Washboard Band*, Folkways FA 2006; and Courlander *The Drum and the Hoe*, pp. 199–201, and illustrations 79, 80, 81.

2. Lydia Parrish, *Slave Songs of the Georgia Sea Islands*, p. 16.

3. See Fernando Ortiz, *Los Instrumentos de la Música Afrocubana*, Vol. II, illustrations on pp. 203–5, 207–9, 212–13, 238ff.; Courlander, "Musical Instruments of Cuba," p. 230; Courlander, *The Drum and the Hoe*, plate 45.

4. See Parrish, *op. cit.*, p. 16.

5. Observed by the author, 1942–44.

6. *Drums and Shadows*, *op. cit.*, p. 176.

7. *Ibid.*, p. 174.   8. *Ibid.*, p. 155.   9. *Ibid.*, p. 155.

10. *Ibid.*, pp. 149–50.   11. *Ibid.*, p. 148.   12. *Ibid.*, p. 62.

13. George W. Cable, "The Dance in Place Congo," in *Creoles and Cajuns*, pp. 369ff.

14. See Courlander, introduction to the record album *African and Afro-American Drums*, Ethnic Folkways Library FE 4502.

15. George W. Cable, "Creole Slave Songs," in *Creoles and Cajuns*, p. 426.

16. Juan Liscano, *Folklore y Cultura*, plates 15 and 16 following p. 103.

17. B. H. B. Latrobe, *Impressions Respecting New Orleans*, pp. 49–51.

18. Thomas Jefferson, *Notes on the State of Virginia*, p. 19.

19. Courlander, *The Drum and the Hoe*, pp. 128, 202.

20. *Drums and Shadows*, p. 154.

21. Cable, "The Dance in Place Congo," in *Creoles and Cajuns*, p. 370.

22. Percy A. Scholes, *The Oxford Companion to Music*, 1938 edition, p. 73.

23. Brownie McGhee quoted by Charles Edward Smith in introduction to Folkways record album FA 2030.

24. See "Old John Booker" as sung by Gus Cannon in Folkways album FA 2610; and performance on *halam* in Ethnic Folkways Library album FE 4461, *Wolof Music of Senegal and the Gambia*.

25. Cable, "The Dance in Place Congo," in *Creoles and Cajuns*, pp. 369–70.

26. Courlander, "Musical Instruments of Cuba," p. 239 and plate IV facing p. 239.

27. Courlander, *The Drum and the Hoe*, p. 201 and photos 83 and 85; and George Simpson's introduction to the record album *Cult Music of Jamaica*, Ethnic Folkways Library FE 4461.

28. See record album *Sounds of the South*, recorded by Alan Lomax, Atlantic 1346.

29. Cable, "The Dance in Place Congo," in *Creoles and Cajuns*, p. 371.

30. See record album *Sounds of the South*, op. cit.

31. Cable, "The Dance in Place Congo," in *Creoles and Cajuns*, p. 378.

32. See Courlander, "Musical Instruments of Cuba," p. 234 and plate XI facing p. 229; also "Abakwa Meeting in Guanabacoa," *Journal of Negro History*, Vol. XXIX, 1944, p. 466.

33. Latrobe, *op. cit.*, pp. 49–50.

34. *Ibid.*, pp. 49–51.   35. Kemble, *op. cit.*, p. 159.

Bibliography

Allen, William F., C. P. Ware, and L. M. Garrison. Slave Songs of The United States. New York, Simpson, 1867.

Asbury, Herbert. The French Quarter. New York, Knopf, 1936.

Ashe, Thomas. Travels in America. New York, 1811.

Botkin, Benjamin. Lay My Burden Down. Chicago, University of Chicago Press, 1945.

Bradford, Roark. John Henry. New York, Harpers, 1931.

Cable, George W. Creoles and Cajuns. Edited by Arlin Turner. New York, Doubleday, 1959.

—— "The Dance in Place Congo," Century Magazine, February, 1886.

Chase, Gilbert. America's Music. New York, McGraw-Hill, 1955.

—— America's Music from the Pilgrims to the Present. New York, McGraw-Hill, 1958.

Checklist of Recorded Songs in the English Language in the Archive of American Folk Song. 2 vols., A–K and L–Z. Washington, Library of Congress, Music Division, 1942.

Courlander, Harold. "Abakwa Meeting in Guanabacoa," Journal of Negro History, October, 1944.

—— The Drum and the Hoe—Life and Lore of the Haitian People. Berkeley, University of California Press, 1960.

—— Haiti Singing. Chapel Hill, University of North Carolina Press, 1939.

—— Introduction to the record albums, Negro Folk Music of Alabama, Ethnic Folkways Library FE 4417, etc.

—— "Musical Instruments of Cuba," Musical Quarterly, April, 1942.

—— "Musical Instruments of Haiti," Musical Quarterly, July, 1941.

—— Negro Songs from Alabama. Published on a grant by the Wenner-Gren Foundation for Anthropological Research, New York, 1960.

—— Terrapin's Pot of Sense. New York, Holt, 1957.

Doerflinger, William M. Shantymen and Shantyboys: Songs of the Sailor and Lumberman. New York, Macmillan, 1951.

Dorson, Richard M. American Folklore. Chicago, University of Chicago Press, 1959.

Feather, Leonard. The Book of Jazz. New York, Meridian, 1959.

Fortier, Alcée. Louisiana Folk-Tales. Memoirs of the American Folk-Lore Society, Vol. II, New York and Boston, Stechert, 1895.

Gayarre, Charles. History of Louisiana. New York, Widdleton, 1867.

Georgia Writers' Project. Drums and Shadows. Athens, University of Georgia Press, 1940.

Greenway, John. American Folk Songs of Protest. Philadelphia, University of Pennsylvania Press, 1953.

Handy, W. C. Blues: An Anthology. New York, Boni, 1926.

Handy, W. C., and Abbe Niles. A Treasury of the Blues. New York, Boni, 1949.

Hearn, Lafcadio. Selected Writings. Edited by Henry Goodman. New York, Citadel, 1949.

Herskovits, Melville J. The Myth of the Negro Past. New York, Harpers, 1941.

Jackson, George P. White and Negro Spirituals. New York, Augustin, 1943.

James, Willis. "The Romance of the Negro Folk Cry in America," Phylon, first quarter, 1955.

Jefferson, Thomas. Notes on the State of Virginia. Philadelphia, 1803.

Johnson, Guy B. John Henry: Tracking Down a Negro Legend. Chapel Hill, University of North Carolina Press, 1929.

—— "St. Helena Songs and Stories," in T. J. Woofter, Jr., Black Yeomanry, Life on St. Helena Island. New York, Holt, 1930.

Kemble, Frances Anne. Journal of a Residence on a Georgia Plantation. New York, Harpers, 1863.

Krehbiel, H. E. Afro-American Folksongs. New York, Schirmer, 1914.

Latrobe, B. H. B. Impressions Respecting New Orleans. Edited by Samuel Wilson, Jr. New York, Columbia University Press, 1951.

Lawless, Ray M. Folksingers and Folksongs in America. New York, Duell, Sloan, and Pierce, 1960.

Liscano, Juan. Folklore y Cultura. Caracas (no date).

Lomax, John A., and Alan Lomax. Folk Songs: U.S.A. New York, Duell, Sloan, and Pierce, 1947.

—— Our Singing Country. New York, Macmillan, 1941.

Lyell, Sir Charles. A Second Visit to the United States of North America. London, 1849.

Merriam, Alan. "Characteristics of African Music," Journal of the International Folk Music Council, Vol. XI, 1959.

Odum, H. W. Social and Musical Traits of the American Negro. New York, Columbia University Press, 1910.

Odum, Howard, and Guy B. Johnson. Negro Workaday Songs. Chapel Hill, University of North Carolina Press, 1926.

Olmsted, Frederick. Journey in the Seaboard States. New York, Dix and Edwards, 1856.

—— The Slave States before the Civil War. Edited by Harvey Wish. New York, Putnam, 1955.

Ortiz, Fernando. Los Instrumentos de la Música Afrocubana. 3 vols. Havana, Ministry of Education, 1952.

Parrish, Lydia. Slave Songs of the Georgia Sea Islands. New York, Creative Age, 1942.

Ramsey, Frederic Jr., and Charles Edward Smith. Jazzmen. New York, Harcourt Brace, 1939.

Sachs, Curt. Man's Early Musical Instruments, introduction to Ethnic Folkways Library record album FE 4525, 1956.

Saint-Méry, Moreau de. De la Danse. Parma, 1801.

Saxon, Lysle, Edward Dreyer, and Robert Tallant. Gumbo Ya-Ya. Boston, Houghton Mifflin, 1945.

Seeger, Pete. Introduction to the record album, Prison Camp Work Songs, Ethnic Folkways Library FE 4475.

Silber, Irwin. Songs of the Civil War. Piano and guitar arrangements by Jerry Silverman. New York, Columbia University Press, 1960.

Simpson, George Eaton. Introduction to the record album Cult Music of Jamaica, Ethnic Folkways Library FE 4461.

Stearns, Marshall. The Story of Jazz. New York, Oxford University Press, 1956.

Tallant, Robert. Voodoo in New Orleans. New York, Macmillan, 1946.

Tax, Sol. Acculturation in the Americas. Chicago, University of Chicago Press, 1952.

Waterman, Richard A. "African Influences on the Music of the Americas," in Sol Tax, Acculturation in the Americas. Chicago, University of Chicago Press, 1952.

—— Introduction to the record album Tribal, Folk and Café Music of West Africa, recorded by Arthur W. Alberts.

Wittke, Carl. Tambo and Bones. Durham, Duke University Press, 1930.

Woofter, T. J. Black Yeomanry—Life on St. Helena Island. New York, Holt, 1930.

Work, John W. American Negro Songs. New York, Howell, Soskin, and Co., 1940.

Discography

THE following list of recordings—selected U.S. Negro folk music and comparative folk music in the United States, the West Indies, mainland Latin America, and Africa—is not exhaustive, but includes materials which cumulatively give a broad and panoramic view of the Negro folk music scene. Among the items listed are most of the best recordings now available in the United States which relate to the subject. Purely commercial or theatrical performances have been discriminated against in this listing. Some of the items are perhaps tainted with non-folk artifice, but there is enough of the folk substance to justify their inclusion. Understandably, a number of recordings listed below have become difficult to find since the first printing of this book in 1963. But virtually all those on the Folkways, Ethnic Folkways Library, and Disc labels are available on tape from the Folkways Collection of the Smithsonian Institution. Others, if so designated, are to be found in the Music Division of the Library of Congress.

I. Negro Folk Music in the United States

GENERAL COLLECTIONS

Music From the South, recorded in southern states by Frederic Ramsey, Jr., Folkways Records FA 2650, 2651, 2652, 2653, 2654, 2655, 2656, 2657, 2658, 2659. Ten volumes of extremely valuable source material, with notes by the collector.

Afro-American Spirituals, Work Songs, and Ballads, recorded in southern states by John, Ruby T., and Alan Lomax and Ruby Pickens Tartt. Library of Congress AAFS-L3.

Negro Folk Music of Alabama, recorded in Alabama and Mississippi by Harold Courlander, Ethnic Folkways Library FE 4417, 4418, 4471, 4472, 4473, 4474. Six volumes of valuable source material, with notes by the collector.

Folk Music U. S. A., compiled by Harold Courlander, Ethnic Folkways Library FE 4530. Two record set, with notes by Charles Edward Smith.

Sounds of the South, recorded by Alan Lomax, Atlantic Recording 1346.

American Folk Music, Vols. II and III, compiled by Harry Smith, Folkways Records FA 2952, 2953. A general collection containing good Negro examples.

RELIGIOUS

Negro Religious Songs and Services, recorded in southern states by Harold Spivacke, John A., Ruby T., and Alan Lomax, and Lewis Jones, Library of Congress AAFS-L10. Edited by B. A. Botkin.

Spirituals With Dock Reed and Vera Hall Ward, recorded in Alabama by Harold Courlander, Folkways Records FA 2038.

Urban Holiness Service, Elder Charles D. Beck, Folkways Records FR 8901.

Georgia Street Singer, Rev. Pearly Brown, Folk-Lyric FL 108.

Harlem Street Singer, Blind Gary Davis, Prestige 1015.

Blind Willie Johnson, edited by Samuel B. Charters, Folkways FG 3585.

Spirituals, the Gospel Keys (Mother Sally Jones and Emma Daniel), Disc Records 657.

Negro Church Music, recorded by Alan Lomax, Atlantic Recording 1351.

WORK SONGS

Negro Work Songs and Calls, recorded by John A., Ruby T., and Alan Lomax, Herbert Halpert, and Mary Elizabeth Barnicle, Library of Congress AAFS-L8.

Negro Prison Camp Worksongs, recorded in Texas by Toshi and Peter Seeger, John Lomax, Jr., Chester Bower, and Fred Hollerman, Ethnic Folkways Library FE 4475. Notes by Peter Seeger.

Negro Prison Songs, recorded in Mississippi by Alan Lomax, Tradition Records TLP 1020.

BANDS AND STREET MUSIC

American Skiffle Bands, recorded in southern states by Samuel B. Charters, Folkways Records FA 2610.

One Man Band, Paul Blackman, Folkways Records FA 2605.

Sonny Terry's Washboard Band, Folkways Records FA 2006.

The Music of New Orleans—Music of the Streets, recorded by Samuel B. Charters, Folkways Records FA 2461.

The Music of New Orleans—The Eureka Brass Band, recorded by Samuel B. Charters, Folkways Records FA 2462.

BLUES AND RELATED MATERIALS

Lightnin' Hopkins, recorded by Samuel B. Charters, Folkways Records FS 3882.

Lightnin' Hopkins: Country Blues, Tradition Records TLP 1035.

Autobiography in Blues, Lightnin' Hopkins, Tradition Records TLP 1040.

The Country Blues of John Lee Hooker, Riverside Records 12-838.

The Country Blues, compiled by Samuel B. Charters, RBF Records RF 1.

Cat-Iron Sings Blues and Hymns, recorded by Frederic Ramsey, Jr., in Mississippi, Folkways Records FA 2389.

Angola Prisoners' Blues, recorded by Harry Oster and Richard Allen in Louisiana, Louisiana Folklore Society. Notes by Harry Oster and Paul B. Crawford.

Afro-American Blues and Game Songs, recorded in southern states and New York by John A., Ruby T., and Alan Lomax, Ruby Pickens Tartt, Bess Lomax, and John Work, Library of Congress AAFS-L4.

Snooks Eaglin, New Orleans Street Singer, recorded by Harry Oster, Folkways Records FA 2476.

Negro Folk Songs and Tunes, played on guitar and banjo by Elizabeth Cotten, Folkways Records FG 3526.

The Blues Roll On, recorded by Alan Lomax, Atlantic Records 1352.

Roots of the Blues, recorded by Alan Lomax, Atlantic Records 1348.

On the Road, Sonny Terry, J. C. Burris, Sticks McGhee, Folkways Records FA 2369.

Get On Board, Sonny Terry, Brownie McGhee, Coyal McMahan, Folkways Records FA 2028.

The Rural Blues: A Study of the Vocal and Instrumental Sources, edited by Samuel B. Charters, RBF Records RF 2.

Brownie McGhee, Blues, Folkways Records FA 2030.

Blues With Big Bill Broonzy, Sonny Terry, Brownie McGhee, interviewed by Studs Terkel. Folkways Records FS 3817.

Big Bill Broonzy, interviewed by Studs Terkel. Folkways Records FG 3586. Introductory notes by Charles Edward Smith.

Blues in the Mississippi Night, recorded by Alan Lomax, United Artists 4027.

Odetta at the Gates of Horn, Tradition Records 1025.

Classical Folk-Blues by Blind Lemon Jefferson, Riverside Records RLP 12-125.

MISCELLANEOUS

Jazz, Vol. I—the South, compiled and edited by Charles Edward Smith, Folkways Records FJ 2801.

Jazz, Vol. II—the Blues, compiled and edited by Frederic Ramsey, Jr., Folkways Records FJ 2802.

Footnotes to Jazz, Vol. I—Baby Dodds, Folkways Records FJ 2290.
Leadbelly's Last Sessions, Vols. I and II, recorded by Frederic Ramsey, Jr., Folkways Records FA 2941, 2942.
If He Asks You Was I Laughin', recorded by Tony Schwartz, privately pressed.
Street Cries and Creole Songs of New Orleans, Adelaide Van Wey, Folkways Records FA 2202.
Ring Games, Line Games and Play Party Songs of Alabama, recorded by Harold Courlander, Folkways Records FC 7004.

II. Non-Negro Folk Music from the South

Cajun Songs from Louisiana, recorded by I. Bonstein, Ethnic Folkways Library FE 4438.
Folksongs of the Louisiana Acadians, recorded by Harry Oster, Louisiana Folklore Society. Notes by the collector.
A Sampler of Louisiana Folksongs, collected by Harry Oster, Louisiana Folklore Society. Notes by the collector.
Ballads in Colonial America, Jean Ritchie and Tony Kraber, edited by Carleton Sprague Smith, New Records NRLP 2005.
Cumberland Mountain Songs, Paul Clayton, Folkways Records FP 2007.
Cowboy Ballads, Cisco Houston, Folkways Records FA 2022.
Buell Kazee Sings and Plays, recorded by G. Bluestein, Folkways Records FS 3810.
Anglo-American Songs and Ballads, four vols., recorded by various collectors, Library of Congress AAFS-L12, AAFS-L14, AAFS-L20, AAFS-L21.
Play and Dance Songs and Tunes, recorded in southern and midwestern states by Herbert Halpert, Alan, Elizabeth, and John A. Lomax, Fletcher Collins, John W. Work, and Lewis Jones, Library of Congress AAFS-L9.
Anglo-American Ballads, recorded in southern states by Herbert Halpert, Alan Lomax, Elizabeth Lomax, and Fletcher Collins, Library of Congress AAFS-L7.
Anglo-American Ballads, recorded in southern states by John A., Alan, Elizabeth and Bess Lomax, Herbert Halpert, Charles Seeger, and Charles Draves, Library of Congress AAFS-L1.
Anglo-American Shanties, Lyric Songs, Dance Tunes and Spirituals, recorded in southern, midwestern, and western areas by Herbert

Halpert, Peter Seeger, Robert Sonkin, Charles Todd, Alan Lomax, and Elizabeth Lomax, Library of Congress AAFS-L2.

III. West Indies and the Caribbean Mainland

Caribbean Festival—Music of the West Indies (Haiti, Puerto Rico, Surinam, Curaçao, Aruba, Martinique, Trinidad, Guadaloupe, Antigua), recorded by Lisa Lekis, Puerto Rico Visitors' Bureau.

Caribbean Dances (Virgin Islands, Martinique, Guadaloupe, Trinidad, Antigua, Curaçao), recorded by Lisa and Walter Lekis, Folkways Records FW 6840.

Caribbean Rhythms, recorded in San Andrés by Thomas J. Price, Jr., Folkways Records FW 8811.

Gospel Songs, recorded in Nassau, Bahamas, by Marshall Stearns, Folkways Records FW 6824.

Bahaman Songs, French Ballads and Dance Tunes, Spanish Religious Songs, and Game Songs, recorded by Mary Elizabeth Barnicle, Juan B. Rael, John A. and Alan Lomax, Library of Congress AAFS-L5.

Religious Songs and Drums in the Bahamas, recorded by Marshall Stearns, Ethnic Folkways Library FE 4440. Notes by Marshall Stearns and Harold Courlander.

Caribbean Holiday, recorded in the Bahamas, Theme TT-2204.

Music of the Bahamas, recorded by Samuel B. Charters, Folkways FS 3845.

Jamaican Cult Music, recorded by George Eaton Simpson, Ethnic Folkways Library FE 4461. Notes by the collector.

Folk Music of Jamaica, recorded by Edward Seaga, Ethnic Folkways Library FE 4453. Notes by the collector.

Calypso and Meringues, Folkways Records FW 6808.

Creole Songs of Haiti, Emerante de Pradines and Michel Dejean group, Folkways Records FW 6833.

Voices of Haiti, recorded by Maya Deren. Elektra P-5.

Drums of Haiti, recorded by Harold Courlander, Ethnic Folkways Library FE 4403. Notes by the collector.

Folk Music of Haiti, recorded by Harold Courlander, Ethnic Folkways Library FE 4407. Notes by the collector.

Songs and Dances of Haiti, recorded by Harold Courlander and Marshall Stearns, Ethnic Folkways Library FE 4432. Notes by Harold Courlander.

Haitian Dances, Frantz Casseus on guitar, Folkways Records FW 6822.

Haitian Piano, Fabre Duroseau and group, recorded by Harold Courlander, Folkways Records FW 6837.

Haitian Folk Songs, Folkways Records FW 6811.

Cult Music of Cuba, recorded by Harold Courlander, Ethnic Folkways
Library FE 4410. Notes by the collector.

The Big Drum Dance of Carriacou, recorded by Andrew C. Pearse,
Monograph Series, Ethnic Folkways Library FM 4011. Notes by the
collector.

Songs and Dances of Puerto Rico, recorded by William S. Marlens,
Folkways Records FW 8802.

Folk Music of Puerto Rico, recorded by Richard A. Waterman, Library
of Congress AAFS-86-90.

Folk and Street Music of Curaçao, Dial Records 407.

Cavalcade of Calypso, Vol. 2, Dial Records 405.

Carnival in Trinidad, Dial Records 404.

Steel Drum Music (Trinidad), Dial Records 406.

The Black Caribs of Honduras, recorded by Peter Kite Smith, Ethnic
Folkways Library FE 4435. Notes by Doris Stone.

The Music of Honduras, recorded by Doris Stone, Folkways Records
FW 6834. Notes by the collector.

Brazil Carnavalesco, SMC 543

Afro-Bahian Religious Songs from Brazil, recorded by Melville J. and
Frances S. Herskovits, Library of Congress AAFS-61-65.

Folk Music of Venezuela, recorded by Juan Liscano and Charles Seeger,
Library of Congress AAFS-71-75.

Caribbean Folk Music, Vol. I, compiled by Harold Courlander, Ethnic
Folkways Library FE 4533. Notes by the compiler.

World Library of Folk and Primitive Music, Vol. IX—Venezuela,
recorded by Juan Liscano, Columbia Records SL-212.

IV. West and Central Africa (selected examples)

Congo Drums, recorded by Hugh Tracey, London Records LB-828.

Drums of the Yoruba of Nigeria, recorded by William Bascom, Ethnic
Folkways Library FE 4441. Notes by the collector.

Music of the Ituri Forest, recorded by Colin M. Turnbull and Francis
S. Chapman, Ethnic Folkways Library FE 4483. Notes by Colin
Turnbull.

African Coast Rhythms (Guinea, Gold Coast, Ivory Coast, Upper Volta,
Liberia), recorded by Arthur S. Alberts, Riverside Records RLP 4001.

Cover notes based on material by Melville J. Herskovits, Richard Waterman, and Arthur Alberts.

World Library of Folk and Primitive Music, Vol. II—French Africa, compiled and edited by Alan Lomax, André Schaeffner, and Gilbert Rouget. Columbia Records SL-205.

Folk Music of the Western Congo, recorded by Leo A. Verwilghen, Ethnic Folkways Library FE 4427. Notes by the collector.

Music of Equatorial Africa, recorded by André Didier, Ethnic Folkways Library FE 4402. Introductory notes by Harold Courlander and Gilbert Rouget.

Bulu Songs from the Cameroons, recorded by Edwin Cozzens, Ethnic Folkways Library FE 4451. Notes by the collector.

The Topoke People of the Congo, recorded by J. Camps, Ethnic Folkways Library FE 4477. Notes by Pete L. A. van Hest.

Congo Songs and Dances, recorded by Hugh Tracey, London Records LB-831.

Negro Music of Africa and America, compiled by Harold Courlander, Ethnic Folkways Library FE 4500. Notes by Richard A. Waterman and the compiler.

African and Afro-American Drums, compiled by Harold Courlander, Ethnic Folkways Library FE 4502. Notes by the compiler.

Africa South of the Sahara, compiled by Harold Courlander, Ethnic Folkways Library FE 4503. Notes by Alan P. Merriam.

Music of the Belgian Congo, recorded by the Denis-Roosevelt expedition, General Records (no number).

African Music, recorded by Laura Boulton, Folkways Records FW 8852. Notes by the collector.

The Baoule of the Ivory Coast, recorded by Donald Thurow, Ethnic Folkways Library FE 4476. Notes by the collector.

Wolof Music of Senegal and the Gambia, recorded by David Ames, Ethnic Folkways Library FE 4462. Notes by the collector.

Folk Music of Liberia, recorded by Packard L. Okie, Ethnic Folkways Library FE 4465. Notes by the collector.

Music of the Malinké and the Baoule, l'Institut Français d'Afrique Noire and the Musée de l'Homme, Esoteric Records ES-529. Notes by Gilbert Rouget.

Music of the Princes of Dahomey, l'Institut Français d'Afrique Noire and the Musée de l'Homme, Esoteric Records ES-537. Notes by Gilbert Rouget.

Voice of the Congo, recorded by Alan P. and Barbara W. Merriam, Riverside Records 4002.

Sources of Notated Songs

All titles marked with an asterisk (*) were recorded by Harold Courlander; others as indicated.

Page

255   Precious Lord, Take My Hand. Singers, "The Gospel Keys" (Mother Sally Jones and Emma Daniel). Tape recording by Moses Asch.

258   I'm Crossing Jordan River. Singers, "The Gospel Keys" (Mother Sally Jones and Emma Daniel). Tape Recording by Moses Asch.

260   Russia, Let That Moon Alone. Singer, Sister Dora Alexander. Recorded by Samuel Charters. Folkways Records FA 2641.

261   Long John. Singers, "Lightning" and group. Recorded by John A. and Alan Lomax. Library of Congress recording 13 B 1.

262   Rosie. Singers, inmates at Mississippi State Penitentiary. Recorded by Alan Lomax. Tradition Records TLP 1020.

263   She Done Got Ugly.* Singer, Archie Lee Hill. Ethnic Folkways Library FE 4417.

265   Captain Holler Hurry.* Singer, Willie Turner. Ethnic Folkways Library FE 4474.

266   Black Woman.* Singer, Rich Amerson. Ethnic Folkways Library FE 4417.

269   Motherless Children. Singer, Blind Willie Johnson. Folkways Records FG 3585. Original release Columbia 14343.

271   I'm Going Uptown.* Singer, Emanuel (Peelee Hatchee) Jones. Ethnic Folkways Library FE 4474.

272   Careless Love. Singer, Snooks Eaglin. Recorded by Harry Oster. Folkways Records FA 2476.

273   Look Down. Singer, Snooks Eaglin. Recorded by Harry Oster. Folkways Records FA 2476.

274   Meet Me in the Bottoms.* Singer, Davie Lee. Ethnic Folkways Library FE 4474.

275   Old Lady Sally Wants to Jump.* Singers, children of Lilly's Chapel School, York, Alabama. Ethnic Folkways Library FE 4474.

277   Green Green Rocky Road.* Singers, children of Lilly's Chapel School, York, Alabama. Ethnic Folkways Library FE 4474.

278   Little Sally Walker.* Singers, children of Lilly's Chapel School, York, Alabama. Ethnic Folkways Library FE 4417.

278   Watch That Lady.* Singers, children of Lilly's Chapel School, York, Alabama. Ethnic Folkways Library FE 4474.

279   Mary Mack.* Singers, children of Lilly's Chapel School, York, Alabama. Ethnic Folkways Library FE 4474.

Page

280 John Henry (Version I).* Singer, Rich Amerson. Ethnic Folkways Library FE 4471.

282 John Henry (Version II).* Singer, Willie Turner. Ethnic Folkways Library FE 4474.

285 John Henry (Version III). Singer, John Hurt. Under title of
Spike Driver Blues, Folkways Records FA 2953. Original issue
Okeh 8692.

287 Old John Booker. Singer, Gus Cannon. Recorded by Samuel
Charters. Folkways Records FA 2610.

Index

Abakwa secret society rites, use of belt of bells, 218
Aberrational church singing styles, 17
Acadian folk music in Louisiana, 9, 164
Accents: African melodies, 29; European melodies, 29
Accompaniment, forms of, 18
Acculturation in Negro communities, 4
Actions in African music, 1
Adam and Eve story, 43-44
Africa: heritage in U.S. Negro music, 1, 38; musical styles, characteristics, 1-2; traditions in U.S. Negro folk music, 1-2; derived customs visible today in the U.S., 2-3; traits in Negro life in the New World, 3-8; exiles' adjustment to new cultures, 3-4; patterns in New World pidgin English, 7; prototypes of American Negro folk tales, 7; use of tone for semantic purposes, 7; characteristics of American folk music, 8-12; scales, survivals of, in American Negro music, 15; musical culture, 16; melodies, accents of, 29; rhythmic element reflected in American Negro music, 29; music, strong percussive tendency in, 30; social comment song, relation of folk blues to, 34; derived animal tales in Louisiana folklore, 172; dance motifs in music of Georgia Sea Islands, 196; style cult activities of the West Indies, 197; style drum, 210
"Afro-American music," an imprecise term, 13-14
Agogo, 208
Agree, Simon, 292n
"Ain't No More Cane on the Brazos," 132-33
Alberts, Arthur S., 290n
"All God's Children Got Wings," 39
Allen, Richard, and Harry Oster, 294n
"Amasee," 154-55 (*example*)
American folk music, influences of phonograph and radio, 10

American Negro folk tales, prototypes of, 7
Amerson, Richard, 56, 292n
Amerson, Sarah, 292n
"Angelico," 165
Animal sounds produced on harmonica, 216
Animal tales: American Negro oral literature, 7, 172; characters, 172-73
Anthems as oral literature, 35-79
Anthropological studies of African and American cultures, 2, 4, 8, 18
Anticipated beat in Negro church and secular music, 29
Antiphony in gang songs, 94
Anglo-Scottish songs, nature of, 124
Armstrong, Louis, 24
"Art" blues versus folk blues, 34
Ashanti, culture of, 3
Attitudes toward music, 1
Auf der Heide, Ralph, 295n

Babouille dance, 190-91
"Baby Please Don't Go," 108-9 (*example*)
Backsliding, as subject, 73-74
Bad men, ballad subject, 178
Bagpipes, 204-5
Balafons, membranes attached to, 30
Ball the Jack dance, 200
Balladeers, white mountaineer, 177
Ballads, 124, 175-88; European, 124; blues molded out of, 137; French, 164; historical Creole, 168-69; "classical" form, characteristics of, 176; English, 176; public performer, 177
Bamboo zithers of Africa, 213
Bamboula dance, 190-91, 211
Banjos, 30, 212-14, 219; African origin, 212-13; style of playing, 214
Banza, 212, 219
Baptismal rites, 7
Barn dances, 147
Basic freedoms of folk music, 126

A CATALOG OF SELECTED

DOVER BOOKS

IN ALL FIELDS OF INTEREST

A CATALOG OF SELECTED
DOVER BOOKS
IN ALL FIELDS OF INTEREST

DRAWINGS OF REMBRANDT, edited by Seymour Slive. Updated Lippmann, Hofstede de Groot edition, with definitive scholarly apparatus. All portraits, biblical sketches, landscapes, nudes. Oriental figures, classical studies, together with selection of work by followers. 550 illustrations. Total of 630pp. 9⅛ × 12¼.
21485-0, 21486-9 Pa., Two-vol. set $29.90

GHOST AND HORROR STORIES OF AMBROSE BIERCE, Ambrose Bierce. 24 tales vividly imagined, strangely prophetic, and decades ahead of their time in technical skill: "The Damned Thing," "An Inhabitant of Carcosa," "The Eyes of the Panther," "Moxon's Master," and 20 more. 199pp. 5⅜ × 8½. 20767-6 Pa. $4.95

ETHICAL WRITINGS OF MAIMONIDES, Maimonides. Most significant ethical works of great medieval sage, newly translated for utmost precision, readability. Laws Concerning Character Traits, Eight Chapters, more. 192pp. 5⅜ × 8½.
24522-5 Pa. $4.50

THE EXPLORATION OF THE COLORADO RIVER AND ITS CANYONS, J. W. Powell. Full text of Powell's 1,000-mile expedition down the fabled Colorado in 1869. Superb account of terrain, geology, vegetation, Indians, famine, mutiny, treacherous rapids, mighty canyons, during exploration of last unknown part of continental U.S. 400pp. 5⅜ × 8½. 20094-9 Pa. $7.95

HISTORY OF PHILOSOPHY, Julián Marías. Clearest one-volume history on the market. Every major philosopher and dozens of others, to Existentialism and later. 505pp. 5⅜ × 8½. 21739-6 Pa. $9.95

ALL ABOUT LIGHTNING, Martin A. Uman. Highly readable nontechnical survey of nature and causes of lightning, thunderstorms, ball lightning, St. Elmo's Fire, much more. Illustrated. 192pp. 5⅜ × 8½. 25237-X Pa. $5.95

SAILING ALONE AROUND THE WORLD, Captain Joshua Slocum. First man to sail around the world, alone, in small boat. One of great feats of seamanship told in delightful manner. 67 illustrations. 294pp. 5⅜ × 8½. 20326-3 Pa. $4.95

LETTERS AND NOTES ON THE MANNERS, CUSTOMS AND CONDITIONS OF THE NORTH AMERICAN INDIANS, George Catlin. Classic account of life among Plains Indians: ceremonies, hunt, warfare, etc. 312 plates. 572pp. of text. 6⅛ × 9¼. 22118-0, 22119-9, Pa., Two-vol. set $17.90

ALASKA: The Harriman Expedition, 1899, John Burroughs, John Muir, et al. Informative, engrossing accounts of two-month, 9,000-mile expedition. Native peoples, wildlife, forests, geography, salmon industry, glaciers, more. Profusely illustrated. 240 black-and-white line drawings. 124 black-and-white photographs. 3 maps. Index. 576pp. 5⅜ × 8½. 25109-8 Pa. $11.95

THE BOOK OF BEASTS: Being a Translation from a Latin Bestiary of the Twelfth Century, T. H. White. Wonderful catalog of real and fanciful beasts: manticore, griffin, phoenix, amphivius, jaculus, many more. White's witty erudite commentary on scientific, historical aspects enhances fascinating glimpse of medieval mind. Illustrated. 296pp. 5⅜ × 8¼. (Available in U.S. only)   24609-4 Pa. $6.95

FRANK LLOYD WRIGHT: Architecture and Nature with 160 Illustrations, Donald Hoffmann. Profusely illustrated study of influence of nature—especially prairie—on Wright's designs for Fallingwater, Robie House, Guggenheim Museum, other masterpieces. 96pp. 9¼ × 10¾.   25098-9 Pa. $8.95

FRANK LLOYD WRIGHT'S FALLINGWATER, Donald Hoffmann. Wright's famous waterfall house: planning and construction of organic idea. History of site, owners, Wright's personal involvement. Photographs of various stages of building. Preface by Edgar Kaufmann, Jr. 100 illustrations. 112pp. 9¼ × 10.
23671-4 Pa. $8.95

YEARS WITH FRANK LLOYD WRIGHT: Apprentice to Genius, Edgar Tafel. Insightful memoir by a former apprentice presents a revealing portrait of Wright the man, the inspired teacher, the greatest American architect. 372 black-and-white illustrations. Preface. Index. vi + 228pp. 8¼ × 11.   24801-1 Pa. $10.95

THE STORY OF KING ARTHUR AND HIS KNIGHTS, Howard Pyle. Enchanting version of King Arthur fable has delighted generations with imaginative narratives of exciting adventures and unforgettable illustrations by the author. 41 illustrations. xviii + 313pp. 6⅛ × 9¼.   21445-1 Pa. $6.95

THE GODS OF THE EGYPTIANS, E. A. Wallis Budge. Thorough coverage of numerous gods of ancient Egypt by foremost Egyptologist. Information on evolution of cults, rites and gods; the cult of Osiris; the Book of the Dead and its rites; the sacred animals and birds; Heaven and Hell; and more. 956pp. 6⅛ × 9¼.
22055-9, 22056-7 Pa., Two-vol. set $21.90

A THEOLOGICO-POLITICAL TREATISE, Benedict Spinoza. Also contains unfinished *Political Treatise*. Great classic on religious liberty, theory of government on common consent. R. Elwes translation. Total of 421pp. 5⅜ × 8½.
20249-6 Pa. $7.95

INCIDENTS OF TRAVEL IN CENTRAL AMERICA, CHIAPAS, AND YUCATAN, John L. Stephens. Almost single-handed discovery of Maya culture; exploration of ruined cities, monuments, temples; customs of Indians. 115 drawings. 892pp. 5⅜ × 8½.   22404-X, 22405-8 Pa., Two-vol. set $17.90

LOS CAPRICHOS, Francisco Goya. 80 plates of wild, grotesque monsters and caricatures. Prado manuscript included. 183pp. 6⅜ × 9⅜.   22384-1 Pa. $5.95

AUTOBIOGRAPHY: The Story of My Experiments with Truth, Mohandas K. Gandhi. Not hagiography, but Gandhi in his own words. Boyhood, legal studies, purification, the growth of the Satyagraha (nonviolent protest) movement. Critical, inspiring work of the man who freed India. 480pp. 5⅜ × 8½. (Available in U.S. only)
24593-4 Pa. $6.95

ILLUSTRATED DICTIONARY OF HISTORIC ARCHITECTURE, edited by Cyril M. Harris. Extraordinary compendium of clear, concise definitions for over 5,000 important architectural terms complemented by over 2,000 line drawings. Covers full spectrum of architecture from ancient ruins to 20th-century Modernism. Preface. 592pp. 7½ × 9⅝. 24444-X Pa. $15.95

THE NIGHT BEFORE CHRISTMAS, Clement C. Moore. Full text, and woodcuts from original 1848 book. Also critical, historical material. 19 illustrations. 40pp. 4⅝ × 6. 22797-9 Pa. $2.50

THE LESSON OF JAPANESE ARCHITECTURE: 165 Photographs, Jiro Harada. Memorable gallery of 165 photographs taken in the 1930s of exquisite Japanese homes of the well-to-do and historic buildings. 13 line diagrams. 192pp. 8⅝ × 11¼. 24778-3 Pa. $10.95

THE AUTOBIOGRAPHY OF CHARLES DARWIN AND SELECTED LETTERS, edited by Francis Darwin. The fascinating life of eccentric genius composed of an intimate memoir by Darwin (intended for his children); commentary by his son, Francis; hundreds of fragments from notebooks, journals, papers; and letters to and from Lyell, Hooker, Huxley, Wallace and Henslow. xi + 365pp. 5⅜ × 8. 20479-0 Pa. $6.95

WONDERS OF THE SKY: Observing Rainbows, Comets, Eclipses, the Stars and Other Phenomena, Fred Schaaf. Charming, easy-to-read poetic guide to all manner of celestial events visible to the naked eye. Mock suns, glories, Belt of Venus, more. Illustrated. 299pp. 5¼ × 8¼. 24402-4 Pa. $8.95

BURNHAM'S CELESTIAL HANDBOOK, Robert Burnham, Jr. Thorough guide to the stars beyond our solar system. Exhaustive treatment. Alphabetical by constellation: Andromeda to Cetus in Vol. 1; Chamaeleon to Orion in Vol. 2; and Pavo to Vulpecula in Vol. 3. Hundreds of illustrations. Index in Vol. 3. 2,000pp. 6⅛ × 9¼. 23567-X, 23568-8, 23673-0 Pa., Three-vol. set $41.85

STAR NAMES: Their Lore and Meaning, Richard Hinckley Allen. Fascinating history of names various cultures have given to constellations and literary and folkloristic uses that have been made of stars. Indexes to subjects. Arabic and Greek names. Biblical references. Bibliography. 563pp. 5⅜ × 8½. 21079-0 Pa. $8.95

THIRTY YEARS THAT SHOOK PHYSICS: The Story of Quantum Theory, George Gamow. Lucid, accessible introduction to influential theory of energy and matter. Careful explanations of Dirac's anti-particles, Bohr's model of the atom, much more. 12 plates. Numerous drawings. 240pp. 5⅜ × 8½. 24895-X Pa. $6.95

CHINESE DOMESTIC FURNITURE IN PHOTOGRAPHS AND MEASURED DRAWINGS, Gustav Ecke. A rare volume, now affordably priced for antique collectors, furniture buffs and art historians. Detailed review of styles ranging from early Shang to late Ming. Unabridged republication. 161 black-and-white drawings, photos. Total of 224pp. 8⅜ × 11¼. (Available in U.S. only) 25171-3 Pa. $14.95

VINCENT VAN GOGH: A Biography, Julius Meier-Graefe. Dynamic, penetrating study of artist's life, relationship with brother, Theo, painting techniques, travels, more. Readable, engrossing. 160pp. 5⅜ × 8½. (Available in U.S. only) 25253-1 Pa. $4.95

CATALOG OF DOVER BOOKS

HOW TO WRITE, Gertrude Stein. Gertrude Stein claimed anyone could understand her unconventional writing—here are clues to help. Fascinating improvisations, language experiments, explanations illuminate Stein's craft and the art of writing. Total of 414pp. 4⅝ × 6⅜. 23144-5 Pa. $6.95

ADVENTURES AT SEA IN THE GREAT AGE OF SAIL: Five Firsthand Narratives, edited by Elliot Snow. Rare true accounts of exploration, whaling, shipwreck, fierce natives, trade, shipboard life, more. 33 illustrations. Introduction. 353pp. 5⅜ × 8½. 25177-2 Pa. $9.95

THE HERBAL OR GENERAL HISTORY OF PLANTS, John Gerard. Classic descriptions of about 2,850 plants—with over 2,700 illustrations—includes Latin and English names, physical descriptions, varieties, time and place of growth, more. 2,706 illustrations. xlv + 1,678pp. 8½ × 12¼. 23147-X Cloth. $75.00

DOROTHY AND THE WIZARD IN OZ, L. Frank Baum. Dorothy and the Wizard visit the center of the Earth, where people are vegetables, glass houses grow and Oz characters reappear. Classic sequel to *Wizard of Oz*. 256pp. 5⅜ × 8.
24714-7 Pa. $5.95

SONGS OF EXPERIENCE: Facsimile Reproduction with 26 Plates in Full Color, William Blake. This facsimile of Blake's original "Illuminated Book" reproduces 26 full-color plates from a rare 1826 edition. Includes "The Tyger," "London," "Holy Thursday," and other immortal poems. 26 color plates. Printed text of poems. 48pp. 5¼ × 7. 24636-1 Pa. $3.95

SONGS OF INNOCENCE, William Blake. The first and most popular of Blake's famous "Illuminated Books," in a facsimile edition reproducing all 31 brightly colored plates. Additional printed text of each poem. 64pp. 5¼ × 7.
22764-2 Pa. $3.95

PRECIOUS STONES, Max Bauer. Classic, thorough study of diamonds, rubies, emeralds, garnets, etc.: physical character, occurrence, properties, use, similar topics. 20 plates, 8 in color. 94 figures. 659pp. 6⅛ × 9¼.
21910-0, 21911-9 Pa., Two-vol. set $15.90

ENCYCLOPEDIA OF VICTORIAN NEEDLEWORK, S. F. A. Caulfeild and Blanche Saward. Full, precise descriptions of stitches, techniques for dozens of needlecrafts—most exhaustive reference of its kind. Over 800 figures. Total of 679pp. 8⅛ × 11. 22800-2, 22801-0 Pa., Two-vol. set $23.90

THE MARVELOUS LAND OF OZ, L. Frank Baum. Second Oz book, the Scarecrow and Tin Woodman are back with hero named Tip, Oz magic. 136 illustrations. 287pp. 5⅜ × 8½. 20692-0 Pa. $5.95

WILD FOWL DECOYS, Joel Barber. Basic book on the subject, by foremost authority and collector. Reveals history of decoy making and rigging, place in American culture, different kinds of decoys, how to make them, and how to use them. 140 plates. 156pp. 7⅞ × 10¾. 20011-6 Pa. $8.95

HISTORY OF LACE, Mrs. Bury Palliser. Definitive, profusely illustrated chronicle of lace from earliest times to late 19th century. Laces of Italy, Greece, England, France, Belgium, etc. Landmark of needlework scholarship. 266 illustrations. 672pp. 6⅛ × 9¼. 24742-2 Pa. $16.95

ILLUSTRATED GUIDE TO SHAKER FURNITURE, Robert Meader. All furniture and appurtenances, with much on unknown local styles. 235 photos. 146pp. 9 × 12. 22819-3 Pa. $8.95

WHALE SHIPS AND WHALING: A Pictorial Survey, George Francis Dow. Over 200 vintage engravings, drawings, photographs of barks, brigs, cutters, other vessels. Also harpoons, lances, whaling guns, many other artifacts. Comprehensive text by foremost authority. 207 black-and-white illustrations. 288pp. 6 × 9. 24808-9 Pa. $9.95

THE BERTRAMS, Anthony Trollope. Powerful portrayal of blind self-will and thwarted ambition includes one of Trollope's most heartrending love stories. 497pp. 5⅜ × 8½. 25119-5 Pa. $9.95

ADVENTURES WITH A HAND LENS, Richard Headstrom. Clearly written guide to observing and studying flowers and grasses, fish scales, moth and insect wings, egg cases, buds, feathers, seeds, leaf scars, moss, molds, ferns, common crystals, etc.—all with an ordinary, inexpensive magnifying glass. 209 exact line drawings aid in your discoveries. 220pp. 5⅜ × 8½. 23330-8 Pa. $5.95

RODIN ON ART AND ARTISTS, Auguste Rodin. Great sculptor's candid, wide-ranging comments on meaning of art; great artists; relation of sculpture to poetry, painting, music; philosophy of life, more. 76 superb black-and-white illustrations of Rodin's sculpture, drawings and prints. 119pp. 8⅜ × 11¼. 24487-3 Pa. $7.95

FIFTY CLASSIC FRENCH FILMS, 1912–1982: A Pictorial Record, Anthony Slide. Memorable stills from Grand Illusion, Beauty and the Beast, Hiroshima, Mon Amour, many more. Credits, plot synopses, reviews, etc. 160pp. 8¼ × 11. 25256-6 Pa. $11.95

THE PRINCIPLES OF PSYCHOLOGY, William James. Famous long course complete, unabridged. Stream of thought, time perception, memory, experimental methods; great work decades ahead of its time. 94 figures. 1,391pp. 5⅜ × 8½. 20381-6, 20382-4 Pa., Two-vol. set $25.90

BODIES IN A BOOKSHOP, R. T. Campbell. Challenging mystery of blackmail and murder with ingenious plot and superbly drawn characters. In the best tradition of British suspense fiction. 192pp. 5⅜ × 8½. 24720-1 Pa. $4.95

CALLAS: Portrait of a Prima Donna, George Jellinek. Renowned commentator on the musical scene chronicles incredible career and life of the most controversial, fascinating, influential operatic personality of our time. 64 black-and-white photographs. 416pp. 5⅜ × 8¼. 25047-4 Pa. $8.95

GEOMETRY, RELATIVITY AND THE FOURTH DIMENSION, Rudolph Rucker. Exposition of fourth dimension, concepts of relativity as Flatland characters continue adventures. Popular, easily followed yet accurate, profound. 141 illustrations. 133pp. 5⅜ × 8½. 23400-2 Pa. $4.95

HOUSEHOLD STORIES BY THE BROTHERS GRIMM, with pictures by Walter Crane. 53 classic stories—Rumpelstiltskin, Rapunzel, Hansel and Gretel, the Fisherman and his Wife, Snow White, Tom Thumb, Sleeping Beauty, Cinderella, and so much more—lavishly illustrated with original 19th-century drawings. 114 illustrations. x + 269pp. 5⅜ × 8½. 21080-4 Pa. $4.95

CATALOG OF DOVER BOOKS

SUNDIALS, Albert Waugh. Far and away the best, most thorough coverage of ideas, mathematics concerned, types, construction, adjusting anywhere. Over 100 illustrations. 230pp. 5⅜ × 8½. 22947-5 Pa. $5.95

PICTURE HISTORY OF THE NORMANDIE: With 190 Illustrations, Frank O. Braynard. Full story of legendary French ocean liner: Art Deco interiors, design innovations, furnishings, celebrities, maiden voyage, tragic fire, much more. Extensive text. 144pp. 8⅞ × 11¾. 25257-4 Pa. $10.95

THE FIRST AMERICAN COOKBOOK: A Facsimile of "American Cookery," 1796, Amelia Simmons. Facsimile of the first American-written cookbook published in the United States contains authentic recipes for colonial favorites—pumpkin pudding, winter squash pudding, spruce beer, Indian slapjacks, and more. Introductory Essay and Glossary of colonial cooking terms. 80pp. 5⅜ × 8½. 24710-4 Pa. $3.50

101 PUZZLES IN THOUGHT AND LOGIC, C. R. Wylie, Jr. Solve murders and robberies, find out which fishermen are liars, how a blind man could possibly identify a color—purely by your own reasoning! 107pp. 5⅜ × 8½. 20367-0 Pa. $2.95

ANCIENT EGYPTIAN MYTHS AND LEGENDS, Lewis Spence. Examines animism, totemism, fetishism, creation myths, deities, alchemy, art and magic, other topics. Over 50 illustrations. 432pp. 5⅜ × 8½. 26525-0 Pa. $8.95

ANTHROPOLOGY AND MODERN LIFE, Franz Boas. Great anthropologist's classic treatise on race and culture. Introduction by Ruth Bunzel. Only inexpensive paperback edition. 255pp. 5⅜ × 8½. 25245-0 Pa. $6.95

THE TALE OF PETER RABBIT, Beatrix Potter. The inimitable Peter's terrifying adventure in Mr. McGregor's garden, with all 27 wonderful, full-color Potter illustrations. 55pp. 4¼ × 5½. (Available in U.S. only) 22827-4 Pa. $1.75

THREE PROPHETIC SCIENCE FICTION NOVELS, H. G. Wells. *When the Sleeper Wakes, A Story of the Days to Come* and *The Time Machine* (full version). 335pp. 5⅜ × 8½. (Available in U.S. only) 20605-X Pa. $8.95

APICIUS COOKERY AND DINING IN IMPERIAL ROME, edited and translated by Joseph Dommers Vehling. Oldest known cookbook in existence offers readers a clear picture of what foods Romans ate, how they prepared them, etc. 49 illustrations. 301pp. 6⅛ × 9¼. 23563-7 Pa. $7.95

SHAKESPEARE LEXICON AND QUOTATION DICTIONARY, Alexander Schmidt. Full definitions, locations, shades of meaning of every word in plays and poems. More than 50,000 exact quotations. 1,485pp. 6½ × 9¼. 22726-X, 22727-8 Pa., Two-vol. set $31.90

THE WORLD'S GREAT SPEECHES, edited by Lewis Copeland and Lawrence W. Lamm. Vast collection of 278 speeches from Greeks to 1970. Powerful and effective models; unique look at history. 842pp. 5⅜ × 8½. 20468-5 Pa. $12.95

THE BLUE FAIRY BOOK, Andrew Lang. The first, most famous collection, with many familiar tales: Little Red Riding Hood, Aladdin and the Wonderful Lamp, Puss in Boots, Sleeping Beauty, Hansel and Gretel, Rumpelstiltskin; 37 in all. 138 illustrations. 390pp. 5⅜ × 8½.   21437-0 Pa. $6.95

THE STORY OF THE CHAMPIONS OF THE ROUND TABLE, Howard Pyle. Sir Launcelot, Sir Tristram and Sir Percival in spirited adventures of love and triumph retold in Pyle's inimitable style. 50 drawings, 31 full-page. xviii + 329pp. 6½ × 9¼.   21883-X Pa. $7.95

THE MYTHS OF THE NORTH AMERICAN INDIANS, Lewis Spence. Myths and legends of the Algonquins, Iroquois, Pawnees and Sioux with comprehensive historical and ethnological commentary. 36 illustrations. 5⅜ × 8½.
                                                                                          25967-6 Pa. $8.95

GREAT DINOSAUR HUNTERS AND THEIR DISCOVERIES, Edwin H. Colbert. Fascinating, lavishly illustrated chronicle of dinosaur research, 1820s to 1960. Achievements of Cope, Marsh, Brown, Buckland, Mantell, Huxley, many others. 384pp. 5¼ × 8¼.   24701-5 Pa. $7.95

THE TASTEMAKERS, Russell Lynes. Informal, illustrated social history of American taste 1850s–1950s. First popularized categories Highbrow, Lowbrow, Middlebrow. 129 illustrations. New (1979) afterword. 384pp. 6 × 9.
                                                                                          23993-4 Pa. $8.95

DOUBLE CROSS PURPOSES, Ronald A. Knox. A treasure hunt in the Scottish Highlands, an old map, unidentified corpse, surprise discoveries keep reader guessing in this cleverly intricate tale of financial skullduggery. 2 black-and-white maps. 320pp. 5⅜ × 8½. (Available in U.S. only)   25032-6 Pa. $6.95

AUTHENTIC VICTORIAN DECORATION AND ORNAMENTATION IN FULL COLOR: 46 Plates from "Studies in Design," Christopher Dresser. Superb full-color lithographs reproduced from rare original portfolio of a major Victorian designer. 48pp. 9¼ × 12¼.   25083-0 Pa. $7.95

PRIMITIVE ART, Franz Boas. Remains the best text ever prepared on subject, thoroughly discussing Indian, African, Asian, Australian, and, especially, Northern American primitive art. Over 950 illustrations show ceramics, masks, totem poles, weapons, textiles, paintings, much more. 376pp. 5⅜ × 8.   20025-6 Pa. $7.95

SIDELIGHTS ON RELATIVITY, Albert Einstein. Unabridged republication of two lectures delivered by the great physicist in 1920–21. *Ether and Relativity* and *Geometry and Experience*. Elegant ideas in nonmathematical form, accessible to intelligent layman. vi + 56pp. 5⅜ × 8½.   24511-X Pa. $3.95

THE WIT AND HUMOR OF OSCAR WILDE, edited by Alvin Redman. More than 1,000 ripostes, paradoxes, wisecracks: Work is the curse of the drinking classes, I can resist everything except temptation, etc. 258pp. 5⅜ × 8½.   20602-5 Pa. $4.95

ADVENTURES WITH A MICROSCOPE, Richard Headstrom. 59 adventures with clothing fibers, protozoa, ferns and lichens, roots and leaves, much more. 142 illustrations. 232pp. 5⅜ × 8½.   23471-1 Pa. $3.95

CATALOG OF DOVER BOOKS

PLANTS OF THE BIBLE, Harold N. Moldenke and Alma L. Moldenke. Standard reference to all 230 plants mentioned in Scriptures. Latin name, biblical reference, uses, modern identity, much more. Unsurpassed encyclopedic resource for scholars, botanists, nature lovers, students of Bible. Bibliography. Indexes. 123 black-and-white illustrations. 384pp. 6 × 9. 25069-5 Pa. $8.95

FAMOUS AMERICAN WOMEN: A Biographical Dictionary from Colonial Times to the Present, Robert McHenry, ed. From Pocahontas to Rosa Parks, 1,035 distinguished American women documented in separate biographical entries. Accurate, up-to-date data, numerous categories, spans 400 years. Indices. 493pp. 6½ × 9¼. 24523-3 Pa. $10.95

THE FABULOUS INTERIORS OF THE GREAT OCEAN LINERS IN HISTORIC PHOTOGRAPHS, William H. Miller, Jr. Some 200 superb photographs capture exquisite interiors of world's great "floating palaces"—1890s to 1980s: *Titanic, Ile de France, Queen Elizabeth, United States, Europa,* more. Approx. 200 black-and-white photographs. Captions. Text. Introduction. 160pp. 8⅜ × 11¼. 24756-2 Pa. $9.95

THE GREAT LUXURY LINERS, 1927–1954: A Photographic Record, William H. Miller, Jr. Nostalgic tribute to heyday of ocean liners. 186 photos of *Ile de France, Normandie, Leviathan, Queen Elizabeth, United States,* many others. Interior and exterior views. Introduction. Captions. 160pp. 9 × 12. 24056-8 Pa. $10.95

A NATURAL HISTORY OF THE DUCKS, John Charles Phillips. Great landmark of ornithology offers complete detailed coverage of nearly 200 species and subspecies of ducks: gadwall, sheldrake, merganser, pintail, many more. 74 full-color plates, 102 black-and-white. Bibliography. Total of 1,920pp. 8⅜ × 11¼. 25141-1, 25142-X Cloth., Two-vol. set $100.00

THE SEAWEED HANDBOOK: An Illustrated Guide to Seaweeds from North Carolina to Canada, Thomas F. Lee. Concise reference covers 78 species. Scientific and common names, habitat, distribution, more. Finding keys for easy identification. 224pp. 5⅜ × 8½. 25215-9 Pa. $6.95

THE TEN BOOKS OF ARCHITECTURE: The 1755 Leoni Edition, Leon Battista Alberti. Rare classic helped introduce the glories of ancient architecture to the Renaissance. 68 black-and-white plates. 336pp. 8⅜ × 11¼. 25239-6 Pa. $14.95

MISS MACKENZIE, Anthony Trollope. Minor masterpieces by Victorian master unmasks many truths about life in 19th-century England. First inexpensive edition in years. 392pp. 5⅜ × 8½. 25201-9 Pa. $8.95

THE RIME OF THE ANCIENT MARINER, Gustave Doré, Samuel Taylor Coleridge. Dramatic engravings considered by many to be his greatest work. The terrifying space of the open sea, the storms and whirlpools of an unknown ocean, the ice of Antarctica, more—all rendered in a powerful, chilling manner. Full text. 38 plates. 77pp. 9¼ × 12. 22305-1 Pa. $4.95

THE EXPEDITIONS OF ZEBULON MONTGOMERY PIKE, Zebulon Montgomery Pike. Fascinating firsthand accounts (1805-6) of exploration of Mississippi River, Indian wars, capture by Spanish dragoons, much more. 1,088pp. 5⅜ × 8½. 25254-X, 25255-8 Pa., Two-vol. set $25.90

CATALOG OF DOVER BOOKS

A CONCISE HISTORY OF PHOTOGRAPHY: Third Revised Edition, Helmut Gernsheim. Best one-volume history—camera obscura, photochemistry, daguerreotypes, evolution of cameras, film, more. Also artistic aspects—landscape, portraits, fine art, etc. 281 black-and-white photographs. 26 in color. 176pp. 8⅜ × 11¼.
25128-4 Pa. $14.95

THE DORÉ BIBLE ILLUSTRATIONS, Gustave Doré. 241 detailed plates from the Bible: the Creation scenes, Adam and Eve, Flood, Babylon, battle sequences, life of Jesus, etc. Each plate is accompanied by the verses from the King James version of the Bible. 241pp. 9 × 12. 23004-X Pa. $9.95

WANDERINGS IN WEST AFRICA, Richard F. Burton. Great Victorian scholar/adventurer's invaluable descriptions of African tribal rituals, fetishism, culture, art, much more. Fascinating 19th-century account. 624pp. 5⅜ × 8½. 26890-X Pa. $12.95

FLATLAND, E. A. Abbott. Intriguing and enormously popular science-fiction classic explores the complexities of trying to survive as a two-dimensional being in a three-dimensional world. Amusingly illustrated by the author. 16 illustrations. 103pp. 5⅜ × 8½. 20001-9 Pa. $2.50

THE HISTORY OF THE LEWIS AND CLARK EXPEDITION, Meriwether Lewis and William Clark, edited by Elliott Coues. Classic edition of Lewis and Clark's day-by-day journals that later became the basis for U.S. claims to Oregon and the West. Accurate and invaluable geographical, botanical, biological, meteorological and anthropological material. Total of 1,508pp. 5⅜ × 8½.
21268-8, 21269-6, 21270-X Pa., Three-vol. set $29.85

LANGUAGE, TRUTH AND LOGIC, Alfred J. Ayer. Famous, clear introduction to Vienna, Cambridge schools of Logical Positivism. Role of philosophy, elimination of metaphysics, nature of analysis, etc. 160pp. 5⅜ × 8½. (Available in U.S. and Canada only) 20010-8 Pa. $3.95

MATHEMATICS FOR THE NONMATHEMATICIAN, Morris Kline. Detailed, college-level treatment of mathematics in cultural and historical context, with numerous exercises. For liberal arts students. Preface. Recommended Reading Lists. Tables. Index. Numerous black-and-white figures. xvi + 641pp. 5⅜ × 8½.
24823-2 Pa. $11.95

HANDBOOK OF PICTORIAL SYMBOLS, Rudolph Modley. 3,250 signs and symbols, many systems in full; official or heavy commercial use. Arranged by subject. Most in Pictorial Archive series. 143pp. 8⅛ × 11. 23357-X Pa. $7.95

INCIDENTS OF TRAVEL IN YUCATAN, John L. Stephens. Classic (1843) exploration of jungles of Yucatan, looking for evidences of Maya civilization. Travel adventures, Mexican and Indian culture, etc. Total of 669pp. 5⅜ × 8½.
20926-1, 20927-X Pa., Two-vol. set $11.90

DEGAS: An Intimate Portrait, Ambroise Vollard. Charming, anecdotal memoir by famous art dealer of one of the greatest 19th-century French painters. 14 black-and-white illustrations. Introduction by Harold L. Van Doren. 96pp. 5⅜ × 8½.
25131-4 Pa. $4.95

PERSONAL NARRATIVE OF A PILGRIMAGE TO AL-MADINAH AND MECCAH, Richard F. Burton. Great travel classic by remarkably colorful personality. Burton, disguised as a Moroccan, visited sacred shrines of Islam, narrowly escaping death. 47 illustrations. 959pp. 5⅜ × 8½.
21217-3, 21218-1 Pa., Two-vol. set $19.90

PHRASE AND WORD ORIGINS, A. H. Holt. Entertaining, reliable, modern study of more than 1,200 colorful words, phrases, origins and histories. Much unexpected information. 254pp. 5⅜ × 8½.
20758-7 Pa. $5.95

THE RED THUMB MARK, R. Austin Freeman. In this first Dr. Thorndyke case, the great scientific detective draws fascinating conclusions from the nature of a single fingerprint. Exciting story, authentic science. 320pp. 5⅜ × 8½. (Available in U.S. only)
25210-8 Pa. $6.95

AN EGYPTIAN HIEROGLYPHIC DICTIONARY, E. A. Wallis Budge. Monumental work containing about 25,000 words or terms that occur in texts ranging from 3000 B.C. to 600 A.D. Each entry consists of a transliteration of the word, the word in hieroglyphs, and the meaning in English. 1,314pp. 6⅜ × 10.
23615-3, 23616-1 Pa., Two-vol. set $35.90

THE COMPLEAT STRATEGYST: Being a Primer on the Theory of Games of Strategy, J. D. Williams. Highly entertaining classic describes, with many illustrated examples, how to select best strategies in conflict situations. Prefaces. Appendices. xvi + 268pp. 5⅜ × 8½.
25101-2 Pa. $6.95

THE ROAD TO OZ, L. Frank Baum. Dorothy meets the Shaggy Man, little Button-Bright and the Rainbow's beautiful daughter in this delightful trip to the magical Land of Oz. 272pp. 5⅜ × 8.
25208-6 Pa. $5.95

POINT AND LINE TO PLANE, Wassily Kandinsky. Seminal exposition of role of point, line, other elements in nonobjective painting. Essential to understanding 20th-century art. 127 illustrations. 192pp. 6½ × 9¼.
23808-3 Pa. $5.95

LADY ANNA, Anthony Trollope. Moving chronicle of Countess Lovel's bitter struggle to win for herself and daughter Anna their rightful rank and fortune—perhaps at cost of sanity itself. 384pp. 5⅜ × 8½.
24669-8 Pa. $8.95

EGYPTIAN MAGIC, E. A. Wallis Budge. Sums up all that is known about magic in Ancient Egypt: the role of magic in controlling the gods, powerful amulets that warded off evil spirits, scarabs of immortality, use of wax images, formulas and spells, the secret name, much more. 253pp. 5⅜ × 8½.
22681-6 Pa. $4.50

THE DANCE OF SIVA, Ananda Coomaraswamy. Preeminent authority unfolds the vast metaphysic of India: the revelation of her art, conception of the universe, social organization, etc. 27 reproductions of art masterpieces. 192pp. 5⅜ × 8½.
24817-8 Pa. $6.95

CHRISTMAS CUSTOMS AND TRADITIONS, Clement A. Miles. Origin, evolution, significance of religious, secular practices. Caroling, gifts, yule logs, much more. Full, scholarly yet fascinating; non-sectarian. 400pp. 5⅜ × 8½.
23354-5 Pa. $6.95

THE HUMAN FIGURE IN MOTION, Eadweard Muybridge. More than 4,500 stopped-action photos, in action series, showing undraped men, women, children jumping, lying down, throwing, sitting, wrestling, carrying, etc. 390pp. 7⅞ × 10⅝.
20204-6 Cloth. $24.95

THE MAN WHO WAS THURSDAY, Gilbert Keith Chesterton. Witty, fast-paced novel about a club of anarchists in turn-of-the-century London. Brilliant social, religious, philosophical speculations. 128pp. 5⅜ × 8½.
25121-7 Pa. $3.95

A CÉZANNE SKETCHBOOK: Figures, Portraits, Landscapes and Still Lifes, Paul Cézanne. Great artist experiments with tonal effects, light, mass, other qualities in over 100 drawings. A revealing view of developing master painter, precursor of Cubism. 102 black-and-white illustrations. 144pp. 8¾ × 6⅜.
24790-2 Pa. $6.95

AN ENCYCLOPEDIA OF BATTLES: Accounts of Over 1,560 Battles from 1479 B.C. to the Present, David Eggenberger. Presents essential details of every major battle in recorded history, from the first battle of Megiddo in 1479 B.C. to Grenada in 1984. List of Battle Maps. New Appendix covering the years 1967–1984. Index. 99 illustrations. 544pp. 6½ × 9¼.
24913-1 Pa. $14.95

AN ETYMOLOGICAL DICTIONARY OF MODERN ENGLISH, Ernest Weekley. Richest, fullest work, by foremost British lexicographer. Detailed word histories. Inexhaustible. Total of 856pp. 6½ × 9¼.
21873-2, 21874-0 Pa., Two-vol. set $19.90

WEBSTER'S AMERICAN MILITARY BIOGRAPHIES, edited by Robert McHenry. Over 1,000 figures who shaped 3 centuries of American military history. Detailed biographies of Nathan Hale, Douglas MacArthur, Mary Hallaren, others. Chronologies of engagements, more. Introduction. Addenda. 1,033 entries in alphabetical order. xi + 548pp. 6½ × 9¼. (Available in U.S. only)
24758-9 Pa. $13.95

LIFE IN ANCIENT EGYPT, Adolf Erman. Detailed older account, with much not in more recent books: domestic life, religion, magic, medicine, commerce, and whatever else needed for complete picture. Many illustrations. 597pp. 5⅜ × 8½.
22632-8 Pa. $8.95

HISTORIC COSTUME IN PICTURES, Braun & Schneider. Over 1,450 costumed figures shown, covering a wide variety of peoples: kings, emperors, nobles, priests, servants, soldiers, scholars, townsfolk, peasants, merchants, courtiers, cavaliers, and more. 256pp. 8⅜ × 11¼.
23150-X Pa. $9.95

THE NOTEBOOKS OF LEONARDO DA VINCI, edited by J. P. Richter. Extracts from manuscripts reveal great genius; on painting, sculpture, anatomy, sciences, geography, etc. Both Italian and English. 186 ms. pages reproduced, plus 500 additional drawings, including studies for *Last Supper, Sforza* monument, etc. 860pp. 7⅞ × 10¾. (Available in U.S. only) 22572-0, 22573-9 Pa., Two-vol. set $31.90

CATALOG OF DOVER BOOKS

THE ART NOUVEAU STYLE BOOK OF ALPHONSE MUCHA: All 72 Plates from "Documents Decoratifs" in Original Color, Alphonse Mucha. Rare copyright-free design portfolio by high priest of Art Nouveau. Jewelry, wallpaper, stained glass, furniture, figure studies, plant and animal motifs, etc. Only complete one-volume edition. 80pp. 9⅜ × 12¼. 24044-4 Pa. $10.95

ANIMALS: 1,419 Copyright-Free Illustrations of Mammals, Birds, Fish, Insects, Etc., edited by Jim Harter. Clear wood engravings present, in extremely lifelike poses, over 1,000 species of animals. One of the most extensive pictorial sourcebooks of its kind. Captions. Index. 284pp. 9 × 12. 23766-4 Pa. $10.95

OBELISTS FLY HIGH, C. Daly King. Masterpiece of American detective fiction, long out of print, involves murder on a 1935 transcontinental flight—"a very thrilling story"—NY Times. Unabridged and unaltered republication of the edition published by William Collins Sons & Co. Ltd., London, 1935. 288pp. 5⅜ × 8½. (Available in U.S. only) 25036-9 Pa. $5.95

VICTORIAN AND EDWARDIAN FASHION: A Photographic Survey, Alison Gernsheim. First fashion history completely illustrated by contemporary photographs. Full text plus 235 photos, 1840–1914, in which many celebrities appear. 240pp. 6½ × 9¼. 24205-6 Pa. $8.95

THE ART OF THE FRENCH ILLUSTRATED BOOK, 1700–1914, Gordon N. Ray. Over 630 superb book illustrations by Fragonard, Delacroix, Daumier, Doré, Grandville, Manet, Mucha, Steinlen, Toulouse-Lautrec and many others. Preface. Introduction. 633 halftones. Indices of artists, authors & titles, binders and provenances. Appendices. Bibliography. 608pp. 8⅜ × 11¼. 25086-5 Pa. $24.95

THE WONDERFUL WIZARD OF OZ, L. Frank Baum. Facsimile in full color of America's finest children's classic. 143 illustrations by W. W. Denslow. 267pp. 5⅜ × 8½. 20691-2 Pa. $7.95

FOLLOWING THE EQUATOR: A Journey Around the World, Mark Twain. Great writer's 1897 account of circumnavigating the globe by steamship. Ironic humor, keen observations, vivid and fascinating descriptions of exotic places. 197 illustrations. 720pp. 5⅜ × 8½. 26113-1 Pa. $15.95

THE FRIENDLY STARS, Martha Evans Martin & Donald Howard Menzel. Classic text marshalls the stars together in an engaging, nontechnical survey, presenting them as sources of beauty in night sky. 23 illustrations. Foreword. 2 star charts. Index. 147pp. 5⅜ × 8½. 21099-5 Pa. $3.95

FADS AND FALLACIES IN THE NAME OF SCIENCE, Martin Gardner. Fair, witty appraisal of cranks, quacks, and quackeries of science and pseudoscience: hollow earth, Velikovsky, orgone energy, Dianetics, flying saucers, Bridey Murphy, food and medical fads, etc. Revised, expanded In the Name of Science. "A very able and even-tempered presentation."—The New Yorker. 363pp. 5⅜ × 8. 20394-8 Pa. $6.95

ANCIENT EGYPT: Its Culture and History, J. E. Manchip White. From predynastics through Ptolemies: society, history, political structure, religion, daily life, literature, cultural heritage. 48 plates. 217pp. 5⅜ × 8½. 22548-8 Pa. $5.95

SIR HARRY HOTSPUR OF HUMBLETHWAITE, Anthony Trollope. Incisive, unconventional psychological study of a conflict between a wealthy baronet, his idealistic daughter, and their scapegrace cousin. The 1870 novel in its first inexpensive edition in years. 250pp. 5⅜ × 8½. 24953-0 Pa. $6.95

LASERS AND HOLOGRAPHY, Winston E. Kock. Sound introduction to burgeoning field, expanded (1981) for second edition. Wave patterns, coherence, lasers, diffraction, zone plates, properties of holograms, recent advances. 84 illustrations. 160pp. 5⅜ × 8¼. (Except in United Kingdom) 24041-X Pa. $3.95

INTRODUCTION TO ARTIFICIAL INTELLIGENCE: Second, Enlarged Edition, Philip C. Jackson, Jr. Comprehensive survey of artificial intelligence—the study of how machines (computers) can be made to act intelligently. Includes introductory and advanced material. Extensive notes updating the main text. 132 black-and-white illustrations. 512pp. 5⅜ × 8½. 24864-X Pa. $10.95

HISTORY OF INDIAN AND INDONESIAN ART, Ananda K. Coomaraswamy. Over 400 illustrations illuminate classic study of Indian art from earliest Harappa finds to early 20th century. Provides philosophical, religious and social insights. 304pp. 6⅜ × 9⅜. 25005-9 Pa. $11.95

THE GOLEM, Gustav Meyrink. Most famous supernatural novel in modern European literature, set in Ghetto of Old Prague around 1890. Compelling story of mystical experiences, strange transformations, profound terror. 13 black-and-white illustrations. 224pp. 5⅜ × 8½. (Available in U.S. only) 25025-3 Pa. $6.95

PICTORIAL ENCYCLOPEDIA OF HISTORIC ARCHITECTURAL PLANS, DETAILS AND ELEMENTS: With 1,880 Line Drawings of Arches, Domes, Doorways, Facades, Gables, Windows, etc., John Theodore Haneman. Sourcebook of inspiration for architects, designers, others. Bibliography. Captions. 141pp. 9 × 12. 24605-1 Pa. $7.95

BENCHLEY LOST AND FOUND, Robert Benchley. Finest humor from early 30s, about pet peeves, child psychologists, post office and others. Mostly unavailable elsewhere. 73 illustrations by Peter Arno and others. 183pp. 5⅜ × 8½. 22410-4 Pa. $4.95

ERTÉ GRAPHICS, Erté. Collection of striking color graphics: *Seasons, Alphabet, Numerals, Aces* and *Precious Stones*. 50 plates, including 4 on covers. 48pp. 9⅜ × 12¼. 23580-7 Pa. $7.95

THE JOURNAL OF HENRY D. THOREAU, edited by Bradford Torrey, F. H. Allen. Complete reprinting of 14 volumes, 1837–61, over two million words; the sourcebooks for *Walden*, etc. Definitive. All original sketches, plus 75 photographs. 1,804pp. 8½ × 12¼. 20312-3, 20313-1 Cloth., Two-vol. set $130.00

CASTLES: Their Construction and History, Sidney Toy. Traces castle development from ancient roots. Nearly 200 photographs and drawings illustrate moats, keeps, baileys, many other features. Caernarvon, Dover Castles, Hadrian's Wall, Tower of London, dozens more. 256pp. 5⅜ × 8¼. 24898-4 Pa. $6.95

CATALOG OF DOVER BOOKS

AMERICAN CLIPPER SHIPS: 1833–1858, Octavius T. Howe & Frederick C. Matthews. Fully-illustrated, encyclopedic review of 352 clipper ships from the period of America's greatest maritime supremacy. Introduction. 109 halftones. 5 black-and-white line illustrations. Index. Total of 928pp. 5⅜ × 8½.
25115-2, 25116-0 Pa., Two-vol. set $17.90

TOWARDS A NEW ARCHITECTURE, Le Corbusier. Pioneering manifesto by great architect, near legendary founder of "International School." Technical and aesthetic theories, views on industry, economics, relation of form to function, "mass-production spirit," much more. Profusely illustrated. Unabridged translation of 13th French edition. Introduction by Frederick Etchells. 320pp. 6⅛ × 9¼.
(Available in U.S. only) 25023-7 Pa. $8.95

THE BOOK OF KELLS, edited by Blanche Cirker. Inexpensive collection of 32 full-color, full-page plates from the greatest illuminated manuscript of the Middle Ages, painstakingly reproduced from rare facsimile edition. Publisher's Note. Captions. 32pp. 9⅜ × 12¼. 24345-1 Pa. $5.95

BEST SCIENCE FICTION STORIES OF H. G. WELLS, H. G. Wells. Full novel *The Invisible Man*, plus 17 short stories: "The Crystal Egg," "Aepyornis Island," "The Strange Orchid," etc. 303pp. 5⅜ × 8½. (Available in U.S. only)
21531-8 Pa. $6.95

AMERICAN SAILING SHIPS: Their Plans and History, Charles G. Davis. Photos, construction details of schooners, frigates, clippers, other sailcraft of 18th to early 20th centuries—plus entertaining discourse on design, rigging, nautical lore, much more. 137 black-and-white illustrations. 240pp. 6⅛ × 9¼.
24658-2 Pa. $6.95

ENTERTAINING MATHEMATICAL PUZZLES, Martin Gardner. Selection of author's favorite conundrums involving arithmetic, money, speed, etc., with lively commentary. Complete solutions. 112pp. 5⅜ × 8½. 25211-6 Pa. $3.50

THE WILL TO BELIEVE, HUMAN IMMORTALITY, William James. Two books bound together. Effect of irrational on logical, and arguments for human immortality. 402pp. 5⅜ × 8½. 20291-7 Pa. $8.95

THE HAUNTED MONASTERY and THE CHINESE MAZE MURDERS, Robert Van Gulik. 2 full novels by Van Gulik continue adventures of Judge Dee and his companions. An evil Taoist monastery, seemingly supernatural events; overgrown topiary maze that hides strange crimes. Set in 7th-century China. 27 illustrations. 328pp. 5⅜ × 8½. 23502-5 Pa. $6.95

CELEBRATED CASES OF JUDGE DEE (DEE GOONG AN), translated by Robert Van Gulik. Authentic 18th-century Chinese detective novel; Dee and associates solve three interlocked cases. Led to Van Gulik's own stories with same characters. Extensive introduction. 9 illustrations. 237pp. 5⅜ × 8½.
23337-5 Pa. $5.95

Prices subject to change without notice.

Available at your book dealer or write for free catalog to Dept. GI, Dover Publications, Inc., 31 East 2nd St., Mineola, N.Y. 11501. Dover publishes more than 175 books each year on science, elementary and advanced mathematics, biology, music, art, literary history, social sciences and other areas.